"The real reason Kelman, despite his stature and reputation, remains something of a literary outsider is not, I suspect, so much that great, radical Modernist writers aren't supposed to come from working-class Glasgow, as that great, radical Modernist writers are supposed to be dead. Dead and wrapped up in a Penguin Classic: that's when it's safe to regret that their work was underappreciated or misunderstood (or how little they were paid) in their lifetimes. You can write what you like about Beckett or Kafka and know they're not going to come round and tell you you're talking nonsense or confound your expectations with a new work. Kelman is still alive, still writing great books, climbing."

—James Meek, *London Review of Books*

"A true original. . . . A real artist. . . . It's now very difficult to see which of his peers can seriously be ranked alongside Kelman without ironic eyebrows being raised."

—Irvine Welsh, *Guardian*

"Probably the most influential novelist of the post-war period."

—*The Times*

"Kelman has the knack, maybe more than anyone since Joyce, of fixing in his writing the lyricism of ordinary people's speech. . . . Pure aesthete, undaunted democrat—somehow Kelman manages to reconcile his two halves."

—*Esquire* (London)

"Kelman has always been a true and honest writer, which is why he is one of the fairly few who really matter."

—*Scotsman*

KAIROS

In ancient Greek philosophy, *kairos* signifies the right time or the "moment of transition." We believe that we live in such a transitional period. The most important task of social science in time of transformation is to transform itself into a force of liberation. Kairos, an editorial imprint of the Anthropology and Social Change department housed in the California Institute of Integral Studies, publishes groundbreaking works in critical social sciences, including anthropology, sociology, geography, theory of education, political ecology, political theory, and history.

Series editor: Andrej Grubačić

Recent and featured Kairos books:

Mutual Aid: An Illuminated Factor of Evolution by Peter Kropotkin, illustrated by N.O. Bonzo

Asylum for Sale: Profit and Protest in the Migration Industry edited by Siobhán McGuirk and Adrienne Pine

Building Free Life: Dialogues with Öcalan edited by International Initiative

The Art of Freedom: A Brief History of the Kurdish Liberation Struggle by Havin Guneser

The Sociology of Freedom: Manifesto of the Democratic Civilization, Volume III by Abdullah Öcalan

Facebooking the Anthropocene in Raja Ampat by Bob Ostertag

In, Against, and Beyond Capitalism: The San Francisco Lectures by John Holloway

Re-enchanting the World: Feminism and the Politics of the Commons by Silvia Federici

Practical Utopia: Strategies for a Desirable Society by Michael Albert

Autonomy Is in Our Hearts: Zapatista Autonomous Government through the Lens of the Tsotsil Language by Dylan Eldredge Fitzwater

For more information visit www.pmpress.org/blog/kairos/

Between Thought and Expression Lies a Lifetime

Why Ideas Matter

Noam Chomsky and James Kelman

KAIROS

PM

Between Thought and Expression Lies a Lifetime: Why Ideas Matter

ISBN: 978-1-62963-880-5 (paperback)
ISBN: 978-1-62963-886-7 (hardcover)
ISBN: 978-1-62963-900-0 (ebook)
Library of Congress Control Number: 2020952228

Cover by Drohan DiSanto
Interior design by briandesign

10 9 8 7 6 5 4 3 2 1

PM Press
PO Box 23912
Oakland, CA 94623
www.pmpress.org

Printed in the USA.

Acknowledgments
Thanks to Gus John and the George E. Davie Estate for their generosity in permitting the use of their work, and to the others whose correspondence is included. All proceeds from the Scottish end of the production go towards the Spirit of Revolt archive.

For all those volunteers, participants, and
audience members who took part in the
Self-Determination & Power event, Govan, 1990

Contents

Introduction
James Kelman

My correspondence with Noam Chomsky began earlier than documented here. There was the first letter I wrote him, and there may have been a second. I don't have these. This was early 1988, and I was working on typewriter and rarely kept copies of letters. I had been commissioned for a review of *The Chomsky Reader* by Peter Kravitz, then editor of *Edinburgh Review*.* The review just got longer and longer as the ideas expanded, and Peter was happy with that. Space was not a consideration. Later he heard through friends that Chomsky was visiting London to give a public lecture.† We wanted to invite him north to give another in Glasgow and attended the lecture at Battersea Town Hall, hoping to make the invitation in person.

John Pilger attended the same meeting and recalls "the incident . . . when (Chomsky) defended the right of a neo-fascist to heckle him."‡ I remember this too, and very clearly. The man had travelled from France to attend the lecture, expressly to confront Chomsky. He was so close to the platform had he fired a gun he could hardly have missed. The significance of that stayed with me. During his subsequent visit to Glasgow, I

* Noam Chomsky, *The Chomsky Reader*, ed. James Peck (New York: Pantheon Books, 1987.

† Especially Mark Ainley of Honest Jon's record store in Portobello Road. Mark was involved in organizing the Battersea event.

‡ John Pilger, *Distant Voices* (London: Vintage, 1992), 344.

mentioned it to Chomsky. He shrugged. It was nothing new and there was little he could do about it.

When we issued the original invitation to him, the idea was that he visit Glasgow to deliver a lecture. Nothing else was planned. When he agreed to come that one lecture developed into what became the Self-Determination & Power event, held over two days. This book is not a record of that, nor of its organization, and I make no attempt to present either, although they are a part of it.

The value of debate and exchanging points of view was in evidence during the organization. People were ignorant of the work of George Davie and could not fathom why he should have been sharing the second-day platform with Noam Chomsky. A few were for, and a few were against. Others knew nothing of any of it. Readers of the *Edinburgh Review* knew more than most. Peter Kravitz was one of Davie's graduate students and had been publishing his essays there. He was also commissioning editor at Polygon Books, publishing wing of Edinburgh University Students Union. The students involved were responsible for galvanizing contemporary Scottish literature during the 1980s. They were also responsible for bringing Davie's work to the attention of the wider public.* In so doing, they were introducing to them the philosophical tradition of their own country.

As late as the 1980s the Common Sense tradition in philosophy as it applied in Scotland was unknown to most people who lived in the place. Some who were aware were hostile. Their hostility may have derived from a colonial mentality, and that vague sense of shame. (Don't give us a showing-up in front of the grown-ups, i.e., the imperialists.) The phrase *Democratic Intellect* appears regularly in association with the Scottish tradition. People on the left were irritated particularly by that.

---

* Notably with George E. Davie, *The Crisis of the Democratic Intellect* (Edinburgh: Polygon Books 1986).

Those who spoke positively of the tradition were derided for arguing that once upon a time Scotland was truly democratic, truly egalitarian; non-elitist, anti-hierarchical and so on; a free society in a free country where people lived freely. Nobody argued any such thing. Nevertheless, they were so accused.

A more pragmatic side of the hostility derived from people with decent salaries. They were less troubled spending them if it could be shown that the anglophone centrality to Scottish society extended through all areas of the intellect and was therefore justified, on the grounds that without it we would have nothing at all, doomed to disappear into the mists of the Celtic twilight and sink thereunto—unto what? a primeval swamp presumably, floundering amid a shoal of kilted Roman Catholics and tartan-trousered Free Kirk Protestants. In Scotland we know this as the Brit or Brūt syndrome. Those who maintain the anti-assimilationist struggle on behalf of *liberté* and indigeneity are of the latter persuasion: *Viva le Brūt!*

The "distinctive" Scottish tradition in philosophy was said to have arisen in opposition to David Hume's skepticism but the only side of the debate most anyone knew, let alone studied, was that of Hume himself. So what opposition were they talking about? Only one side of the argument was up for discussion. No Scottish context existed. The ideas and arguments of Hume's contemporaries and peers were either ignored, marginalized, misunderstood, or unknown. People were in ignorance, even in Scotland. Hume's path was the Brit path, not the true path but the *only* path. His work stood alongside Descartes, Newton, Locke, Berkeley, Rousseau and Kant. The Scottish philosophers of that time were excluded, they were outside the discourse.

Two of the three lecturers in philosophy from my old course at the University of Strathclyde, attended the Self-Determination event. One came to me towards the end of the second day.* He had taken to heart what he had learned of

* Hywell Thomas, and the other was Christopher Long; both deceased.

the Scottish philosophical tradition and its absence from the course of study and felt that he should apologize, and he did apologize.

But what should he have known? Why should he have known anything about "the tradition"? What tradition?

There was no department of philosophy when I attended the University of Strathclyde, it was a wee section overseen by the three lecturers, subsumed within the Department of English Studies. Nowadays even that has gone. The study of philosophy has been withdrawn from this university altogether. Imagine a university without philosophy. (The last sentence demands an exclamation mark but doesn't deserve one.)

Why should we expect the Scottish tradition in philosophy to have a place within the Scottish education system? Only one university in the country has a Department of Scottish Literature.

As a living artform the existence of non-anglophone English-language literatures has been a matter of opinion, whether any lived or not an irrelevance; their only value historical. Prose fiction and poetry not conforming to the standard imposed by ruling authority is unacceptable, always inferiorized. But writers keep using language as it is used by people.

In former times, foreign students with an interest in the "genre" were directed to a broom cupboard in the lower basement of the Department of English Studies. Inside a wizened old fellow in full Highland regalia guarded musty copies of this and that and the next thing. Insert a coin and off he spun with recitations of "the Scotch Ballads," the "dialect verse" of Rabbie Burns, while displaying pictures of Sir Walter Scott bowing to the King of the United Kingdom.

Students who wanted more than that were invited to check out the addenda pages of the British Council Annual Report where sightings of indigenous exotica are itemized, *quod nullo sensu percipi potest,** and appeared in the section entitled Lost Forms of the Celt.

And the mark of the beast is with them, my son, those who work in the unassimilated voices of the lower orders for they are the tradition-bearers, borne through older linguistic forms, denying the linguistic supremacy of Standard English Imperial form.

Value-systems are controlled by the occupying force. Those who assimilate receive the reward: they pass. People who speak in the voice of authority have made a career decision. The greatest praise is to be advised that they don't sound Scottish, but in this context "Scottish" describes the condition of uneducated working class, what they call white trash in the US. It never had anything to do with "Scottishness," whatever that happens to be. Self-determination should not be confused with nationalism. There never was any one language, no one culture. That notion of unity is absurd. It only makes sense to the imperialist.

Many who attended the Self-Determination & Power event did not see beyond the question of Scotland as a self-governing country, freely determining its own future. It was up to them. They were free to believe what they wished.

This event was also a place to seek out difference in concepts such as "self-determination" and "nationalism." In doing so they would embark on a discussion essential to the radical politics of several decades earlier. At the 1922 General Election, twenty-nine Scottish socialists were elected to the Westminster Parliament. They belonged to the vast numbers of left-wing optimists who had come to believe that infrastructural change is possible within a political system founded and controlled by the State. Radicals, revolutionaries, activists, and intellectuals from other parts of the world were in agreement, influenced in

* In English this reads: "removed from the sphere of the senses."

particular by V.I. Lenin and the Communist Party's arguments on internationalism and participation in government.

The anarchist and the anti-parliamentarian left were consigned to the margins, along with other anti-imperialist positions that activists had fought for, and died. The situation in Ireland was significant. The British State had murdered James Connolly and other perceived leaders of the 1916 rising by due process of rules and procedures laid down by gloved fist and described to the world as "execution." Connolly was born in Edinburgh and Scottish socialists considered him to be one of them, as indeed he was by birth and upbringing, the first full-time employee of the Scottish Labour Party and one of the leading Marxist theorists of the time. He had many friends on Clydeside, among the not-so radicals as well as the revolutionaries.

The State-approved route to self-determination was tried in 1918. This was a General Election. If the population win enough votes, it is said, they can act to change the system. The majority of the Irish people accepted the idea and voted in favor of Home Rule by an overwhelming majority. Their party of choice was Sinn Féin. Roughly translated into the language of the British colonizer, *Sinn Féin* is *we go it alone, we shall do it by ourselves, we shall determine our own existence*. Sinn Féin accepted the results of the General Election as a mandate to form an Irish government, and this they did in Ireland, their own country. The British State responded in the manner of most other occupying forces. They outlawed the local parliament and criminalized the legitimate party of government.

There were many areas under discussion at the Self-determination Event. New ideas and fresh takes on old ones were to be explored in meetings, in corridors, cafes, and bars.

When I asked his permission to embark on this book, Professor Chomsky was immediately supportive and sent me a version of his original keynote paper, which now amounts to 100 pages. I edited this, keeping in front of me the original transcript, as it appeared in the book *Chomsky on Anarchism* (AK Press, 2005). It was appropriate that AK Press should have published the original. In those days, Ramsey Kanaan was centrally involved. He was the founder of AK Press, which was based in his mother's home in Stirling, He didn't have a car. He had a tall and sturdily framed backpack stuffed with books, flyers, posters, and assorted printed matter. This towered upright on his shoulders. In windier weather he walked at an angle and on foggier evenings cut a strange figure disappearing into the distance. Later, he moved the AK base to a wee flat in Edinburgh. His living quarters continued as storeroom and office. A friend assembled and joined his front door to open out the way, such that "forced entry" was less available to the heavy boot of HM the polis, a lesson learned from peddlers of authentic political discourse by aspiring dope dealers.

His initial contact with Noam Chomsky happened in my flat in Glasgow the night before Day One. Many of the conference contributors and organizers were there that evening. Ramsey wondered if Chomsky might allow AK Press to publish the keynote paper, or if not something else. I suggested he go and ask the man himself which is what he did. Chomsky agreed immediately. This became his first book with AK and is reprinted here.* It derives from a paper he delivered at the University of Edinburgh for which he somehow managed to find time during the conference. I had prepared a second introductory talk for Day Two of the conference, but there was no time to deliver it properly. Ramsey Kanaan had asked if I would contribute a preface to the book, and I used some of the Day Two paper as the basis of my preface.†

News of Professor Chomsky's visit spread quickly. Was it true that one of the world's leading intellectuals was coming to

* Noam Chomsky, *Terrorizing the Neighborhood: American Foreign Policy in the Post-Cold War Era*, preface by James Kelman (San Francisco: AK Press, 1991).

† Ibid.

Govan, Glasgow, to take part in an event organized by a raggle-taggle assortment of activists, anarchists and wayward artists? The BBC World Service heard and approached for an interview with him. By this time the two-day event had sold out. Professor Gus John was among those travelling north from England, in company with Roxy Harris, John La Rose and Iain MacDonald QC. These four were crucially involved in the UK struggles against racism. The BBC World Service asked if Gus John might do the interview. He agreed and also agreed that this interview be published here. It is instrumental to see some of the points covered in regard to what we might call the Americanization of the United Kingdom; the withdrawal of health and welfare, the repression of labor, attacks on human rights, on civil rights, on citizens' rights.

Other media interviews occurred during the conference and less formal ones too, plus workshops, discussion groups and an unknown number of free-ranging dialogues. Poets and writers gave readings, and there was music too. Video recordings exist of some of those. Malcolm Dickson,* a founder member of Transmission Gallery, went around with a video camera and managed to film decent portions of the event. Some of this may be accessed online.

Others who attended the two-day event have tales to tell and it would be great if they told them. Professor Chomsky regrets that there is not more of it in this book. I can only repeat that this is not "a book of the event." His memories, and those of other folk I know, are vivid and appreciative; he refers expressly to the "merriment" of the last night ceilidh and how wonderful were the readings, hearing Gaelic spoken and so on. I have no such recollections, unfortunately, I was too involved in the organizational minutiae. I took no part in workshops and discussion groups. When there was time to relax I hid away, steering clear of the local pub. If I had succumbed I

* Current director of Street Level Gallery, Glasgow.

would have been lost. I wasn't alone in that. A few others from the organizing team remember little, barely hearing any of the platform contributions. What they recall is shifting tables and chairs, carrying books to help set up or close down bookstalls, and guiding people here and there.

A note on the text is necessary: in correspondence the writer is in direct communication with other human beings and makes use of oral as well as literary methods. Basic punctuation markers such as commas, semi-colons, colons, dashes, ellipses, and so on, are employed not only as standard grammatical practice but as an expression of breath-pause and to produce particular emphases. Grammatical rules and procedures are applied with caution. If implemented as a general rule then levels of meaning and nuance are lost, and the individuality of the unique voice is in danger of being extinguished altogether. This applies in the transcription of verbal interviews and "talks." Within the pages of this book one example of the issue is the talk delivered on Day Two by George E. Davie. This was in response to the paper delivered by Professor Chomsky on Day One. What we have here is Davie's transcription of his own talk, with minor editing. It is a great paper. Readers should use the punctuation as an aid to discovering its richness.

My aim in this book has been to make available what remains accessible to me (including myself). In making available my contact with Noam Chomsky in this context I hope the possibility of change is emphasized. In my own case I am strongly aware of his influence, that to be "in touch with Noam Chomsky" is to be in touch with the thought of Noam Chomsky and what that might amount to; not just his work in the academic sense but as a field of action, a philosophy of action and how this leads into the thought of other people, into communication with other people. He places the obligation, the burden of proof, on the shoulders of his academic colleagues as well as the politicians, and perhaps the rest of us too, and this is why he is punished. He handles it in the proper fashion. At the age of eighty-eight he takes on a new job, and moves half way across country to resume contact with a new bunch of students.

Change does not happen of its own accord. It is up to the individual. Chomsky presents us with the basis; how things are, and we do with it what we can. For most of his working life he has blasted his way through academia, insisting on truth, the place of justice, the assumption of the right to freedom. It has been exciting to engage with his thought, and a privilege to assemble this book.

Correspondence One

May 23, 1988

Dear Mr. Kelman,

Thanks very much for your invitation to visit Glasgow, and also for the collection of short stories, which I am very pleased to have and look forward to reading when the pace relaxes slightly in a few weeks.

The idea of visiting the Free University, and Scotland generally, is very appealing, and your letter made it more so. I've been trying to see if my very tight schedule can be juggled to allow it to work out somehow. Unfortunately, there doesn't seem to be any way. I'd planned to be in England for only three days (not ten, as you heard—a ten-day trip abroad is an almost unheard of luxury for me for the past twenty years; just too many demands here). Unfortunately, I can't extend it at either end, because of other commitments here. Demands for speaking in particular are extraordinarily heavy, more than ever before, because of the combination of defection of intellectuals to the right (therefore, few speakers) and substantial growth of popular groups all over the place (who need outside speakers, both for information and discussion, or even for organizing purposes—an excuse to bring people together and bring in new people). I'm booked up into late 1990, solidly. Within the three days, it is pretty tight. I'm afraid I don't see any way to work it out, to my regret. I'd like to try to arrange it sometime. Maybe there'll be another occasion. If you don't mind, I'll file your letters away and if I do manage another trip to Britain before too long, will contact you to see if we can work something out.

February 12, 1989

Dear Mr. Kelman,

Thanks to some rearrangements, cancellations, and reschedulings, I have finally been able to arrange to visit Glasgow next January, about the 10th. I wonder if we could pick up the ideas we were discussing some time back?

February 23, 1989

Dear Professor Chomsky,

Many thanks for your letter. That's good news, and this is simply a note to confirm that we here in Glasgow shall be delighted to have you visit. Let's keep things fairly open at this point, including the precise dates, which we can fill in later at your own convenience.

I'm not sure whether I mentioned in my initial letter that I was involved in an essay deriving from your work and the philosophy of Common Sense. It began as a review of the "Reader" published by Serpents Tail Press in London, but since I have some basic grasp of your work in linguistics and philosophy generally I felt it would be of value to go a bit further than a review, and try to link in certain of the more theoretical aspects; and being a layperson myself I could only attempt to do so for a lay readership—rather bold I suppose, but I hope in keeping with the tradition itself. However, I would like to take the liberty—not of sending you my essay—but of sending you on some of my reading for it; specifically, writings by the contemporary Scottish philosopher George Davie that I think shall interest you. He is now in his mid-seventies but very little known, not even here in Scotland. At this point I have the enclosed pamphlet copy of a lecture to spare. Unless you indicate otherwise, I would like to send you a few of his other things.

Once again, very many thanks for accepting our invitation.

Best regards to you, I hope things go well and that you are managing to find time for your own work.

ps You'll no doubt receive a copy of my novel *A Disaffection*, from my publisher in New York. There is no moral obligation to open the pages!

April 20, 1989

Dear Professor Chomsky,

Please find enclosed some work by the Scottish philosopher George Davie which as I mentioned previously I think you'll find interesting; there is a line traced through Hume and Husserl which may be especially so. What I find so important and exciting myself, is the link-in from Rousseau and this line in Hume and other later Scottish philosophers, primarily his great rival Thomas Reid but also via later folk like Ferrier, to libertarian theory through a Common Sense philosophy differing from the Cartesian, the link in through learning theory—all as I understand it, and as purely and simply as perhaps only a nonacademic can state with such confidence.

A ramble: I'm working on a play just now about an insurrection in Scotland around 1819 when three weavers were executed for high treason. The attempted dissemination of knowledge for more than twenty years previously via Mechanics Institutes, and discussion groups among craftsmen like the weavers. Of the three executed a man called James Wilson whose nickname was Purly—why? because he invented the purl stitch. He was in his midsixties when executed; as a young man he knew the radical advocate Thomas Muir, read *Black Dwarf*, etc. and was with the United Scotsmen who took their name from the United Irishmen—Berkeleyean influence and the Scottish school again at work there. The weaver poet and great ornithologist Alexander Wilson (no relation) was a contemporary, and a great radical who spent time in gaol back here around the same period before being obliged to emigrate to the US. Bla bla bla.

My publisher in NY should have sent you a copy of my new novel by now. I'm aware that folk send you stuff all the time. Anyway, they're a big firm, and they like nothing better than that I can give a name to send a copy to.

Very best wishes to you and take care.

April 26, 1989

Dear James,

Got both your letter and your book (thanks), the latter set aside for summer reading (actually, it was ripped off at once by Jamie Young, who runs the show here). Arrangements for Glasgow are by now firmed up, for about the 10th–11th. Can we work out something?

I'd be most interested in reading the essay that you didn't send, but thanks for the one you did (Davie's Dow lecture), which I found quite interesting. I'm looking forward to seeing more. The only real disagreement I felt was in (at least the implication of) the final passages. I don't think that Locke's tabula rasa doctrine (borrowed from neo-scholasticism) opens the way to the radical vision he suggests; rather, it bars the way. In contrast, what he regards as the Scottish pessimism opens the way to an optimistic view of human potential, though, to be sure, with the intrinsic limitations that are a logical consequence of capacity to achieve anything nontrivial. I think there has been a great deal of confusion about this, based really on careless reasoning, for reasons I've discussed at length elsewhere.

Best.

May 8, 1989

Dear Mr. Kelman,

Thanks very much for the material, set aside for summer reading. I wish I knew more about the material you discuss. Sounds most interesting, and worth an intense look. Much intrigued to hear about the new play.

About next January, accidents excepted, I'm expecting to be in Glasgow.

I don't know exactly what is scheduled for me, but I'm sure we can work it out. What, exactly, would make sense, from your point of view?

June 7, 1989

Dear Professor Chomsky,

By coincidence, Derek Rodger, the editor of the magazine *Scottish Child*, whom I had never met before, was up in my flat on some other business, when in the course of conversation it transpired he was also in the process of organizing an event centered on the participation of yourself. The outcome is that we shall be working together as far as possible.

We plan a three-day event—strictly nonacademic, although academics who wish to attend on a personal basis will be welcome—set in Glasgow around the theme of "self-Determination & Power," with subheadings of "a life task, a political task" "tradition and existence." We hope for a participating group of around 250 people. There shall be guest speakers alongside yourself; these will include mainly poets and prose writers, but essentially they will be writers engaged in tradition-bearing, where this has become an active political struggle e.g., the Kenyan, Ngugi Wa Thiong'o who now writes only in Gikuyu; his latest novel is banned in his own country (apparently the government attempted to arrest the central character, unaware his life was a fiction) and whose work, along with that of others, in drama, led to the medium itself being banned in a district in Kenya. So far from allowing a person the "right" of self-determination the powers-that-be have proscribed the "right" to self-expression, as is the case in one way or another in almost every country in the world, including Britain. But this sort of struggle has been going on in literature for a long while of course—I noted in the James Peck interview that one writer you did mention was Mendele Mocher Sforim, and I recollect the fight on behalf of "living language" (in this case Yiddish) as a literary form was one he too was engaged in. Unfortunately, the struggle can degenerate from the affirmation of a language and/or culture to the point of tradition at all costs, especially that of the individual, i.e., tradition at the expense of existence, where art becomes simply heritage, from there the path spirals downwards into "blood and soil" politics, the "purity" of the language into the "purity" of the race, and so on.

Another line of interest following from there concerns selfhood into nationhood, "independence," where colonialism is replaced by neocolonialism; a line of thought relevant in a Scottish context at present where the majority of citizens would seem to prefer severing ties with England altogether (out of more than seventy MPs, the Scottish people who did vote at the last election returned only ten Conservatives to the British Parliament; in effect Thatcher's Government has never had a mandate in this country) but many of us are far from convinced by those who wait in the wings.

The majority of the people invited to participate for the three days will be activists of some sort or another, usually in local politics, e.g., tenants' groups, anti-racist groups, and so on. Some will be invited up from England and elsewhere, e.g., I hope to get a poet from the Leningrad '82 group (writers outwith the Writers Union in USSR) as well as representation from the ANC. In this way a number of folk directly involved in diverse self-determining activities will be drawn together; the intention being that space and time is given over to an exchange of knowledge, experience, information etc., that general points will emerge through process.

Bearing in mind that you can allow two days to us, our plan is that you give the key lecture on the Wednesday forenoon—maybe taking for granted that the folk there will also be interested in the Common Sense tradition; a reply or addendum of some sort will come from someone known in Scottish life; someone who is aware not only of your work in politics but who also has a grasp of your work in the study of language and philosophy in general. It may be the case that George Davie will not be up to it physically, although he would be the ideal. But it won't have to be an academic. In fact it is desirable that it isn't an academic at all, thus establishing the "generalist," "democratic intellect" feel to things, the sense that a genuine dissemination of knowledge is in process, and that ordinary people (I mean people who have had no higher education) are not being excluded. After lunch all participants will be sectioned off into groups of around fifteen to twenty individuals—the place we hope to hold the event has many different style rooms and areas where each group/workshop can hold their own forum. With luck, some concrete things will emerge, and with more luck bonds may be formed that go beyond the three-day period. Late afternoon comes a sort of plenary discussion led by an invited speaker. In the evening there will be a concert; musicians but also poets and prose writers performing from their work. The second and third days are programmed in similar fashion.

Would you be willing, not only to give the key speech on the Wednesday, but to participate in one of the small groups and give a brief talk on the Thursday plenary discussion? All invited speakers and the evening guest musicians and writers will also be asked to participate in the groups.

The details are only being worked out by us just now; if anything so far stated is not acceptable to you, or if you have any reservations on particular points, please let myself or Derek Rodger know. Your visit to Glasgow is exciting: it is also the starting basis of the entire project; the last thing we would wish is to put you off coming. We want to do everything possible to make it an enjoyable experience. I think I may have mentioned in the past that I am acquainted with Mark Ainley and Pete Ayrton—they initially invited me to "chair" the night at Battersea Town Hall.

All the best.

I wrote the following letter to Alan Fountain, then of Channel Four, hoping for financial support in return for the Self-determination & Power Event. In return the organizers were offering Channel Four the freedom to make a film of the proceedings for their flagship arts program of the day. In those far-off times Channel Four was attempting a serious engagement with contemporary art and cultural matters. Alan Fountain controlled this side of it. He never replied to the letter (nor did anyone else).

June 8, 1989

Dear Alan Fountain,

I'm not sure whether or not you will know my name. I am a writer (my most recent novel *A Disaffection* received fair publicity). Don Coutts gave me your address and telephone number and recommended I make contact with you as soon as possible on the following matter:

On January 10th, 11th and 12th here in Glasgow myself and others are holding a three-day event—strictly nonacademic though academics attending under their own steam will be as welcome as anyone, almost—under the general heading "Self Determination & Power," subheadings "a life task, a political task" "tradition and existence." The key speech takes place on the Wednesday, and the speaker will be Noam Chomsky with whom I have been corresponding.

We hope for a participating group of some 230 to 300 people, most of whom will be there by invitation. Alongside Chomsky there shall be other guest speakers; it is hoped that these will include such names as Ngugi Wa Thiong'o, George Davie, June Jordan, Jerome Rothenberg, Tom Leonard, Adonis, Christa Woolf; essentially writers who have in common that their work extends towards "tradition-bearing" where this has become an active struggle in one way or another. Ngugi is a good example at present; nowadays he writes exclusively in the language of his own cultural group (Gikuyu), and his latest novel is banned in Kenya—apparently the government there tried to arrest the central character in it, before discovering the life was a fiction. An aspect of this is the line concerning selfhood/nationhood and independence, where colonial rule has been followed by neocolonial rule. So far are the Kenyan authorities from allowing a person the "right" of self-determination the powers that be have proscribed the "right" of the artist to self-expression, but this is the case in most countries of the world. The fight on behalf of cultural "self-determination" has been happening in literature for around two hundred years. Unfortunately, at a later stage the struggle occasionally degenerates from the affirmation of a language and/or culture to the point of tradition at all costs, especially at that of the individual, i.e. tradition at the expense of existence, where art becomes simply heritage; and from there the path spirals downwards into "blood and soil" politics, the "purity" of a language becoming the "purity" of a race, and so on.

The majority of the people invited to participate for the three days (Chomsky is staying for both the Wednesday and the Thursday) will be activists in one way or another, usually in local politics, e.g., tenants' groups, the anti-poll tax organizers, anti-racist groups, women's self-help groups etc.; it will also include people invited from outside Scotland and elsewhere—I hope someone from the Leningrad '82 writers' group (writers who aren't part of the official Writers' Union) will take part, also representatives from UMOJA, the ANC. Thus a number of folk directly involved in diverse self-determining activities will be drawn together, the intention being that space and time are given over to an exchange of knowledge, experience, information etc., that general points will emerge through process.

Once Chomsky has given his key address on the Wednesday forenoon, a reply or addendum of some sort will come from somebody who is fairly well-known in Scottish public life—someone aware not only of Chomsky's work in international politics but who has a grasp of his work in the study of language and philosophy in general. This person won't be an academic, thus consolidating the "generalist," "democratic intellect" feel to things, the sense that a genuine dissemination of knowledge is in process, and that ordinary people (people who have not had higher education) are not being excluded from the discourse. After lunch, all participants, including guest speakers, will be sectioned off into groups of around fifteen to twenty Individuals—the place we are situating the event (the Pearce Institute, Govan) has many different style rooms and areas where each group/workshop can hold their own forum. With luck, some concrete things will emerge, and with more luck, bonds may be formed that go beyond the three-day period. The second and third days are programmed similarly, with the other guests giving the opening talk each morning. In late afternoon, a plenary discussion will also be led by one of the other invited guest speakers. In the evening there will be a concert; not only musicians will take part here but poets and prose writers who are used to performing their work in public—such names as Wally Serote, Kathy Acker, Alasdair Gray, Tom Raworth, Sorley Maclean, Linton Kwesi Johnson, Mahmood Jamal will be invited.

We are still working out the details, but the above represents where we are at present. The reason I have made contact with yourself concerns filming and the backing of it by Channel Four—I should also mention that Don is himself very keen on being involved. It occurred to myself and the other main organizer (Derek Rodger who edits the magazine the *Scottish Child*) that something based on the three-day event would not only be exciting, because of the names involved it would be marketable in countries like Holland, Sweden, West Germany, USA, Canada, possibly Cuba. The ideal slot would be the Eleventh Hour one, and the duration of the program would he around the one-hour-fifteen to -thirty-minute mark. If I was a filmmaker myself, at the risk of presumption, I would be wanting to go about for the three days and nights with the camera on my shoulder, maybe following the process through one or two of the small groups—the musicians and performance poets and prose writers from the evening concerts will also be asked to participate as ordinary group members.

Don has told me that budgets operate on an annual basis and that the year from April '89 to April '90 will already have been accounted for, but he also said there would be contingency funding available, if a project was considered exciting enough to warrant a special effort. We think this project is exactly that, and that it must be recorded; I hope you will give it a full consideration on behalf of Channel Four. I am aware that there is also the possibility of a development budget; is there something through the Scottish connection? Such a budget would allow for the expenses accruing on setting the event up, to include air travel, hotel fees, and so on—around £5 to £8,000, we estimate.

I rarely get to London these days, but towards the middle of next week I shall be there, and if it is convenient for you—and you are interested in discussing the matter further—we could meet for a brief chat about it. Thanks for your attention so far.

Yours sincerely.

June 14, 1989

Dear Mr. Kelman,

Professor Noam Chomsky is away from MIT for the summer months and I am writing for him to let you know that your letter was received here at his office. I am sorry for the form letter but it is the most efficient way we have found to deal with the large volume of mail he receives.

Your letter will be forwarded to Professor Chomsky as soon as possible, however, because of the rerouting it may be several weeks before you receive a response.* We appreciate your patience. In the meantime, if you have any questions that I may be able to answer, feel free to contact me at the address above or by telephone at (617) 253-7819.

Jamie Young
Secretary
MIT Linguistics

---

* Professor Chomsky answered the next day, rather than "several weeks" later. This indicated that he valued the idea and thought it worth pursuing, as he makes clear in the next letter.

June 15, 1989

Dear Jim,

Didn't realize that I hadn't told you that Derek Rodger was arranging my other talk. I thought I'd written that. Sorry. Anyway, glad it turned out to be a small world and you met, and that now things are on track.

The arrangements look fine to me. Sure, I'd be pleased to take part in the Thursday events. Arrange anything that seems reasonable. I'm really looking forward to it.

Hope you have (had) a fine time in Newfoundland.

Best.

June 15, 1989

Dear Professor Chomsky,

Enclosed a copy of the essay I spoke of earlier. I send it with many misgivings, and I hope coyness is more than halfway down the list. When I say that my academic background is the three-year course I spent doing English Lit and Philosophy as an undergraduate, it is not so much an excuse as a pointer towards the difficulties. But part of this whole thing is the implicit affirmation of the validity of the generalist approach, that there must be room for the layperson. Yes, but in such a subject as this one the problems. . . Not least among them the welter of criticism on your work (which aside from John Lyons' book I more or less stayed clear off altogether). This means the person working an essay must jump in always through a mixture of naivety and presumption, and at best this will include a small mixture of faith and arrogance—I remember doing my dissertation on Kafka, and being faced with the fact of the more than ten thousand books on the man already in existence (third in the league table of criticism, behind Shakespeare & Goethe). But this jump will have to be made in the face of specialism always, for the more you know, the harder it gets and at some point, I think, the person involved in say following a line of thought in philosophy will end up debating whether or not to embark on a "history of philosophy" instead.

From your position, you will be used to seeing criticism on your work. I am also sent most of the reviews and criticism on my own work, and I suppose one of the more irritating factors is when a dubious not to say totally false statement is made, where it is obvious that the critic has generalized without a true knowledge of the work as a whole—which does not require every last word to be read. And it makes matters worse when the critic in question is employed as teacher or lecturer in an educational establishment, thus you feel hordes of young folk are getting this hopelessly wrong picture of you, or else it appears in print—and the right of reply doesn't really exist, you just end up looking foolish.

However, I have to say to you that I would not have missed being obliged to get into what I had to get into in order to write the enclosed, not for anything; it took me into the heart of philosophy in a way that I never had been previously, and that has been truly exciting.

All the best to you.

A Reading from Noam Chomsky and the Scottish Tradition in the Philosophy of Common Sense

James Kelman

In 1982 polls indicated that 70 percent of the US population believed the Vietnam War to have been "fundamentally wrong and immoral"[1] whereas "virtually none of the really educated class or articulate intelligentsia ever took that position."[2]

Thus in the face of more than two decades of relentless media propaganda on behalf of the ruling group the great majority of ordinary people had the wit and the will to judge it for themselves. It is absolutely central to Chomsky's thesis that "there is no body of theory or significant body of relevant information, beyond the comprehension of the layman, which makes policy immune from criticism."[3] Everybody can know and everybody can judge. Unless we are mentally ill or in some other way disadvantaged, all of us have the analytic skills and intelligence to attempt an understanding of the world. It just is not good enough "to be bad at mathematics."

The skills demanded of an elderly person playing several cards of bingo simultaneously or for studying thoroughly the form for a big sprint handicap in the heavy going at Ayr Racetrack in an effort to pick the winner; the skills demanded of parents on welfare trying to cope with a family of young children, just seeing they stay healthy from one week to the next: all such skills are there to be developed and could be applied to any subject whatsoever, including subjects like a country's foreign policy or, nearer home, the correlation between cuts in welfare and infant mortality; between cuts in welfare and suicide; cuts in welfare and death from hypothermia; cuts in welfare and local crime and violence; cuts in welfare and drug abuse, alcohol abuse, gambling abuse, prostitution, madness.

No matter the subject under scrutiny certain factors remain the same, we apply our reasoning devices and these devices are interdisciplinary. We apply them in physics, in astronomy, in domestic economy, in horse racing, in joinery, in the creation of art. Logic is a reasoning device; so too is mathematics. They are also activities. We engage in them to find solutions to problems all the time. They are also skills; they can be refined and improved.

By approaching different kinds of problems we apply our reasoning skills in different kinds of ways. We start reflecting on how we use them and see how other folk are faring; we make comparisons and connections, construct theories. This is why poets can discuss methodology with people involved in sculpting marble or rigging up electrical circuits. If we are restricted to one subject only, then our ability to reason may stagnate; it will become difficult to reflect on what other folk are doing when they are engaged on subjects not directly related to our own; we will forego the opportunity of keeping an eye on "the experts."

Although his name had been known to me, I first became aware of Chomsky's work while at university as a mature student but my reading was confined to what he was doing in linguistics, and I did not persist; the technicalities of the subject did not interest me especially, nor do I find them especially interesting at the present time.

One of his earliest works was published in Holland when he was twenty-nine years of age; this was entitled *Syntactic Structures* and it

> revolutionised the scientific study of language . . . the revolutionary step that (he) took . . . was to draw upon

> (finite automata theory and recursive function theory) and to apply it to natural languages, like English, rather than to the artificial languages constructed by logicians and computer scientists. . . . He [further] made an independent and original contribution to the study of formal systems from a purely mathematical point of view.[4]

Both finite automata theory and recursive function theory are crucial not only in abstract disciplines like mathematics and logic but in disciplines such as physics, economics, botany, art theory, anthropology. They are also central to the analytic method known as "structuralism."

But an understanding of these theories is not at all necessary to appreciate Chomsky's demonstration that an argument used by the US Congress in 1984 with regard to "the right to bomb Nicaragua" could be adopted by the USSR with regard to "the right to bomb Denmark."

There again but it is good to know things, not to let ourselves be put off by technical phrases like "finite automata theory." We don't have to go away and look up a dictionary, we just keep such stuff in quotation marks.

I want to know about physics. By knowing about physics people have split "the atom." Most people do not know what an "atom" actually is, yet by splitting "it" the world can be destroyed. The worlds of Nagasaki and Hiroshima have already been destroyed, an event described by the Thirty-third President of the United States of America as the "greatest thing in history."[5] I want to know why the most powerful figure on Earth can say that, and if there is any connection between it and the fact that by the end of World War II the nation of which he is supposedly the boss owned 50 percent of the planet's wealth. Yet this same nation has only 6 percent of the planet's population. And of that 6 percent (some 220 million folk), about 90 percent would have owned next to nothing at all. So, in other words, if we take the 6 percent and divide it by 100 and multiply that by 90, and so on, we see that less than 0.6 percent of the world's population owned half of the world's entire wealth and material resources. This was back in 1945. I wonder what the figures are now. Maybe also, if I had been given examples like that in primary school, instead of things like apples in baskets and quantities of water in leaky tubs, maybe I might have become "good at mathematics." Who knows.

Chomsky's boyhood in New York City had been spent hanging around his uncle's news-stand at 72nd Street and Broadway

> which was sort of a radical center . . . in part Jewish working class . . . Communists . . . very much involved in the politics of the Depression . . . all night discussions and arguments . . . Freud, Marx, the Budapest String Quartet, literature. . . . [From adolescence he was] deeply interested . . . in radical politics with an anarchist or left-wing [anti-Leninist] Marxist flavor, and even more deeply interested in Zionist affairs and activities—or what was then called "Zionist," though the same ideas and concerns are now called "anti-Zionist." [He] was interested in socialist binationalist options for Palestine, and in the kibbutzim and the whole cooperative labor system that had been developed in the Jewish settlement there . . . but had never been able to come close to the Zionist youth groups that shared these interests because they were either Stalinist or Trotskyite and [he] had always been strongly anti-Bolshevik.

His father had been a linguist and up to the age of twelve he was put to an experimental, progressive school. His years at college and university were also noncomformist. He came under the influence of the philosopher and mathematician Nelson Goodman. And also Zellig Harris, one of the foremost names in linguistics, although Chomsky has said that "it was really his sympathy with Harris's political views that led him to work as an undergraduate" in the subject. Apparently Harris used to conduct his lectures in a cafe and continue them during the evening back in his flat.

These details can be decisive; so-called background or personal information is often the difference between taking us into the work of somebody or not. Just knowing that Zellig Harris had "political views," that his lectures and personality could keep students stimulated for hours; it's interesting stuff. What kind of a man was he? What was it about linguistics that drew him to the field? The way most present-day educational systems operate, we are to study the work and leave the somebody out of it. Never you mind if that literary critic does happen to be a fascist. You are hereby sentenced to spend the following year studying his theoretical work on the art of poetry. And for the rest of your life you are duty-bound to take it into account whenever the topic of literature arises.

During a series of lectures Chomsky was asked about his method of investigation,[6] given that he appears "to reject Marxism and materialism (and) investigation involves" both. While denying that he does reject them, Chomsky demonstrates the often irrelevant and stultifying effect of fixing labels to ideas. Ideas are not static; they do not belong to anybody, they are simply the outcome of the "common intellectual background of reasonable people trying to understand the world." "Marxism" consists of an indefinite number of ideas and in terms of the history of ideas "it" has already been incorporated. And as for "dialectical materialism," he "personally, has never understood it (but) if other people find it useful then fine, use it."

Chomsky went on to say that he has no particular method of investigation at all, what he does is "look hard at a serious problem and try to get some ideas as to what might be the explanation for it, meanwhile keeping an open mind about all sorts of other possibilities."

Such a statement might sound surprising, almost like an exercise in mystification, as though he is trying to make what he has achieved accessible but the route by which he travelled inaccessible. This is common amongst professionals and "experts" generally, including many so-called teachers. We try to follow the process by which they arrived at a solution, then discover the destination becomes as mysterious as the route.

It is a serious problem. Whole areas of experience and knowledge are hived off from ordinary men and women and children. Society is controlled by those who are "paid to know," the specialists. In recent years the most famous international expert on global affairs has probably been Henry Kissinger, someone whose downright "ignorance and foolishness" Chomsky describes as a "phenomenon."

Nevertheless, when sponsored by the might of the US military, the power exercised by such a person is life or death—as in Angola, for example, where he "tried to foment and sustain a civil war simply to convince the Russians that the American tiger could still bite." Human suffering is of no account and the economic cost is next to irrelevant, since in political affairs of state such costs "are always public" anyway; only the "profits are private." All talk of morality as a value is naive. If morality does exist it is to be regarded as a separate field of endeavor, like experimental physics or mechanical engineering or opera. Even genocide is consigned to the realm of tactics and becomes "wrong" only when its "effects are debatable and are likely to provoke hostile reactions in world capitals."

But at its official level international reaction is fairly predictable. It depends on who is doing what and to whom, and the profit involved. In 1974 the country of East Timor, with a population less than that of Glasgow, was attempting to determine its own existence; like Angola, this was after the horrors of Portuguese fascist colonization. Four years later a quarter of its people had been massacred after an invasion by Indonesia, 90 percent of whose military supplies came directly from the USA:

> but while (they were) the major foreign participant in the slaughter, the others tried to profit as they could and kept their silence. In Canada, the major Western investor in Indonesia, the government and the press were silent [while in France] *Le Monde* reported in 1978 that the French government would sell arms to Indonesia while abstaining from any U.N. discussion of the invasion and in general doing nothing to place "Indonesia in an embarrassing position."

This is only one instance from an enormous number cited by Chomsky. But after a time statistics dull the senses, including those concerned with wholesale slaughter, as he reminds us:

> You see what they mean when you look more closely at the refugees' reports: for example, a report by a few people who succeeded in escaping from a village in Quiche province [Guatemala] where the government troops came in, rounded up the population and put them in the town building. They took all the men out and decapitated them. Then they raped and killed the woman. Then they took the children and killed them by bashing their heads with rocks.

Reports of atrocities by refugees are difficult to cope with. We are not used to such testimony, not unless, perhaps, the refugees are in flight from the same ideological enemy as ourselves.

If Chomsky has a specialist subject, then it might be argued that it is not linguistics, nor the philosophy of language, rather it is US global policy, with particular reference to the dissemination of all related knowledge. When he says he has no "method of investigation," we would be as well asking to what the term could refer. Is having a "method of investigation" the same thing as having a system of rules and procedures worked out in advance so that we know how to proceed in problem solving? Should we be thinking of "induction" or "deduction" or "dialectics" or "structuralism"? What do these things mean? Before going off to investigate something are we supposed to go away and learn a method of investigation?

Maybe by "method" some people just mean they prefer working with a fresh pot of tea at the ready, a packet of cigarettes within reach and soft music in the background. They might even be referring to a preference for observation and experimentation as opposed to sitting about chatting and thinking aloud, in the style of some old Greek philosophers (and some contemporary ones as well, not just from Greece). What seems clear is that restricting yourself to one particular method will just make life more difficult. Everything and anything should be available, including intuition. Einstein was a staunch believer in intuition. Without such a reasoning device a great many scientific advances would not occur. It is the ability people have to soar above the boundaries of one field and land not in another field but in a street.

In his introduction to Chomsky's work in linguistics John Lyons suggests that it is necessary to meet him "on his own ground." This can imply the need to embark on a concentrated study of linguistics or the philosophy of language. But an insight into the technical, the formal problems confronted by Chomsky, may be possible without that. It also may be possible to see where these formal problems impinge on matters of more general, political concern.

Rousseau is an important thinker for Chomsky. It was what Rousseau perceived as the strength of the will to self-determination that led him to propose "the struggle for freedom [as] an essential human attribute." Rousseau also concluded that "the uprising that ends by strangling a sultan is as lawful an act as those by which he disposed, the day before, of the lives and goods of his subjects." The sultan has no inherent rights. Beyond civil society, there is an authority to which he is as subject as the retinue of men who helped him dress for breakfast that morning. This authority does not derive from outwith the realms of humankind. It is not God. It is not superhuman in any form. This is the authority of natural law which inheres in every woman and child and man.

Rousseau sent the essay in which that appeared to Voltaire whom he much admired, aside from his atheism, which he detested. But Voltaire did not appreciate the argument at all; he said it made him feel like "walking on all fours."[7] He thought the essay was affirming some sort of "golden age" where primitive folk would be free to be primitive once the shackles of civilization were burst asunder.

But Rousseau's argument is more powerful than that. When he saw "multitudes of entirely naked savages scorn European voluptuousness and endure hunger, fire, the sword, and death to preserve only their independence" he was seeing a basic premise that had to be true beyond any shadow of doubt: it is "from human nature that the principles of natural right and the foundations of social existence must be deduced . . . the essence of human nature is human freedom and the consciousness of this freedom." Human freedom is so inalienable a right that it can scarcely be described as a "right" at all, it is the very essence of what it is to be a person.

When Chomsky started in linguistics he accepted the orthodox view which was that semantics had nothing to do with the subject. Semantics involves "meanings," the way that people actually use language, whereas linguistics was to concern language as it already exists. In other words, the subject was restricted to the study of syntax and phonology. To start bringing in "meaning" was very risky, since it implied "mentalism," having to get involved with events and activities that take place in the mind; and this was awkward, things that happen in the mind are not readily available to observation—we cannot see into minds.

Earlier linguists like Zellig Harris and Leonard Bloomfield had sought to provide a collection of procedures which would "yield the correct grammatical analysis of (any) language once applied to the raw data.[8] But a formal difficulty in this presents itself over the idea of "the correct analysis": how can we ever know for certain that the analysis we have is the correct one? Maybe it will just turn out to be one of many.

There is a proposition by Ludwig Wittgenstein, that "when all possible scientific questions have been answered the problems of life remain completely untouched."[9] At a glance this could suggest a separation between science and life of a kind that will lead to mysticism; but at the core of the proposition and of Wittgenstein's "picture-theory" in general lies the theory of structure. Two central features of any "structure" are: 1) that they are not theoretical constructs (they are not "man-made" but "natural"); and 2) that they are sealed off from description.

In this sense, no science can ever hope to describe life; it is not possible. "Man is uniquely beyond the bounds of physical explanation" and will aye remain so.[10] There is even a mathematical proof we can offer as a demonstration of this courtesy of a theorem formulated by an Austrian mathematician, Kurt Gödel. His theorem makes use of both finite automata theory and recursive function theory.

Chomsky was well aware of Gödel's Theorem. Even back when he accepted the orthodox view of linguistics—that semantics should be excluded from the study—he had his own distinctive approach:

> a linguistic theory should not be identified with a manual of useful procedures, nor should it be expected to provide mechanical procedures for the discovery of grammars.... We cannot hope to say whether a particular description of the data is correct, in any absolute sense, but only that it is more correct than some alternative description of the same data.... The most that can be expected is that linguistic theory should provide criteria [an evaluative procedure] for choosing between alternative grammars.

In comparison to the Bloomfield/Harris objective, as John Lyons points out, Chomsky's objective here seems quite unassuming, but ultimately it is more ambitious. Einstein's physical system is greater than Newton's because it is more powerful, it copes more adequately with the raw data of the universe. His system can do what Newton's can do, but it can do a great deal more. Yet nowadays we know enough about systems in general to appreciate also that the Einstein version is not the last word, not in any absolute sense. Eventually another system will come to supersede it. Once this point is realized Chomsky's ambitions become clearer, he is seeking a form of ultimate criteria, universal principles by which different grammars may be evaluated.

At least one trap was lying in wait for those social scientists who saw nothing peculiar in isolating language from people; it becomes exposed through the following statement by Bloomfield:

> although we could, in principle, foretell whether a certain stimulus would cause someone to speak and, if so, exactly what he would say, in practice we could make the prediction "only if we knew the exact structure of his body at the moment."[11]

Those who assume freedom as the natural right of all people should reject the statement *intuitively*. The extended line of thought is instanced again and again by Chomsky, straight from the annals of imperialism, where as late as the mid-1960s a "think tank" of eminent, mainstream intellectuals—US scientists—had to go to their work in order to arrive at the startling conclusion that "you cannot isolate (counterinsurgency) problems from people."

Bloomfield's position does recognize that every human being is unique; he knows that no one can ever hope to fully comprehend anyone else. But his particular brand of behaviorism can make no allowance for any genuine freedom in the way a person handles language; there is no room for linguistic creativity. What remains is a kind of pathology, where syntactical components and phonemes are assembled so that eventually a body of language gets constructed, but any resemblance between it and a living force is very slight indeed; the introduction of semantics is akin to the breath of life.

In one of his more illustrious book reviews Chomsky attacked the extreme branch of behaviorism as it appears in the shape of B.F. Skinner and that approach to psychology which seeks to affirm that "what a person does is fully determined by his genetic endowment and history of reinforcement." Chomsky can barely conceal his contempt: "It would be hard to conceive of a more striking failure to comprehend even the rudiments of scientific thinking."

But it is integral to his approach that you should not halt at the point where something is revealed as false: from there you will make further discoveries by asking "what social or ideological needs" are being served by such a theory.

In the case of Skinner-style behaviorism, this is quite straightforward; in fact Skinner himself has suggested that "the control of the population as a whole must be delegated to specialists—to police, priests, owners, teachers, therapists and so on, with their specialized reinforcers and their codified contingencies."

Yet a tacit acceptance of this sort of behavioral approach is a feature of those who exercise the controlling interest in Western society. It lies at the core of the dogma of imperialism and the unswerving belief that a colonized people has neither the wit nor the will to determine its own existence. Every insurrection becomes the effect of foreign infiltration. There is no such thing as a self-motivating populist movement. Ordinary working people never go on strike except when hypnotized into it by crazed external agitators who have penetrated the shop floor. Within the terms of this argument, folk like Arthur Scargill,[12] like Castro, Allende, Mandela, are always puppets of a foreign regime. It is inconceivable that they might create strategies of their own, close to a logical contradiction.

Chomsky offers a great example of this in the person of Ho Chi Minh. For years a variety of Western intelligence agencies tried to establish his connection with Moscow but it could never be done. Such a connection could never be discovered, but to suggest the connection might not exist would have required a mammoth leap of the imagination. Instead came the following:

> No evidence has yet turned up that Ho Chi Minh is receiving current directives either from Moscow, China, or the Soviet legation in Bangkok.... It may be assumed that Moscow feels that Ho and his lieutenants have had sufficient training and experience and are sufficiently loyal to be trusted to determine their day-to-day policy without supervision.

It is only by an extension of the same logic that the fortieth president of the United States—Ronald Reagan—began to wonder, apparently in all sincerity, if Auld Nick, the very Devil himself, could be responsible for the current wrongdoing in the world. It is scarcely credible yet consistent. The global policy of his government has presupposed the existence of an international conspiracy forever engaged in novel methods of advancing its own "Communist interests while preserving the fiction of 'autonomous' national liberation movements." Thus, if the authorities are never brought any evidence of "spying" they are entitled to suppose their intelligence agents are falling down on the job. If eventually they are forced to concede that their agents are doing their work properly, then they will have to look elsewhere for an answer. At this stage, instead of reexamimining the actual premise of the argument—the existence of an international Communist conspiracy—the authorities go veering off into the outer reaches of the theory: enter the alien infiltrator, the superhuman force of evil, he of the cloven hoof. It may be the stuff of comic books, but the logic is consistent.

Generally, both logic and mathematics operate as systems of deductive reasoning; they begin from assuming the truth of one fundamental premise or set of premises, and from there any number of statements or propositions can be produced. And all of these statements or propositions will be true for as long as that original premise, or set of premises, itself remains true. But once they start showing too many signs of collapse there is no point trying to shore them all up; the entire edifice probably needs to be reconstructed, and that means a new foundation, one that will hold everything together.

Philosophers have been preoccupied for centuries by the search for that one thing they could see to be true beyond any shadow of doubt. It was this search that led René Descartes to his *cogito, ergo sum* (I think therefore I am), the one statement about the world he felt able to rely upon absolutely. It made no difference what he was thinking about, just that he was thinking; this was the fact. From that one foundation he went on to demonstrate the existence of God.

The years previous had been difficult in Europe; among other people Galileo, Kepler and Copernicus were discovering things about the physical world that did not seem compatible with the prevailing wisdom, especially that which held the earth to be the center of the universe. The implications for the Church by this modern line of reasoning were all too apparent to the ecclesiastical authorities of the day—the history of persecution is probably the history of the defense of false premises.

Just about the first move any dictatorship makes on procuring power is to have its right to that power placed beyond challenge. It is achieved by diverse methods; one such is by having the right established not simply in law or by force of arms, but as an actual "fact of nature," i.e., a law set beyond the reach of mere mortals. Thus comes about the divine right of kings and the infallibility of religious leaders.

The less blatant method is to frame the right in a constitution and have as its first principle that all challenges to The Constitution shall be deemed "unconstitutional." In South Africa, at the time of writing,[13] the African National Congress was the representative voice of the overwhelming majority of women and men who lived there; but that voice was always excluded the "right" to be heard when any "official" talks began. Yet if the racist group who held power there were to include the ANC in these talks, in effect, they would have been conceding their own illegitimacy; their "right" to power was premised solely on their appropriation of the right not to recognize the overwhelming majority of people who live in the country.

And civilized Western societies like Great Britain and the USA were content to concede them that right, as they always are, and allow the argument from tyranny to reign supreme; so yet another murderous dictatorship is entitled to do whatever it likes, it can change or not change but in the last analysis it is entirely up to itself.

During his revolutionary work in *Syntactic Structures* Chomsky abandoned a purely behaviorist approach and accepted the primacy of semantics in the study of language.[14] Some of the universal principles he sees as part of "human nature" are grammatical, e.g., rules of transformation, and these he had worked out before his movement away from orthodoxy. But once the way in which language is actually used by people is introduced into linguistics, the full complexity of the study becomes apparent, for the matter is thrown right back to what Chomsky calls "Plato's Problem." This is where

> Socrates demonstrates that an untutored slave boy knows the principles of geometry by leading him, through a series of questions, to the discovery of theorems of geometry. This experiment raises a problem that is still with us: How was the slave boy able to find truths of geometry without instruction or information?

In his own attempt at solving the problem of how folk seem to know things they have never before experienced, Plato landed in other worlds and previous existences, along with other thinkers, both before and since. An extension of the problem concerns creativity in language—not the creativity of people involved in literary art-forms, but the daily creativity of men and women and children as they go about their daily business:

> in normal speech one does not merely repeat what one has heard but produces new linguistic form—often new in one's experience or even in the history of the language—and there are no limits to such innovation.

The importance of this fact for any theory of knowledge is underlined by Chomsky. Language is so rich and sophisticated, capable of such an infinite variety of possibilities, that no strictly empirical approach can hope to account for its existence. Once we are engaged in its study at this level we are in at the heart of the study of mind; "linguistics, psychology and philosophy are no longer to be regarded as separate and autonomous disciplines."

The step Chomsky takes around this point is very bold, very courageous; it leads him away from the vanguard of contemporary linguistics. In philosophical terms he becomes, like Plato himself, a "rationalist": somebody who believes there are a priori forms of knowledge, i.e., forms of knowledge available to people outwith any experience they may have gained from being in the world. This allows of a solution to "Plato's Problem" and also to the "creativity" extension of it referred to above, which derives from another rationalist, René Descartes.

The problem is knowledge, how to give a satisfactory account for its acquisition and for the unique application each one of us makes of it. There are some things we know from our experience of being in the world, but there are other things we seem to know just by the workings of our own individual minds—mathematical truths, for example, the kind of "truths" that the "untutored slave boy" knew.

But there are other sorts of similar truths, such as the "properties" of God, i.e., "goodness," "perfection," "immortality"; then too there is our knowledge of the connecting links and relations between things and events, for example, our certain knowledge that the sun will rise tomorrow morning, etc. For Chomsky, these a priori forms of knowledge will include certain principles of universal grammar; these principles enable human beings to use the language or languages of whatever culture they chance to be born within.

Through the Middle Ages society had been segmented. In matters of the intellect, individual disciplines were inclined to keep themselves to themselves, the physical world consisting largely of a confused jumble of raw data and it was up to each to make what sense of it they could. Alongside the breakthroughs being made in the sciences from the latter part of the fifteenth century onwards, there developed a critical interest in mathematical reasoning. Also, communication was becoming more public; discussions were taking place between people. Then a hundred years or so later Descartes had his tremendous insight into the possibility of one theoretical foundation being provided for all the sciences. Even bolder, a system as powerful as the one he envisaged might provide a way of working out the connecting links and relations between God and men and things.

Yet he could find no foundation of truth in the world about him, the physical world; there was nothing he could perceive there as being true absolutely. Every last thing was open to doubt. The one and only certainty he had (I think, therefore I am) was true by the light of his own reason: Descartes knew that he existed only because he was thinking. There was no evidence for it outside of himself, his own mind. It was a *natural* judgment, one arrived at purely through his own reason, his own common sense.

Nowadays, much of the antagonism towards rationalism results from dogma, straight prejudice against (and confused by) the very idea of "mind" being "a place" where principles of reason are "stored." In his later writings Chomsky refers always to "mind/brain"; this is a way of distinguishing his own conception. It can deflect the confusion that may arise from conventional thinking, where brain is "body" but mind is "mental," somehow "not body" at all. This sort of "dualism" is associated with Descartes and others; it makes a clear separation between body and mind, where body is "physical" and mind is "metaphysical":

> When we speak of the mind, we are speaking at some level of abstraction of yet-unknown physical mechanisms of the brain, much as those who spoke of the valence of oxygen or the benzene ring were speaking at some level of abstraction about physical mechanisms, then unknown.[15]

Arguments against rationalism and the entire idea of innate forms of knowledge usually revolve round the existence or otherwise of metaphysical entities like "mind" and "soul." But in the above Chomsky is carrying the defense a stage beyond, by suggesting that there is no longer any adequate explanation of "body." At the present time of inquiry what we are left with "are a variety of forces, particles that have no mass, and other entities that would have been offensive to the 'scientific common sense' of the Cartesians." He seems to be proposing that if the most elementary "thing" in the physical world is an infinitesimal bundle of energy—instead of an infinitesimal particle of matter—then there may well be "places" where innate forms of knowledge can be located after all.

But that aspect of the problem may well turn out to have no solution at all, which last point provides another sharp distinction between Chomsky's beliefs and those of the great metaphysicians like Descartes for whom it was central that the system he hoped to construct would be powerful enough to supply the answers to everything. Chomsky dismisses that as an illusion; no theoretical construct can ever be capable of such a thing.

A way of avoiding the problem is thought possible by some via the work of other folk involved in theory of structure. Jean Piaget once suggested that Chomsky seemed aware of only two alternatives in the acquisition and application of knowledge: a) innate principles of reason; and b) knowledge that we derive directly from the world about us.[16]

Piaget's comment came in the late 1960s and he refers to a third process, that of "internal equilibration," a process "governed by general laws of organization" which is "self-regulating." Here he cites the findings of a group of French mathematicians ("Nicholas Bourbaki" is the group's pseudonym); in particular their "discovery of three 'parent structures', that is, three not further reducible 'sources' of all other structures." The three structures referred to are : a) Algebraic b) Order; c) Topological. This trio encompasses the kind of activities associated with judgment.

Chomsky was aware of Piaget's line of argument, he rejected it:

> Piaget and I actually took part in a lengthy discussion about these topics a couple of years later. The problem is that there simply is nothing to the third process that he mentions. It's impossible to formulate, and it turns out to be nothing but metaphor and empty rhetoric. By now I think these ideas have largely been abandoned in cognitive psychology simply because they don't get anywhere.[17]

Chomsky sees "libertarian conceptions (being derived) by Rousseau from Cartesian principles of body and mind," then being "developed further in French and German Romanticism" and on through the "libertarian social theory of Wilhelm von

Humboldt." But this view may underestimate the ramifications of the intellectual struggle going on in Britain around that time.

Rousseau was influenced by Andrew Fletcher (1655–1716) who favored the Greek ideal of the little nation whose "seat of government (would) remain in a city small enough to contain a face-to-face community where people could be under one another's eyes most of the time."[18] Fletcher wanted federalism and was strongly opposed to being governed by remote control, whether from London or anywhere else. George Davie points to the influence here of "the reformation ideal of a constitution finely balanced as between church and state."

It is too easy to disregard this from a late twentieth-century Western perspective but the "ideal" can provide a system of checks and balances "through the cooperation of a pair of mutually complementary assemblies, the one concerned with politics and law, the other with the sphere of ethics and faith." If this sounds anachronistic, it should be compared to the present system of Western democracy where voting is usually just a method of "ratifying decisions that have already been made" by one or two people in an office.

In Scotland during the last years of the seventeenth century, between a third and a fifth of the people were reported as "having died or fled" due to the effects of famine.[19] The Darien Scheme had just collapsed and the economy was more or less bankrupt. On a wider intellectual level this was a decade or so after the German thinker Leibnitz and the English thinker Newton—unbeknown to each other—had been locked in the simultaneous creation of differential calculus. Meanwhile, in Edinburgh, certain premises were still not open to challenge and a nineteen-year-old student by the name of Aikenhead was executed for having dared to demand "evidence for the dogma that the moral blindness of natural man can sometimes be overcome by a grace-inspired reading of the bible."[20]

What developed from all of this was a fierce debate on the problem of how to reconcile economic expansion with the moral and intellectual consciousness of the population as a whole. For those unfamiliar with George Davie's work on the Scottish Enlightenment this can appear a rather surprising "problem." It may be thought obvious that the greater the technological and economic progress in a country, the greater the benefits must accrue to the country as a whole. But, in reality, such conclusions are only guaranteed in party political broadcasts.

One clearly defined route to economic expansion lies in the production of highly skilled and trained individuals who are to take on specialized employment. This can lead to the demand for an educational system geared precisely to the production of experts and specialists. Under the influence of John Locke and others, this was happening in England, and many folk north of the border were pushing for the same thing. Andrew Fletcher was not one of them.

Fletcher argued that an educational system devoted to the production of specialists would result in a situation where none of the educated community would be fit to govern the nation, given that being fit to govern the nation entails the capacity for decision-making in general contexts. This capacity involves the power of judgment and critical evaluation, which is developed more potently by the ability to see beyond the limits of your own discipline. If the educational system is to thrust groups of people into separate compartments, then none will be equipped to take the wide view necessary. No longer does it become possible for the poet to discuss methodology with sculptors and electricians. Reasoning devices like mathematics, logic, and intuition will stagnate, this being abetted by the decline in subjects thought to be impractical, e.g., philosophy, the classics, the study of languages and other cultures, these very subjects which encourage a general approach to the world.

In this scenario actual knowledge itself becomes at a premium, cut off from those who are not "specializing." And gradually the majority of men and women and children become divorced from those areas where "experts" reign supreme. What remains is not only repugnant but disastrous:

> a society spiritually split between over-specialized boffins on the one hand and unthinking proles on the other is not merely repellent from a moral point of view, because of its tolerating or even encouraging the intellectual backwardness of the masses, but at the same time is also inherently an unstable basis for the material progress it seeks to sustain (and) the stultification of the majority (will) affect the mental balance of society as a whole. . .[21]

If there is any irony at work at all in this nightmarish world being envisaged by Davie it could lie in its resemblance to the medieval order of ignorance which Descartes had sought to eradicate by constructing his unified system of knowledge. At the root of the matter is the segmentation of knowledge, the push for individual disciplines to keep themselves to themselves; and in line with that the creation of "experts: and "keepers-of-the-faith" (priests, owners, teachers, therapists and so on, with their specialized reinforcers and their codified contingencies), whether they be monks in a monastery or members of a government planning department.

As far as Fletcher could see, once Scotland became incapable of creating its own governing elite it would cease to be free, it would become an intellectual desert, having to import an elite from the English upper classes. He advocated a return to the "solider sorts of learning,"[22] as in Oxford and Cambridge, for it is to be noted that both these seats of higher education continued as before, prior to the new approach and altered curriculum, designed to hasten economic progress. It could be argued, perhaps, that the classical approach being so rigorously defended by the Oxbridge traditionalists was devoted to that most subtle of all specializations, the production of a leadership class. This class dominated most of the English-speaking world then, and for folk who live in countries connected to the former Empire very little has changed, certainly not in Scotland.

The continued erosion of the generalist approach to education ensures that the entire system comes to exist as a straight reinforcement of the prevailing right-wing authority. Beyond Oxbridge about the best we can hope for is the paternalistic liberalism of a William Cobbett, whose "ideas of democratic or mass education seem to have been drawn from his experiences in the army. The model of mass education is for him the NCO explaining the 'naming of the parts' to the recruits."[23] And it is within this context, no matter how well intentioned are its orthodox left-liberal principles, that the educational system comes to be nothing more than "a reification of the notion that culture is synonymous with property. And the essentially acquisitive attitude to culture, "education" and "a good accent" is simply an aspect of the competitive, status-conscious class structure of . . . society as a whole."[24]

Thus, across the mainstream political spectrum, from "hardline" left to "extremist" right, different games are being played with the same set of rules. The end product is hierarchy, whether it be a form of meritocracy or a mix of that with the usual hereditary privileges for rank and/or riches.

This is a world where the skepticism of Locke, Berkeley, Hume, and the rest has led to the ideological behaviorism of those responsible for the global and domestic policies of Western civilization during the past couple of hundred years. It is a world where there are no universal principles, whether of freedom or anything else. People are "blank slates" upon which anything is to be scraped by those who have assumed the right to power. Knowledge gets doled out in the form of rewards and punishment exercises. Those who have been produced to govern on behalf of the rulers decide the curriculum: history will concern the lives and loves of famous personalities;

politics is a field of endeavor best left to those who specialize in it, i.e. Members of Parliament and Members of the Media; poverty and deprivation become the concepts of social science, death and disease the experience of the medical profession.

Both the Cartesian Common Sense tradition as developed by Chomsky and the Common Sense tradition developed in Scotland are premised on forms of natural reason. In the former, this becomes grounds for rationalism whereas in the Scottish philosophical tradition such a necessity does not arise, there is no need to become involved in innateness hypotheses. Each shares a belief in fundamental principles that are inherent in all people. These include the faculty of judgment which lies at the heart not only of reason, but of the will to freedom. This faculty is neither learned nor is it taught. But neither is it a "thing," whether material or immaterial.

The skills involved in judgment are mathematical, logical, intuitive; they can be refined and improved, or else they can remain fallow. It does not follow that highly educated folk will prove more capable of good judgment than those who "fail" within the mainstream educational system.

Chomsky destroys any presuppositions about the relationship between higher education and the ability to think clearly and critically. The educated classes have more access to information than the vast majority of ordinary men and women, but it is rarely in their own economic interest to seek it out and see what it amounts to. This does not have to imply a deliberate policy, let alone the existence of a conspiracy:

> the intellectual elite is the most heavily indoctrinated sector [of society], for good reasons. It's their role as secular priesthood to really believe the nonsense they put forth. Other people can repeat it, but it's not that crucial that they believe it because, after all, they are the guardians of the faith. Except for the very rare person who's just an outright liar, it's hard to be a convincing

exponent of the faith unless you've internalized it and come to believe it.

An interesting example of this is the novelist Saul Bellow, "a propagandist's delight," according to Chomsky in his review of Bellow's *To Jerusalem and Back*,[25] which he describes as "a catalogue of What Every Good American Should Believe, as compiled by the Israeli Information Ministry." He concludes the review by referring to the "critical acclaim (the book) has received (as) revealing, with regard to the state of American intellectual life."

But that applies equally to Great Britain, where Saul Bellow is always being pushed by the mainstream literary establishment, including the "radical" younger writers who defer to him as the one infallible source of American integrity and clarity of vision. When a fine introduction to Chomsky's political writings was published, the London *Independent* newspaper gave it for review to Auberon Waugh, a right-wing author and journalist of the day. Waugh was perceived as a sort of no-nonsense skeptic, just the man to debunk pretentious left-wing upstarts such as Noam Chomsky. Elsewhere Waugh was revealed as an "occasional mouthpiece for some highly sensitive "gossip" or "intelligence smears" by covert agencies within the British State.[26]

Finding new ways of denying reality is a key function of the mainstream intelligentsia. Language provides unlimited opportunity for it. Before it is possible to enter any debate about the unspeakable atrocities being perpetrated on people every day of the week, in all parts of the world, a slow trudge through semantics has to begin. What do we mean by *pain*? What do we mean by *suffering*? Around this point the very words get surrounded, captured by inverted commas—e.g., what do we mean by "torture"—thus throwing into doubt the very existence of the experience. A distinction is created between the actual experience and the "concept of the experience." In creating this distinction, a closed system is put into operation: only those who specialize in discussing concepts will be admitted. The actual experience of atrocity becomes redundant. It becomes the predicate instead of the subject; we no longer refer to "atrocity," we refer to the "concept of atrocity," where concept is subject and atrocity predicate. Refugees' reports are excluded. So too are folk who are likely to be affected by such reports:

> The ardently opinionated, the ardent in all forms, the raisers of voices, the thumpers on the table, the "swearers," the passionate, those who burst into tears—these are all absent. . . . For the "professional" exists through a language that acquits him of personal involvement . . ."[27]

Such specialists are paid for their experience of experiences they never encounter, their experience is conceptual. They get paid for their experience of every concept under the sun; from the concept of happiness to the concept of torture, from the concept of malnutrition to the concept of dampness in council housing and its relation to the concept of death from lung disease. They exclude the actual experience from the terms of the argument; they "categorise in the absence of that which is being categorised,"[28] they get rid of the premise.

One year after the European Convention on Human Rights had "found the British Government guilty of 'torture, inhuman and degrading treatment,'" a famous judgment was delivered, soon known as the "Torturers' Charter";

> after a torture case had been brought against the Greek Colonels . . . the Commission defined "inhuman treatment" as "at least such treatment as deliberately causes severe suffering, mental or physical." 'Torture' was "inhuman treatment which has a purpose, such as the obtaining of information or confession, or the infliction of punishment, and it is generally an aggravated form of inhuman treatment." "Degrading treatment"

> was "treatment or punishment of an individual which grossly humiliates him before others or drives him to act against his will."[29]

which gives us a fair idea of what the Callaghan-led Labour Government had been found guilty in 1976.

But this judgment occurred one year afterwards, when four men and one woman found themselves in front of the Belfast City Commission. One of the four men was a boy of sixteen who complained of Assault During Interview by the RUC. The experiences he complained of included being "struck thirty times mostly to the stomach and having his hair pulled" during the first interview; receiving "dozens of blows" during the second interview; while in the third

> he said he had been punched in the stomach, the kidneys, and the back more than fifty times and slapped around the face with an open hand. He said that his mouth had been burnt with a lighted cigarette, that he had been made to strip, and was struck in the testicles and around the kidneys.

A report by a refugee. . . But a report of what? Torture? Rough treatment? Hard luck? Interrogation? Being interviewed?

Defining experiences are notoriously difficult, especially those endured by other people. State authority thinks it a job best left to the experts. In this particular instance the expert was Lord Justice McGonigal, "former Second World War commando and a founder of the SAS." He was quick to indicate that "a certain roughness of treatment" was allowed by the *European Commission* according to the above definition; and this could take the form of slaps or blows of the hand on the head or face and also underlines the fact that the point up to which prisoners and the public may accept physical violence as being neither cruel nor excessive varies between different societies and even between different sections of them.

Such equivocation allowed Lord Justice McGonigal to draw that wee bit closer to the elimination of the experience altogether when he did his own exercise in semantics: "Inhuman treatment is . . . treatment causing severe suffering. Torture is an aggravated form of inhuman treatment and degrading conduct is conduct which grossly humiliates." At which point experts who specialize in encountering concepts can instigate a further debate on the meaning of "grossness" or "severity," or the meaning of the concept "aggravation."

This kind of dualist thinking has a long tradition, reminiscent of an ancient line of thought which believed every single thing in the world had its own tiny god. It also lands us back with Descartes and the rationalists in one corner, the British empiricists in the other. While in between is the problem of knowledge and how to connect reason with experience, thought with extension (mind with body), essence with existence.

The argument given on behalf of the British Labour Government above is in sharp opposition to common sense and natural reason. It amounts to the following: people who have been tortured do not have valid grounds for knowing what torture is.

When refugees' reports are heeded, it is usually as an aid to apportioning blame, to discover which individual is responsible. During this, the position of the victims will be brought into question: Are they innocent or guilty? Are they innocent victims or guilty victims? It so happens that in the case mentioned above the sixteen-year-old boy was released. It was conceded that he might have been treated roughly but, if so, then any statements made by him were "not admissible in evidence," which not only refers to any so-called confession, it also refers to the complaints he made concerning the RUC and their Assault During Interview.

The relativist position of the European Commission should be kept also in mind. By extension, there is one legal system for the powerful and another legal system for the powerless. But nobody expects anything else anyway, not even the powerless themselves, and that seems the only justification. "Terror and torture" governments should just exercise caution occasionally, lest they "provoke hostile reactions in world capitals."

The crucial feature of skepticism is that it subjects premises and principles to scrutiny. Nothing is taken for granted: "truths" are no longer allowed to be assumed, they must be put to the test and verified. This has obvious dangers for metaphysical theories to do with "mind" as also for truths connected with religious belief and faith. But in the early eighteenth century, people in Scotland wanted to fight clear of the dogmatic prejudice that resulted in the state killing of the student who dared to demand "evidence."

The critical method of John Locke and others seemed to offer this possibility through its rejection of innate forms of knowledge. Nothing would be admitted as true unless it was seen to be true. Unlike Descartes, they did not want to construct one unifying system to yield ultimate knowledge of all the mysteries of the universe. They were content to clear away the muddle of conventional thought, thereby allowing the scientists to get on with the real work, applying the proper methods of observation and experimentation. Unfortunately, formal problems over the "two" kinds of knowledge still arose.

Empiricist approaches become bogged down in the theory of knowledge, tending as they do towards "atomism," the belief that suggests it is possible to discover the nature of the whole by a strict examination of the parts. The ancient form of this philosophy centered on the notion that "the whole visible universe has arisen by the cohesion of small invisible particles, the atoms." This further applied to the mind which was composed of "very smooth, delicate and round (atoms); or, as Lucretius put it . . . the smallest, roundest and most mobile that there are."[30]

But if we do come to know things only piecemeal, via our sensory experience, then "Plato's Problem" must crop up sooner or later. How can we know the properties of a triangle if triangles do not exist in the world? How do we know about the connecting links and relations between things if none of those links or relations can be discovered as things in the world about us? And if we learn about the whole by assembly of the parts, how are we able to recognize the whole when it is complete? Davie points to the influence of Irish philosophy as decisive on the Scottish tradition here, in particular the work of George Berkeley (although Francis Hutcheson is also of importance).

There is a vague echo of Chomsky when instead of worrying over the existence of "mind" Berkeley proceeds to dispense with "body"; he rejects the existence of matter altogether. A body exists only when it is being perceived. We never know any objects in the physical world at all, only our own perceptions of them. But this does not mean that bodies come in and out of existence, or that the world disappears when we close our eyes—common charges against him, still being levelled against him into the twentieth century, such that "we have not so much reason to admire the strength of Berkeley's genius, as his boldness in publishing to the world an opinion which the unlearned would be apt to interpret as the sign of a crazy intellect."[31]

His influence in Scotland was primary, none left a greater mark on the Scottish Enlightenment. He personally wrote to congratulate a group of youths from the Edinburgh Students' Society on their understanding of his "system" and his paradoxical and provocative argument that there was perhaps less difference between Locke and his illiberal opponents, whether Scottish or otherwise, than was generally supposed, and that, properly sifted and consistently developed, the experimental pragmatic principle which was Locke's greatest contribution was likely to lead men back to a God-centered philosophy not unlike that of Halyburton.[32]

But one of the most powerful voices raised in opposition to the Irish philosopher was not of the "unlearned" section of society, rather it was the "learned" Dr. Johnson. Johnson held the Ghàidhlig language in contempt; while visiting Scotland he scoffed at the very idea that it might also have had a written form. Rather than telling him to fuck off, Scots in the vicinity offered arguments, which the "learned doctor" refused to accept. Of course it was not the "unlearned" of whom Berkeley was so scathing but his colleagues and peers, the "learned," in the areas of philosophy and science; those unable to trust "their own senses . . . and [who] after all their labouring . . . are forced to own that . . . self-evident or demonstrative knowledge of the existence of sensible things" is just not possible.[33] Their work led to "forlorn Scepticism," foundering on the belief that we know our ideas of reality but never reality itself. If what these "learned" believed were true then it is impossible for us ever to know the world at all, we are doomed to remain in a state of ignorance for all eternity. The "illiterate bulk of mankind . . . walk the high-road of plain, common sense . . . governed by the dictates of nature, for the most part easy and undisturbed."[34] This because their belief in God is absolute, as with Berkeley himself.

Berkeley was answering John Locke, who had distinguished between "primary ideas" as representative of "primary qualities" existent in the world, e.g., size, shape, extension, and "secondary" ideas representative of "secondary qualities" that cannot exist in themselves, e.g., smells or sounds. The existence of these "secondary qualities" is dependent upon the agency of an active being, e.g., a thing smells only if it is being smelled, the wind sounds only when it is being heard.

But Berkeley demonstrated that "primary qualities"—qualities as they are in themselves—can never be represented truly by our ideas of them. He further argued that "primary qualities" are every bit as dependent on the perception of an active being as are "secondary qualities." Nothing at all exists, said Berkeley, not unless perceived by an active being or itself a being capable of perceiving. He was a Bishop of the Anglican Church in Ireland, based firstly at Derry City, then later at Cloyne, and his solution to the problem lies in the existence of God: matter is always and eternally being perceived by the Almighty.

The existence of God is the premise of his philosophy; the world is always in His presence. It is a line of thought in the tradition of the concept of Divine Illumination—there is never a time when we are not in the presence of God, through Him the world is revealed, and so on—and can be traced back to Augustine and earlier neo-Platonists, Christian and not Christian. Berkeley argued that we experience the world "immediately," as brute data; there is nothing between us and it. And, further, that these brute data are elements of a divine language, the language of God Himself. Science may describe the world but not explain it. He formulated a theory of vision and an alternative approach to geometry, stressing "touch" as distinct from "sight," leading

> the way in shewing how we learn to perceive the distance of an object from the eye. . . . He made the distinction between that extension and figure which we perceive by sight only, and that which we perceive by touch; calling the first, visible, the last, tangible extension and figure.[35]

As far as he is concerned "the externality we attribute to the objects of our senses consists simply in the fact that our 'sensations occur in groups, held together by a permanent law.'"[36] In terms of straight empiricism, this offers good progress in the theory of knowledge, but his position still lapses into atomism; the gap between our sensory experience of the world and our actual knowledge of the world remains as wide as ever.

An escape from the difficulty appears through the work of the Scottish philosopher Thomas Reid whose insight is of significance in the development of theory of structure:

> Every operation of the senses, in its very nature, implies judgment or belief, as well as simple apprehension. . . . When I perceive a tree before me, my faculty of seeing gives me not only a notion or simple apprehension of the tree, but a belief of its existence, and of its figure, distance and magnitude; and this judgment or belief is not got by comparing ideas, it is included in the very nature of perception. [These] original and natural judgments . . . make up what is called the common sense of mankind.[37]

Our knowledge of the world does not derive from singular sensations of brute physical data. It comes about through an elementary synthesis. Knowledge begins from judgment. When we sense something, we are perceiving it at one and the same time. There is no gap between coming into sensory contact with something and the knowledge of what contact with the something amounts to. And this "knowledge of what contact with the something amounts to" includes an understanding of connecting links and relations such as must be essential for "a belief of [something's] existence, and of its figure, distance and magnitude."

This strand of thought distinguishes Reid not only from Berkeley but from his great rival, David Hume. Hume was opposed to the idea that experience could ever bring knowledge of connecting links or causal relations. We cannot experience these "necessary connections"; what happens is that we "feel" such things to be true.

But in common to both Scottish philosophers is an acceptance of a form of natural reason. In the case of Hume this seems to end at "instinct"; Reid goes further, common sense is a faculty of judgment held in common by all members of humankind. The Common Sense tradition, whether of Chomsky, Descartes, Reid, or Rousseau, is not a question of instinct, not unless by instinct we mean something that can comprise logic, mathematics, and intuition.

The key feature of Reid's position is irreducibility; it is in opposition to any form of atomism. If it is at all possible to discuss a reductive process, then it can only be something along the lines of the "Bourbaki" "parent-structures," the algebraic, order, and topological. These are the processes of understanding, of thought. And in terms of further exploratory work here, it is of interest to note that if we stick to mathematics in the slipstream of Thomas Reid then, we enter the field of spherical geometry in which he was engaged some fifty years ahead of his time.[38] The concepts of time and space have loomed into view, not only in the world of science but in the world of ideas generally.

And for the politics of late eighteenth-century Scotland a philosophical context is also set for the libertarian consciousness that was developing through thinkers like John Millar and Dugald Stewart, both of whom believed in the general dissemination of knowledge.

George Davie describes this period as the "pinnacle" of Scottish philosophy, when came the creation of its many great textbooks. There are obvious parallels here with what was happening in France, with the rise of discussion groups among tradesmen and craftsmen, inextricably bound in with the basic notion that if people can think for themselves they can also determine their own existence. In Paris, around the turn of last century, it was not uncommon for the great mathematicians of the time to lecture to as many as 1,200 folk at a sitting.

Needless to say, radical lines of thought were not confined to any single field of endeavor. How could they be when the very essence of the argument concerned the universalizability of knowledge, that no boundaries were to exist. Ideas of freedom and self-determination, the attempted unshackling of bolts and chains, were being discussed in different parts of Great Britain. The work of the poets was of significance, not only that of Robert Burns,[39] but also poets like Robert Tannahill, Sandy Rodgers, and Alexander Wilson—the last two of whom were gaoled at different times for sedition. Both Tannahill and Wilson were weavers to trade; eventually the latter was under so much pressure from the authorities that he emigrated from Paisley to the USA, where he went on, in the best generalist tradition, to become the co-founder of American ornithology.[40]

Wilson had been tossed into the dungeon for lampooning local politicians. When he landed in the USA, he took various jobs, including schoolteacher. He later developed his interest in art, in particular drawing birds, and nowadays is regarded as the "grandfather" of American ornithology. In his lifetime, he published seven of the final nine volumes of his collection of the birds of America. He travelled throughout the country, where possible drawing the birds in their habitat, whereas Audubon had the birds brought to him. All of Wilson's collection eventually was published in four complete volumes, and this beautiful work can be seen, with permission, in Paisley Central Library, Renfrewshire. At the same location, also with permission, you can see that other beautiful work, James Audubon's, in four mammoth volumes.

Another weaver by the name of Wilson was in communication with Thomas Muir, the radical lawyer, and involved in organizing discussion groups with other workers. Thirty years later, while in his mid-sixties, he was hanged at Glasgow Green, at the foot of Saltmarket, in front of a crowd said to number twenty thousand. He was James "Purly" Wilson, so-called through his invention of the purl stitch. Official history for the next 150 years described him as an illiterate half-wit, that he had been led astray by infiltrators.[41]

Aside from Thomas Muir he was in contact with John Baird, the Condorrat weaver hanged at Stirling alongside Andrew Hardie. The three men were executed for their part in the Scottish Insurrection; there were eighty-eight counts of high treason in Scotland during that one year alone (1820). Instead of honoring these men, the political establishment in Scotland continues to pay its public respect to the so-called

"Merchants," individuals who made extreme fortunes in the slave trade and in the tobacco industry by the employment of an enslaved workforce.

The name of "the Ettrick Shepherd" might sound unlikely in the above context. Yet in a sense the work of James Hogg is every bit as crucial in this generalist, common sense tradition as is the life of Alexander Wilson. As well as being a noted poet he published a great deal of prose. His novel *The Private Memoirs and Confessions of a Justified Sinner* appeared in 1824 and is his masterpiece. But within mainstream Departments of English literature, this novel is regarded as a fluke—that is, when it is being regarded at all. If evaluated solely within this restricted field the novel seems destined to remain a fluke forever.[42]

Nowhere else is there to be found even a suggestion of that strange and deadliest of ironies which Hogg perpetrates, bending reality, in the latter pages of the story. This is the point where real-life members of the contemporary literati of Edinburgh are suddenly introduced into the tale, thereby offering an illusion of "natural reality," while lending their own personal weight to the "authenticity" of the narrative. The literati being portrayed by Hogg were in the main contemptuous of his inferior social standing. As well as being a famous poet, he had spent much of his life as a shepherd (until his late teens he was close to illiterate) and he spoke in the language of his own cultural background. There was a tendency among his peers to patronize the poetry while failing to appreciate the prose. Hogg's novel is written in the ordinary standard English literary form of the period. When he brings the literati into the story, he has them speak in that same standard form.

But then he introduces himself into the story and this "self" is the man who is employed at wheeling and dealing in ewes, lambs and rams at country markets; not the "self" as writer. He has this shepherd "self" speak in the phoneticized language of someone who, by English literary standards, is a certain social inferior. The irony works on different levels but the most hair-raising one of the lot is that which is structured on the premise that somebody who speaks in a "culturally debased" linguistic form could not conceivably create this prose masterpiece in the imperial language of English.

But such preposterous elitism is still rampant in contemporary literary circles where in a recent interview with the poet Craig Raine it was yet another example of "the intellectual elite (as) the most indoctrinated sector" of society. In a discussion of the medium in which he works in relation to his "working-class" background Raine was quite willing to concede that the actual artform itself, poetry, belonged to the upper reaches of society. But the folk from his own "working-class" background do have their own artforms, he was at pains to point out, his father for instance had been a "fine raconteur."[43]

This kind of myopic nonsense is extraordinary. All it takes to disprove the point is a walk into the local library—although from there you might have a search, of course; the poetry written by people who "fail" our educational system is likely to be discovered in the "local history" section.[44]

The year after the publication of Hogg's novel the French mathematician and astronomer, Pierre Laplace, had summarized "the development of deterministic mechanics"[45] as follows:

> We must envisage the present state of the universe as the effect of its previous state, and as the cause of that which will follow. An intelligence that could know, at a given instant, all the forces governing the natural world, and the respective position of the entities which compose it, if in addition it was great enough to analyze all this information, would be able to embrace in a single formula the movements of the largest bodies in the universe and those of the lightest atoms: nothing would be uncertain for it, and the future, like the past, would be entirely present to its observation.

With slight adjustments here and there, this could be turned into a textbook approach to semantics-free linguistics or, perhaps, for any purely behavioral approach to the study of mind. And with other slight adjustments it becomes an argument on behalf of the existence of God. But the God so conceived would stand in brooding opposition to human creativity and the principle of natural reason, utterly opposed to any puny demonstrations of self-determined activity and the will to freedom. It is a conception of God abhorrent not only to such as George Berkeley but also to William Blake and Søren Kierkegaard.

The Anglo-American tradition approves of David Hume the great empiricist and skeptic but is less certain of the Hume "who spoke of those parts of our knowledge that are derived 'from the original hand of nature' and that are 'a species of instinct.'"[46]

Chomsky does pick up on that side of him but without being aware of him in the context of Scottish Common Sense philosophy. The thing that excited Immanuel Kant about Hume's thought concerns the theory of knowledge and the Scotsman's denial of "the existence of necessary connections in nature" and his severing of any "logical relations from those of the real world." But this also influenced thinkers of a diametrically opposed view, e.g., the Christian mystic Johan Hamann, whose regard for Hume is somewhat reminiscent of Rousseau's regard for Voltaire.

Hamann's own influence on Kierkegaard and existentialism can be readily appreciated from the following:

> Nature is no ordered whole: so-called sensible men are blinkered beings who walk with a fine treat because they are blind to the true and profoundly disturbing character of reality, sheltered by it from their man-made contraptions; if they glimpsed it as it is—a wild dance—they would go out their minds. How dare these

> pathetic pedants impose on the vast world of continuous, fertile, unpredictable, divine creation their own narrow, desiccated categories?[47]

The important factor being derived here is the ultimate unknowability of the brute physical data of reality. For people like Hamann, a return is now sanctioned to that conception of God that is premised on absolute, and logical, incomprehensibility.

In the same year Laplace died, 1827, another blow was being struck against deterministic mechanics and its "anti-existential" implications. A Scottish botanist from Montrose by the name of Robert Brown observed

> the behavior of pollen grains—particles from various plants which . . . measured something like 1/5000 of an inch—when immersed in water. What he discovered was that these particles perform a constant, agitated, and apparently erratic motion which has nothing to do with any currents moving in the water. . . . "These motions were such as to satisfy me, after frequently repeated observation, that they arose neither from currents in the fluid, nor from its gradual evaporation, but belonged to the particle itself."[48]

As with Reid's elemental judgment there is an "irreducibility" being posited here, a structure that simply cannot be broken down into any "constituent parts." The particle is a network of impulses or motions of a self-determining/self-regulatory kind, i.e., it seems to be governed by itself and for itself (but a confusion here could lead to the difficulty Descartes had and the split between "I" and "I think").

This phenomenon has become known in the world of science generally as "Brownian Motion" and was the subject of a decisive paper by Einstein which finally "convinced the skeptics of the existence of atoms." These atoms differ from those of the ancient materialists; they are structures as opposed to elemental, indivisible "bits": when these atoms have been "split" worlds have blown up.

People confined by the parameters of their own specialization probably assume Einstein discovered his physical system by a close reading of the collected works of Isaac Newton, but ideas develop and shift in innumerable ways. The concepts of "irreducibility" and "elementary synthesis" are implicit in some remarks of the Spanish cubist painter, Juan Gris:

> the architectural abstraction of the elements in a picture must be explored by the painter as if he were his own spectator. . . . Until the work is completed he must remain ignorant of its appearance as a whole. To copy a preconceived appearance is like copying the appearance of a model. . . . From this it is clear that the subject does not materialise in the appearance of the picture, but that the subject, in materialising, gives the picture its appearance.[49]

At this level the technical problems to be resolved by the artist concern space and time. These have been the preoccupations of, among others, artists like Cezanne, Claude Monet, Gertrude Stein, James Joyce, Franz Kafka, Carlos Williams, and also W.S. Graham and Samuel Beckett. Tom Leonard writes of the last two named and

> that area of present-time consciousness [they] give to their personae; and their personae in turn pass it on to the reader. It's a very political thing to do, since it seems to assume that the only—and equal—value that can be placed on any human being is in the fact that the human being actually exists.[50]

The most crucial aspect of James Hogg's achievement is linked to this "present-time consciousness" and the way in which he succeeded in embellishing himself in the text. Any attempt to isolate him from the "reality" of his "fiction" leaves the reader stranded in strange loops and warps; a technical term for this is "recursiveness."

In the summary of deterministic mechanics given by Pierre Laplace, a formal problem arises. Is the "intelligence" he refers to capable of "embracing itself" while "embracing the universe"? If the "intelligence" is itself a part of the universe then that should go without saying. This means it must "embrace itself" while "embracing the universe," as it "embraces itself" "embracing the universe" "embracing itself" "embracing the universe" and so on *ad infinitum* throughout the spiral of all eternity. If the "intelligence" is not of "this" universe, then the concept "universe" requires redefining. Perhaps one solution will be to create a second universe, one more powerful than the first, so that the "intelligence" can belong to it and be capable of embracing the smaller one.

When that happens a separation takes place between "intelligence" and "universe." But probably the first implication concerns the power of the "intelligence"; it simply cannot be as powerful as we thought, since it is bound to run up against the "embracing itself" problem and can never become capable of embracing this second, more powerful universe. Maybe a third universe is the answer.

This sort of problem turns up in various disciplines and involves finite automata theory and recursive function theory. It was central to the theorem formulated by Kurt Gödel and published in 1931 as a response to *Principia Mathematica*,[51] a three-volume work on mathematical logic by A.E. Whitehead and Bertrand Russell. One thing demonstrated is that if there is any "system comprehensive enough to (embrace) the whole of arithmetic,"[52] then there cannot be any method of proving it—not unless the proof can employ rules and procedures different to the actual system itself. But if a different set of rules and procedures is allowed then how are we to find out if the set is valid or not? If there is no possibility of proving a correct analysis to be the correct analysis, then perhaps we would be as well dispensing with the search for one altogether.

Sir William Hamilton edited the works of Thomas Reid. In his day he was a famous and controversial Common Sense philosopher, whose "notorious hostility to algebra" was no doubt influenced by Reid's rejection of atomism and experimental work in the "space and time" of spherical geometry.[53] Two of Hamilton's pupils have to be mentioned here. The first is James Clerk Maxwell, one of the greatest mathematicians of all time; he has been likened to Michael Faraday, as "Newton was to Galileo and Kepler."[54] There is an interesting personal detail provided by Faraday, where the old physicist compliments Maxwell—who was forty years his junior—on his ability to break down even the most esoteric formulae in such a way that somebody who is not a specialist is able to comprehend the issues involved. The second pupil was James Ferrier (poet and philosopher), and it is Ferrier who

> sorts out with a sure hand, the incredible complexities of the empirically based self-knowledge which lies at the root of common sense . . . combining with this Wittgensteinian aperçu the complementary insights, due to Sartre and Merleau-Ponty . . . [on] the relation of sight and touch.[55]

that aspect of David Hume's thought which is known to have influenced the phenomenology of Edmund Husserl.[56]

The development of the Common Sense tradition in Scotland allows for an escape from rationalism while managing to keep that fundamental will to freedom, the very heart of natural reason. And this should be borne in mind when, in reference to his overall view of the study of mind,[57] Chomsky speaks of

> studies by British Neoplatonists of the seventeenth century that explored the categories and principles of

> perception and cognition along lines that were later extended by Kant and that were discovered, independently in twentieth-century gestalt psychology.[58]

When he dispenses with the search for "the correct analysis," Chomsky brings in the search for an "evaluative procedure" that will enable us to "choose between alternative grammars." The question may then be asked: How will we know that the "evaluative procedure" is valid? It will be valid if it is capable of doing the job; and it will prove its power if it can achieve what the last one achieved, and then achieve a little bit more. In reference to his "critique of the structuralist approach," Chomsky points out that it

> really has nothing to do with incompleteness. The problem is that Harris, Bloomfield, and others were seeking a system of analytic taxonomic procedures that could carry them from a text from some language to a description of that language, and we now know that such procedures simply do not exist. My critique was essentially based on that observation.[59]

Arguments from human nature and fixed principles are usually regarded as reactionary by the orthodox left. They take it to lead to hierarchy, people being born to rule or to serve; people being born lazy or talented, being born good at mathematics, or at dancing or painting pictures, or being born selfish, etc. Such arguments are thought to suggest that we are not born free at all but are chained to our essential selves and thus have our lives, and the lives of our children, determined for us in ways that are forever beyond our own control. There may be elements of this that can be framed validly. Chomsky looks on "human nature . . . as a system of a sort familiar in the biological world, a system of 'mental organs.'" Against the "left-liberal spectrum" his defense takes the following course:

Human talents vary considerably, within a fixed framework that is characteristic of the species and that permits ample scope for creative work, including the creative work of appreciating the achievements of others. This should be a matter for delight rather than a condition to be abhorred. Those who assume otherwise must be adopting the tacit premise that people's rights or social reward are somehow contingent on their abilities.

But for most mainstream intellectuals a true democracy is a form of meritocracy, a system whereby highly educated specialists will be rewarded in accordance with the quantity of knowledge they have consumed in their specialist subject; in this kind of society a twenty-three-year-old university graduate will begin his or her working life at a salary some two to three times that of a woman or man who has spent the past thirty years working on a factory production line. As Chomsky has said, meritocracies "insofar as they exist at all, are simply a social malady to be overcome much as slavery had to be eliminated at an earlier stage of human history."

The basic principle of humankind is freedom, the right to not be tortured, the right to not be raped, the right to not be violated, the right to not be colonized in any way whatsoever. It is an inalienable right; whether it is deduced or whether it has to be discovered in any other manner is not of great significance—such questions can only be of ultimate interest to those whose ideological position is served by obscuring the issue. Either we do battle on behalf of the basic principle or we do not. This seems to me to be Chomsky's position. It is not a new one but it remains as dangerous as ever. I cannot conceive of someone reading deeply on Chomsky's work and failing to be moved by it. His writings are banned in some countries and anathema to the ruling minorities of most of the rest.

NB All the quotations not referred to by footnote number are taken from *The Chomsky Reader*, edited by James Peck. There is a fine essay by P.G. Lucas, *Some Speculative and Critical Philosophers (1600–1750)*, which helped greatly to clear my head. It is crucial to mention the conversations I've had with Tom Leonard over the past fifteen years or so, and here with particular reference to the "existential voice" in literature and related problems of time and space. I thank Noam Chomsky for his response and comments. This essay developed from a book review for which I had been commissioned. It took over my working life for several months.

Notes

1 This and other uncredited quotations are from Noam Chomsky, *The Chomsky Reader*, ed. James Peck (New York: Pantheon Books, 1987).

2 Peter Kravitz, editor of *Edinburgh Review*, reminded me that there had been "tremendous opposition to the war on university campuses (at Berkeley, etc.) partly inspired by Chomsky . . ."

3 John Lyons, *Chomsky* (New York: Fontana Press, 1970).

4 Ibid.

5 Harry S. Truman.

6 The Managua lectures comprise Noam Chomsky, *On Power and Ideology: The Managua Lectures* (Boston: South End Press, 1987); Noam Chomsky, *Language and Problems of Knowledge: The Managua Lectures* (Cambridge, MA: MIT Press, 1988).

7 See the discussion of Rousseau in Bertrand Russell, *History of Western Philosophy* (New York: Simon & Schuster, 1945).

8 Lyons, *Chomsky*.

9 Ludwig Wittgenstein, *Tractatus Logico-Philosophicus* (London, Kegan Paul, 1922), 6.52.

10 J.R. Lucas, *The Freedom of the Will* (Oxford: Clarendon Press, 1970).

11 Lyons, *Chomsky*.

12 Then President of the National Union of Mineworkers; famously during the great miners' strike of 1984–1985, when the miners and their families fought so heroically against the British State.

13 This was how it was in 1988, when this essay was written.

14 See the Chomsky letter dated August 15, 1989 on pages 78–79, this volume.

15 Chomsky, *Language and Problems of Knowledge*.

16 Jean Piaget, *Structuralism* (New York: Basic Books, 1970).

17 See the Chomsky letter dated August 15, 1989 on pages 78–79, this volume.

18 See George E. Davie, *The Scottish Enlightenment and Other Essays* (Edinburgh: Polygon Books, 1991).
19 T.C. Smout, A History of the Scottish People 1560–1830, (Glasgow: Collins, 1969).
20 George E. Davie, *The Scottish Enlightenment* (London: London Historical Association, 1981).
21 George E. Davie, "The Social Significance of the Scottish Philosophy of Common Sense" (the Dow Lecture delivered at the University of Dundee, November 30, 1972), in *The Scottish Enlightenment.*
22 Davie, *The Scottish Enlightenment.*
23 Tom Leonard, "The Proof of the Mince Pie," in *Intimate Voices: Selected Work, 1965–1983* (Newcastle, UK: Galloping Dog Press, 1984).
24 Ibid.
25 Noam Chomsky, *Towards a New Cold War: Essays on the Current Crisis and How We Got There* (New York: Pantheon Books, 1982).
26 See *Lobster: The Journal of Parapolitics*, 16, 1988.
27 Tom Leonard, "On Reclaiming the Local or The Theory of the Magic Thing," *Edinburgh Review* 77; republished in Tom Leonard, *Reports from the Present: Selected Work 1982–94* (London: Jonathan Cape, 1995).
28 Tom Leonard, "The Proof of the Mince Pie."
29 For this and the other quotations in this section, see Peter Taylor, "The Rafferty File," in *Beating the Terrorists* (London: Penguin Books, 1980).
30 Cited in Oswald Külpe, *Introduction to Philosophy* (London: Sonnenschein & Co., 1897).
31 Thomas Reid, "Of the Sentiments of Bishop Berkeley," in *Inquiry and Essays*, ed. Ronald E. Beanblossom and Keith Lehrer (Indianapolis: Hackett Publishing Co., 1983), 166.
32 Quoted in Davie, *The Scottish Enlightenment.*
33 See George Berkeley, "Introduction," in *The Principles of Human Knowledge; with Other Writings* (New York: Fontana, 1982).
34 Ibid.
35 Reid, "Of the Sentiments of Bishop Berkeley."
36 J.S. Mill, cited in John Passmore, *A Hundred Years of Philosophy* (London, Penguin Books, 1968 [1917]).
37 See Frederick Copleston, *A History of Philosophy*, vol. 5, part II (New York: Image Books edition, 1964 [1959]).
38 As George E. Davie points out.
39 George E. Davie, *The Crisis of the Democratic Intellect: The Problem of Generalism and Specialisation in Twentieth-Century Scotland* (Edinburgh: Polygon Books 1986) addresses the "well-known lines, in which [the poet] remarks that our blind spots are due to its being impossible for us to see ourselves as others see us, a phrase which he

directly borrows from . . . Adam Smith's *Theory of Moral Sentiments* (a book admired by Burns)."

40 Predating James Audubon.

41 This disinformation, unfortunately, is unchallenged by Peter Mackenzie in his fine history of Glasgow. The poet and activist Freddie Anderson reminded me of the merit of Mackenzie's work.

42 Goethe's work is of interest in this connection, for both his prologue and the later added epilogue to *The Sufferings of Young Werther*. Hogg translated writings by Goethe, who seems also to have been influenced by the Christian mystic Johan Hamann referred to later in this piece. An early unpublished essay by Tom Leonard on Hogg's *Confessions of a Justified Sinner* has been essential to my own appreciation of the novel in this context.

43 March 22, 1988, in a BBC television program.

44 Tom Leonard, introduction to Tom Leonard, ed., *Radical Renfrew: Poetry from the French Revolution to the First World War by Poets Born or Sometime Resident in the County of Renfrewshire* (Edinburgh: Polygon Books, 1990).

45 Jeremy Bernstein, *Einstein* (New York: Fontana, 1973).

46 Cited in Chomsky, *Language and Problems of Knowledge*.

47 Cited in Isaiah Berlin, *Against the Current: Essays in the History of Ideas* (Oxford: Oxford University Press, 1981).

48 Bernstein, *Einstein*.

49 Cited in Mike Weaver, *William Carlos Williams: The American Background* (Cambridge: Cambridge University Press, 1971).

50 Tom Leonard, "On Reclaiming the Local or The Theory of the Magic Thing."

51 Kurt Gödel, *On Formally Undecidable Propositions of Principia Mathematica and Related Systems* (Dover Publishing, Inc., New York, 1992 [1931]).

52 Selected extracts from Ernst Nagel and James R. Newman, *Gödel's Proof* (London: Routledge, 1989).

53 Passmore, *A Hundred Years of Philosophy*.

54 Bernstein, *Einstein*.

55 Davie, "The Social Significance of the Scottish Philosophy of Common Sense."

56 George E. Davie, "Husserl and Reinach on Hume's 'Treatise'" (unpublished essay).

57 Or "epistemology"; the term was first coined by James Ferrier, according to Davie.

58 Chomsky, *Language and Problems of Knowledge*.

59 See the Chomsky letter dated August 15, 1989 on pages 78–79, this volume.

Correspondence Two

August 15, 1989

Dear James,

First of all, apologies for my long delay in getting back to you after your letter of June 15 and the paper that I received from you. I've been in the hospital all summer, ending up finally with back surgery, and have just gotten out a few days ago. I'm now at home beginning what may be a rather lengthy period of recovery, lasting over a couple of months or so. They tell me that I should be getting back to normal function before too long. I very much hope that none of this delays my visit to Glasgow next January. I have had to call off travel over the fall, but I'm keeping my fingers crossed and hoping by January that I'll be up to a transatlantic flight and something like a regular schedule. Be back in touch with you before too long about all of that.

At the moment, I still am unable to sit down at the computer and type a real letter, so this one is coming to you via dictation, and I apologize for the likely incoherence resulting from the unfamiliarity with this art.

I enjoyed and appreciated the paper very much, in particular the parts about the Scottish tradition and its relation to some of the things I've discussed. Most of that is, as you gathered, unfamiliar to me, though I do hope to learn more about it. I had a few comments, not many. On page 9, you say that it was only after *Syntactic Structures* that I abandoned a behaviorist approach and accepted the primacy of semantics in the study of language. That's not quite accurate. *Syntactic Structures* is actually a brief excerpt from a much longer book, which was then unpublishable, entitled *The Logical Structure of Linguistic Theory*. That one in fact came out only twenty years later. At the time, it was considered neither fish nor fowl, and the commentators for the publishers simply said they didn't know what it was and didn't know whether it could or could not be published. But, in any event, even that book, and surely *Syntactic Structures*, did accept the primacy of semantics in the sense that any linguistic theory would have to be judged adequate or inadequate on the basis of its ability to account for semantic facts. In fact, a large part of *Syntactic Structures* is devoted to precisely that question. On page 11, you refer to Piaget's critique. Piaget and I actually took part in a lengthy discussion about these topics a couple of years later. The problem is that there simply is nothing to the third process that he mentions. It's impossible to formulate, and it turns out to be nothing but metaphor and empty rhetoric. By now, I think these ideas have largely been abandoned in cognitive psychology, simply because they don't get anywhere. The last comment has to do with page . . . and my critique of the structuralist approach. This really has nothing to do with incompleteness. The problem is that Harris/Bloomfield and others were seeking a system of analytic taxonomic procedures that could carry them from a text from some language to a description of that language, and we now know that such procedures simply do not exist. My critique was essentially based on that observation.

Hope to be able to get back to you with a more serious letter later on, and I do very much hope that this unpleasant business will not delay my visit to Scotland.

Sincerely.

August 23, 1989

Dear Professor Chomsky,

Thanks for your comments on the essay, which I found impossible to read beyond the most superficial glimpse for a couple of days. However, I can cope with them now and thanks for taking the trouble. In my own work I have various mechanisms to cope with criticism, but nonfiction is different—and in this essay in particular I feel extremely exposed. I was never cut out to be an academic, thank god, I couldn't cope with it, nor with the academics (apart from one or two) that I encounter occasionally. The essay is being published in the *Edinburgh Review* this late autumn-early winter, and if you have no objections I would greatly appreciate being able to append your criticisms; but if you do object there are no hard feelings.

About the same day as your letter arrived, George Davie passed on to me a copy of Harry Bracken's *Mind and Language* essays on Descartes and yourself. Bracken is a mutual friend of you both, as you'll see from his acknowledgments in the foreword, if you have the book to hand. I'm looking forward to reading it, but I'm glad I didn't know of it until now.

I hope your back is healing. I dare say it won't help you to know about the general buzz of excitement around here at the prospect of your visit next January. We are also keeping our fingers crossed that George Davie will manage to be there too, although as I may have mentioned he is now in his mid-seventies and not always up to travelling away from Edinburgh (about fifty miles from here by road).

Take care, and thanks again for taking the trouble to comment on the essay. I am back on my own territory again, short story writing, and enjoying the freedom.

Best regards.

September 13, 1989

Dear James,

Just got your letter. Glad to hear that the essay will appear. About my comments, do as you think best. If you think they're coherent and helpful, then use them, of course. You may have to turn them back into English; as I remember, I was flat on my back at the time, dictating.

I'm improving and am now up and about. I had a post-surgery checkup today and raised the question of flights. They want me to keep away from airplanes for the rest of this year. When I raised the question of a transatlantic flight in January, the answer was a qualified OK, assuming that everything continues as of now, except that they don't want me to fly tourist anymore because of the cramped position. One way or another, I expect to make it. I had originally planned side trips in Iceland and Ireland but cancelled these, so it'll be Glasgow and back. I'm much looking forward to it and hope that there are no problems.

Look forward to seeing the next batch of short stories.

October 28, 1989

Dear Professor Chomsky,

I apologize for the delay in writing. I've been involved here in an aspect of the literary circus, shortlisted for a prize which "I failed to win"; the publicity hype of it all was very wearing and continued for five weeks, interviews and so on, the same words being said all the time; the announcement is made as a sort of imitation of the Hollywood Oscar Ceremony, etc., televised in the London Guild Hall, with shortlisted authors, publishers, and agents feted and feting each other; and "one is supposed" to don Evening Dress for the occasion. I didn't go. But without offering any explanation other than that it was a fairly long trip to go just for a meal, one-thousand-mile-round—once you start negating these publicity publishing hypes in any genuine way you're in trouble, it takes so much energy and time and is exactly what the PR boys are searching for anyway. One striking thing was the venom with which the TV critics went for all of the six shortlisted authors (the Canadian writer Margaret Atwood was one of the six); and the way it turned against myself was in a neo-racist way, but that happens; the T.S. Eliot view of language and the world still pertains as orthodoxy: one way this comes out in terms of language and culture is the logical absurdity produced by juxtaposing High Art and Low Life—or what the critics term "low life." Thus, they only have to mention "the Glasgow dialect" as a cue for a chortle about the ridiculous idea of such a medium being employed for the Higher Intellectual Pursuits, e.g., philosophy, art, politics, etc. Old battles still being waged here.

Enough of that. Things progress here in Glasgow for the event next January, which is creating considerable excitement. I think also the notion that this can be done unofficially—and without institutional funding—causes a bit of eyebrow raising. But the amount of work involved in organizing such an event is not to be underestimated; we only manage it through a network of energetic and committed individuals.

I enclose the booking leaflet and information sheets which were put out in too much of a rush but had to be in order to be included in magazines for a certain date; they shouldn't be taken too seriously, more as a guide, and if there is any problem at all please advise me: we have always wanted the event to be a process anyway. There has been of necessity some changes and general tightening up from earlier plans. As you are aware the event now exists as a joint effort by myself and Derek Rodger, aided by from my side the Free University Group, and on Derek's side, the *Scottish Child* magazine. And as with any joint venture compromises have to be made, although, being very different from each other Derek and myself are probably the ideal team. Both for *Scottish Child* and the majority of the Free University the danger was in involving too many writers and too much philosophy—there is a general wariness not to say hostility for writers among the left here in Britain, which occasionally borders on straight Stalinism, and philosophy suffers from a similar reaction (which maybe only proves how well the right has highjacked both areas). But we've held out as much as we can without alienating folk. The second day of Common Sense and Freedom has the potential of being very exciting indeed. Some of those attending have been actively engaged for years. A great many will have a strong grounding in socialist theory, but the philosophical/libertarian context does shift the ground somewhat, and, in a local sense, the Scottish tradition will be quite an eye-opener, although, in saying that, the same folk are well aware of how the libertarian right (which brought Margaret Thatcher into power here) have been appropriating Scottish thinkers like Adam Smith and Adam Ferguson. The crucial right-wing "think-tank" here is actually called the Adam Smith Institute.

Anyway, we're aware that if your health is not up to this there is no case for taking risks, and please don't even consider it. If your health continues to progress and you can make it please let me know how the air travel is to be arranged and whether and how soon the money should be advanced from here. I hope things are going well for you. On the subject of prizes, a friend told me he had seen or heard you had received some such major thing in China.

All the best.

November 17, 1989

Dear Mr. Davie,

We haven't met before although I have been acquainted with your wife, Elspeth, for a few years; we also have at least two mutual friends, Peter Kravitz and Murdo MacDonald. I write to ask if you would be willing to attend an event I am co-organizing here in Glasgow this coming January, the 10th and 11th. The title of the event is "Self-Determination & Power," and our keynote speaker on both days is Professor Noam Chomsky who has very kindly accepted our invitation to come to Scotland for the two days—assuming that his health allows it.

Some eighteen months ago I undertook a review of a selection of his work entitled *The Chomsky Reader*, but very soon the review became an essay. The prime factor in this was the absence of Chomsky's work in linguistics and philosophy generally within the *Reader*, which I had become acquainted with some years ago while doing a Philosophy of Language course at the University of Strathclyde. As a layperson myself I thought I would like to try giving a general idea of the power and importance of this most central part of his work, in terms that other laypersons might appreciate. This appealed to me for different reasons, one being that the role of the ordinary person as "watchdog," the nonspecialist, is so crucial to Chomsky's political writings and the project of attempting to disseminate something of his more technical work seemed appropriate.

I had lately become aware of the Scottish tradition by way of your own work, firstly through the essays published in *Edinburgh Review*, then by both *The Democratic Intellect*, and *The Crisis of the Democratic Intellect*; I was very struck by certain factors, to the extent that the essay on Chomsky became very much enmeshed with your work on the Scottish "Common Sense" tradition. I later took the liberty of sending Chomsky some of your essays, as well as a copy of *The Democratic*

Intellect; this because it occurred to me that he was not aware of the Scottish context. This proved to be the case and he was pleased to receive your work (although he answered my own argument in the essay more than adequately!). The essay will appear in the forthcoming edition of *Edinburgh Review*. I herewith enclose a copy of it and at some stage I hope you will get round to reading it.

Meanwhile, in the full flush of the writing of the essay, I invited Chomsky to Glasgow. Eventually dates suited and he accepted. I think it certain that the philosophical context has been primary in his acceptance (he had back surgery during the summer and has called off from other overseas engagements). And there is no question that your work has played a supreme part in that. It would be tremendously exciting if you could attend the event, most especially on the Thursday, when the day is entitled "Common Sense and Freedom" and the discussion becomes essentially philosophical. I would also like to take this opportunity of extending an invitation to Elspeth. Sorley MacLean and Hamish Henderson, and Janet Hassan, among others, have agreed to come and with luck, the two days will be special indeed.

I am very aware that your own health is not great. We shall be hiring a minibus for the duration of the event and we would collect and return yourself and Elspeth from Glasgow to your doorstep in Edinburgh and generally ensure that things went as smoothly as possible.

From the enclosed form you will see that your name is already mentioned there. This will seem extremely presumptuous and I accept responsibility for it. It is due to a misjudgment on my own part and I apologize. I wrongly assumed you would have been invited via different channels and only very recently discovered this not to be the case. You may feel even at this stage that you want to decline the invitation. I hope you don't. In fact, there is no need for either yourself or Elspeth to make a decision till much closer the time. I would also like to have a chat with you at some point in the very near future if it is convenient for you; it was my attention to try and do so within the next fortnight in the company of Graham Stalker, a former student of yours, but at the moment I am confined to my home by virtue of a Bad Back. I shall phone you in a few days' time.

Very best wishes to yourself and please pass on my regards to Elspeth.

December 14, 1989

Dear Jim,

I've been holding off answering your letter while I tried to figure out if I was going to be able to make it to Glasgow. Looks right now as though it will be OK. I haven't been allowed to do any plane travel yet, but seems that by January it should be OK. So, looking forward to seeing you then. Hope you are not down with flu, which seems to be devastating the country right now.

December 29, 1989

Dear Noam,

Thanks for your letter and the confirmation that you will be able to manage across to Scotland—in probably about a week's time as you receive this. I hope it means you are recovering from the operation as well as expected. You do so much air travel, you will have your own thoughts on it. I found the flight to Newfoundland last summer really worthwhile because of the solid five hours' reading without interruption—not least my own; here at home my reading is done in my study/workroom, but the problem is that I get unsettled by the proximity of this word processor and my work on it. Therefore, travelling long distances has become a pleasure, even driving, insofar as I can listen to music without feeling guilty, again about my work. But I don't do that much when it comes down to it. Although this coming late spring there is a chance I'll be heading to Zambia for a month, also Frankfurt in May.

I met George Davie for the first time ten days ago; he's a good man. His wife is a short story writer and novelist whom I have known for some years, and I get on well with her. They're a great couple, in fact—she also will be coming to Glasgow for the event. I must say, as Derek Rodger will have mentioned, there is a tremendous interest generally. Also the media, of course, but we have arranged a chap to take care of it; unless you think differently, we thought having a press conference would preempt the hassle—also, by not giving out information on where you will be staying, etc., during the trip. The actual place the event is being held has advantages in this connection. The district, Govan, is the former home of British shipbuilding, quite insular in some ways, very working class, the Red Clydeside, etc., and my grandmother lived seventy years there—myself and four brothers were born and bred there the first years of boyhood; my great aunt was a teacher there too (she taught D.W. Brogan early, maybe nothing to be proud of, though I say it without especially knowing his work). And St. Constantine was here around the sixth century, the church next door to where the event takes place. Also the home of the Glasgow Rangers football (soccer) team, which up until six months ago had an expressly anti–Roman Catholic policy—the situation in Ulster, the religious bigotry and so on, isn't too far away.

I shall stop now to get this posted at once. Everything stops in Scotland for the New Year festivities.

All the very best to you.

At the Self-Determination & Power Event

The Self-Determination & Power event was a two-day conference which took place at the Pearce Institute, Govan, Glasgow in January 1990. It was organized by the Free University Network, with support from the *Scottish Child* magazine. The opening welcome was by Derek Rodger, then editor of *Scottish Child* magazine.

Introducing Day One*

James Kelman

Noam Chomsky is not only a major Western philosopher, he is a major thinker of the left. In one way or another, he has spent most of his life in the struggle against oppression, against greed. There are at least three things I see to put him out on a limb:

1) in philosophical terms he is a rationalist, he believes there are certain kinds of knowledge available to folk right at birth; that is, before they've had any experience gained from living in the actual world; at this present time it seems the most comprehensive way of explaining how it is we are able to know and understand things in the way that we do;
2) as a committed thinker of the left, he insists on discussing politics at almost every opportunity, not only in conversation but on the page; he is as likely to publish an article on the secretive and murderous affairs of state—in particular the US state—as he is to publish an essay on philosophy or aspects of transformational grammar.

The third reason I want to point to is the way he uses his own skills to break down information.

It's not too difficult to imagine the effect of all that on established authority, academic and otherwise—even at a basic

* This is a revised version of the opening talk delivered by James Kelman.

level, by which I mean his colleagues and peers; at least those who share the usual career preoccupations of job-security and the accumulation of personal wealth. Most so-called experts seem to look on their own specialized field of study as a piece of property anyway. This can be seen in terms of this event too, in its informality and unofficial nature, which has put some of them off. Maybe they've gone in the huff. Maybe they wanted a personal invitation, and a brass band to play them up the stairs and along the road from Govan subway station.

The third reason Noam Chomsky can be considered subversive has to with the dissemination of knowledge, the tremendous range of work he does in spreading information, just getting things known to the public at large. It is central to his thesis that everybody can know: "there is no body of theory or significant body of relevant information, beyond the comprehension of the layman, which makes policy immune from criticism."

> Unless we are mentally ill or in some other way mentally disadvantaged, all of us have the analytic skills and intelligence to attempt an understanding of the world. It just isn't good enough to be bad at mathematics; the skills demanded of an elderly person playing several hands of bingo, the skills demanded to get to the supermarket and do a weekly shopping on a limited budget for a large family of young kids—all such skills are there to be developed and applied to any subject whatsoever, including subjects like a country's foreign policy or, nearer home, the correlation between cuts in welfare and infant mortality; between cuts in welfare and suicide, drug abuse, alcohol abuse, prostitution, madness.*

* Quoting from James Kelman, "A Reading from Noam Chomsky and the Scottish Tradition in the Philosophy of Common Sense," see pages 29–75, this volume.

No one should have any illusions about how political this can be. It's probably the basic premise in most countries of the world that everybody can't know.

There's always the risk of sounding paranoiac when you criticize the way information and knowledge is relayed by the mainstream media. But generally speaking they operate on a basis similar to imperialism. If they don't "discover" you, then you don't exist. Once they do discover you, they turn you into a colony. What they do is provide you with their own context, then they give you a name. Take a local example, how the European City of Culture business works.* It means that any piece of art, no matter the medium, created by any artist in Glasgow is instantly transformed into a piece of packaged property and has entered the ownership of those entrepreneurs who nowadays lay claim to the city itself. What happens is you cannot exist beyond the context they've designed for you. It applies across the board. Even this event, the Self-Determination conference, couldn't avoid the tarnish, no matter the pains we took to disassociate ourselves from it: because it takes place in Glasgow in 1990 it takes place in the City of Culture context; you can be for it or against it, but you don't transcend it unless maybe by silence, or by going into exile.

There's never been a time when censorship and suppression didn't exist in this country; information has always been withheld, and specialized knowledge mystified. In the mainstream media names like John Pilger are exceptions, and exceptions only prove the rule. It's always been right in front of our nose. If we haven't seen it, it's because we either haven't looked or else we're operating on that basis of intellectual myopia, which Noam Chomsky essays on so accurately.

---

* The City of Glasgow had purchased the title European City of Culture in 1990.

It is because of the fact of media suppression and distortion that other channels of communication must be available; the need for them has to be assumed. It's just a waste of time to argue about it. The same applies to other forms of knowledge.

When I was at university as a mature student, I had to study his earlier work on linguistics; his political writings were not part of the curriculum. Why was that? One reason is that politics is regarded as irrelevant to the study of language. Our educational system operates on a system of specialist segregation: literature for the literature department, linguistics for the linguistics department, politics for the politics department, and so on.

Once you finish school, college, or university, you are encouraged to stop learning; to stop finding things out: you are trained to leave intellectual matters to the "experts." Even existence itself, you are trained to leave the living of your life to those who specialize in such "concepts," the folk who are paid by the state: they won't live your life for you but they'll determine how it should be lived, they'll let you know what's possible, and what is not possible. The situation of being a child in society is appropriate here, the expert as parent. But so too is the situation of a group or class or an entire race of people under domination or colonization, external or internal; folk who cannot determine their own existence: they are in thrall. The right to self-determination has been taken from them and is kept from them, often by force, by the calculated violence of those in power.

As I recall the Free University project was started by assuming the power of those in control, we didn't really have to argue it out. We wanted a network based on the free exchange of ideas and information; a network of shared experience, shared energy and material resources; a network based on alternative forms even of movement, so that at an event like this one in Govan folk from all over could come and get a crash somewhere. Such networks find ways of supporting one another in trying to live our own lives, define our own context, our own existence. In different parts of the world, there are folk who have been doing that and trying to do that for years.

We should remember that there are people present here in Govan for this two-day event whose commitment to social change has meant they've had to face various degrees of harassment, and personal danger. People are with us who are unable to raise their family within the traditions and customs of their own culture. There are people here this morning who cannot even live in their own country.

Professor Chomsky is wary of links being made between his work on the philosophies of mind and language and his work on politics—and he gives good grounds for that. As he said in a recent interview, "obviously one can't infer anything about politics from what you know about universal grammar, or conversely."

But at the same time there is something implicit in the very fact of our existence as human beings, and that is freedom, the right to self-determination, the right to not be tortured, and the right to not be raped, the right to not be violated—the right to not be colonized in any way whatsoever.

And from my own reading of his work, this is his position, and either we do battle on that basic principle of freedom, or we don't.

The theme of this conference is Self-Determination & Power, how individuals cope in the face of power and authority, ordinary people trying to determine their own day to day existence. We have tried to appeal to local groups and organizations throughout the country, anti-racist groups, homeless people, unemployed centers. People applied for tickets from different parts of Britain and also from abroad. We received enquiries from as far away as Lithuania and Estonia.

Containing the Threat of Democracy: A Keynote Address[1]

Noam Chomsky

In his study of the Scottish intellectual tradition, George E. Davie identifies its central theme as a recognition of the fundamental role of "*natural beliefs* or principles of common sense, such as the belief in an independent external world, the belief in causality, the belief in ideal standards, and the belief in the self of conscience as separate from the rest of one." These principles are sometimes considered to have a regulative character; though never fully justified, they provide the foundations for thought and conception. Some held that they contain "an irreducible element of mystery," Davie points out, while others hoped to provide a rational foundation for them. On that issue, the jury is still out.[2]

We can trace such ideas to seventeenth-century thinkers who reacted to the skeptical crisis of the times by recognizing that there are no absolutely certain grounds for knowledge, but that we do, nevertheless, have ways to gain a reliable understanding of the world and to improve that understanding and apply it—essentially the standpoint of the working scientist today. Similarly, in normal life, a reasonable person relies on the natural beliefs of common sense while recognizing that they may be parochial or misguided and hoping to refine or alter them as understanding progresses.

Davie credits David Hume with providing this particular cast to Scottish philosophy, and, more generally, with having taught philosophy the proper questions to ask. One puzzle that Hume raised is particularly pertinent to the questions we are hoping to address in these two days of discussions. In considering the First Principles of Government, Hume found "nothing more surprising" than to see the easiness with which the many are governed by the few and to observe the implicit submission with which men resign their own sentiments and passions to those of their rulers. When we enquire by what means this wonder is brought about, we shall find, that as Force is always on the side of the governed, the governors have nothing to support them but opinion. It is, therefore, on opinion only that government is founded; and this maxim extends to the most despotic and most military governments, as well as to the most free and most popular.

One dubious feature is the idea that force is on the side of the governed. Reality is more grim. A good part of human history supports the contrary thesis put forth a century earlier by advocates of the rule of parliament against the king, but, more significantly, against the people: that "the power of the Sword is, and ever hath been, the Foundation of all Titles to Government."[3] Nevertheless, Hume's paradox is real. Even despotic rule is commonly founded on a measure of consent, and the abdication of rights is the hallmark of more free societies—a fact that calls for analysis.

The harsher side of the truth is clarified by the successes and the tragedies, fate of the popular movements of the past decade. In the Soviet satellites, the governors had ruled by force, not opinion. When force was withdrawn, the fragile tyrannies quickly collapsed, for the most part with little bloodshed. These remarkable successes are a sharp departure from the historical norm. Throughout modern history, popular forces motivated by radical democratic ideals have sought to combat autocratic rule. Sometimes they have been able to expand the realms of freedom and justice before being brought to heel. Often, they are simply crushed. But it is hard to think of another case when established power simply withdrew in the face of a popular challenge. No less remarkable is the behavior of the reigning superpower, which not only did not bar these developments by force as in the past, but even encouraged them, alongside of significant internal changes.

The historical norm is illustrated by the dramatically contrasting case of Central America, where any popular effort to overthrow the brutal tyrannies of the oligarchy and the military is met with murderous force, supported or directly organized by the ruler of the hemisphere. Ten years ago, there were signs of hope for an end to the dark ages of terror and misery, with the rise of self-help groups, unions, peasant associations, and other popular organizations that might have led the way to democracy and social reform. This prospect elicited a stern response by the United States and its client regimes, supported by Britain and other Western allies, with a campaign of slaughter, torture, and general barbarism on a scale reminiscent of Pol Pot. This violent Western response to the threat of democracy left societies "affected by terror and panic," "collective intimidation and generalized fear," and "internalized acceptance of the terror," in the words of a Church-based Salvadoran human rights organization, well after the shameful elections held to satisfy the consciences and propaganda needs of the masters. Early efforts in Nicaragua to direct resources to the poor majority impelled Washington to economic and ideological warfare, and outright terrorism, to punish these transgressions by reducing life to the zero grade.

Western opinion regards such consequences as a success insofar as the challenge to power and privilege is rebuffed and the targets are properly chosen: killing priests is not clever, but rural activists, union leaders and human rights activists are fair game—and, of course, peasants, Indians, students, and other lowlife generally.

The pattern is uniform. US occupying forces in Panama were quickly ordered to arrest most political activists and union leaders, because they are "bad guys of some sort," the US Embassy told reporters.[4]

The "good guys" to be restored to power are the bankers who were happily laundering drug money in the early 1980s. Then Noriega was also a "good guy," running drugs, killing and torturing and stealing elections—and, crucially, following American orders. He had not yet shown the dangerous streak of independence that transferred him to the category of demon. Apart from tactics, nothing changes over the years, including the inability of educated opinion to perceive that two and two is four.

Central America represents the historical norm, not Eastern Europe. Hume's observation requires this correction. Recognizing that, it remains true, and important, that government is founded on opinion, which brings will submission.

In the contemporary period, Hume's insight has been revived and elaborated, but with a crucial innovation: control of thought is "more" important for governments that are free and popular than for despotic and military states. The logic is straightforward. A despotic state can control its domestic enemy by force, but as the state loses this weapon, other devices are required to prevent the ignorant masses from interfering with public affairs, which are none of their business.

The point is, in fact, far more general. The public must be reduced to passivity in the political realm, but for submissiveness to become a reliable trait, it must be entrenched in the realm of belief as well. The public are to be observers, not participants, consumers of ideology as well as products. Eduardo Galleano writes that "the majority must resign itself to the consumption of fantasy. Illusions of wealth are sold to the poor, illusions of freedom to the oppressed, dreams of victory to the defeated and of power to the weak."[5] That is the essential point.

I will come back to these central themes of modern political and intellectual culture. But let us first have a look at some of the "natural beliefs" that guide our contact and our thought. One such belief is that a crucial element of essential human nature is what Bakunin called "an instinct for freedom." Hume's paradox arises only if we make this assumption. It is the failure to act upon this instinct that Hume found so surprising. The same failure inspired Rousseau's classic lament that people are born free but are everywhere in chains, seduced by the illusions of the civil society that is created by the rich to guarantee their plunder. There have been efforts to ground the instinct for freedom in a substantive theory of human nature. They are not without interest, but they surely come nowhere near establishing the case. Like other tenets of common sense, this belief remains a regulative principle that we adopt or reject on faith. Which choice we make can have large-scale effects for ourselves and others.

Those who adopt the common-sense principle that freedom is our natural right and essential need will agree with Bertrand Russell that anarchism is "the ultimate ideal to which society should approximate." Structures of hierarchy and domination are fundamentally illegitimate. They can be defended only on grounds of contingent need, an argument that rarely stands up to analysis. As Russell went on to observe seventy years ago, "the old bonds of authority" have little intrinsic merit. Reasons are needed for people to abandon their rights, "and the reasons offered are counterfeit reasons, convincing only to those who have a selfish interest in being convinced." "The condition of revolt," he went on, "exists in women towards men, in oppressed nations towards their oppressors, and above all in labour towards capital. It is a state full of danger, as all past history shows, yet also full of hope."[6]

Russell traced the habit of submission in part to coercive educational practices. His views are reminiscent of seventeenth- and eighteenth-century thinkers who held that the mind is not to be filled with knowledge "from without, like a vessel," but "to be kindled and awaked." "The growth of knowledge [resembles] the growth of Fruit; however external causes may in some degree cooperate, it is the internal vigour, and virtue of the tree, that must ripen the juices to their just maturity." Similar conceptions underlie Enlightenment thought on political and intellectual freedom, and on alienated labor, which turns the worker into an instrument for other ends instead of a human being fulfilling inner needs—a fundamental principle of classical liberal thought, though long forgotten, because of its revolutionary implications. These ideas and values retain their power and their pertinence, though they are very remote from realization anywhere. As long as this is so, the libertarian revolutions of the eighteenth century remain far from consummated, a vision for the future.[7]

Hume posed his paradox for both despotic and more free societies. The latter case is by far the more important. As the social world becomes more free and diverse, the task of inducing submission becomes more complex, and the problem of unraveling the mechanisms of indoctrination more challenging. But intellectual interest aside, the case of free societies has greater human significance, because here we are talking about ourselves and can act upon what we learn. It is for just this reason that the dominant culture will always seek to externalize human concerns, directing them to the inadequacies and abuses of others. When US plans go awry in some corner of the Third World, we devote our attention to the defects and special problems of these cultures and their social disorders—not our own. Fame, fortune, and respect await those who reveal the crimes of official enemies; those who undertake the vastly more important task of raising a mirror to their own societies can expect quite different treatment. George Orwell is famous for *Animal Farm* and *1984*, which focus on the official enemy. Had he addressed the more interesting and significant question of thought control in relatively free and democratic societies, it would not have been appreciated, and, instead of wide acclaim, he would have faced silent dismissal or obloquy. Let us nevertheless turn to the more important and unacceptable questions.

Keeping to governments that are more free and popular, why do the governed submit when force is on their side? First, we have to look at a prior question: to what extent *is* force on the side of the governed? Here some care is necessary. Societies are considered free and democratic insofar as the power of the state to coerce is limited. The United States is unusual in this respect; perhaps more than anywhere else in the world, the citizen is free from state coercion, at least, the citizen who is relatively privileged and of the right color, a substantial part of the population.

But it is a mere truism that the state represents only one segment of the nexus of power. Control over investment, production, commerce, finance, conditions of work, and other crucial aspects of social policy lies in private hands and the same is true of articulate expression, largely dominated by major corporations that sell audiences to advertisers and naturally reflect the interests of the owners and their market. The ability to articulate and communicate one's views, concerns, and interests—or even to discover them—is thus narrowly constrained as well.

Furthermore, through familiar mechanisms, private power sets narrow limits on the actions of government. The United States is again unusual in this respect among the industrial democracies. It is near the limit in its safeguards for freedom from state coercion and also in the poverty of its political life. There is essentially one political party, the business party, with two factions. Shifting coalitions of investors account for a large part of political history. Unions, or other popular organizations that might offer a way for the general public to play some role in influencing programs and policy choices, scarcely function apart from the narrowest realm. The ideological system is bounded by the consensus of the privileged. Even elections are largely a ritual form. In congressional elections, virtually all incumbents are returned to office, a reflection of the vacuity of the political system and the choices it offers. There is scarcely a pretense that substantive issues are at stake in the presidential campaigns. Articulated programs are hardly more than a device to garner votes, and candidates adjust their messages to their audiences as public relations tacticians advise. Political commentators ponder such questions as whether Reagan will remember his lines or whether Mondale looks too gloomy or whether Dukakis can duck the slime flung at him by George Bush's speech writers. In the 1984 elections, the two political factions virtually exchanged traditional policies, the Republicans presenting themselves as the party of Keynesian growth and state intervention in the economy, the Democrats as the advocates of fiscal conservatism; few even noticed. Half the population does not bother to push the buttons, and those who take the trouble often consciously vote against their own interest.

These tendencies were accelerated during the Reagan years. The population overwhelmingly opposed the policies of his administration, and even the Reagan voters in 1984, by about three to two, hoped that his legislative program would not be enacted. In the 1980 elections, 4 percent of the electorate voted for Reagan because they regarded him as a "real conservative." In 1984, the percentage dropped to 1 percent. That is what is called "a landslide victory for conservatism" in political rhetoric. Furthermore, contrary to much pretense, Reagan's popularity was never particularly high, and much of the population seemed to understand that he was a media creation who had only the foggiest idea of what government policy might be.[8] It is noteworthy that the fact is now tacitly conceded; the instant that the "great communicator" was no longer of any use as a symbol, he was quietly tucked away. After eight years of pretense about the "revolution" that Reagan wrought, no one would dream of asking its standard bearer for his thoughts about any topic, because it is understood, as it always was, that he has none. When Reagan was invited to Japan as an elder statesman, his hosts were surprised—and given the fat fee, a bit annoyed—to discover that he could not hold press conferences or talk on any subject. Their discomfiture aroused some amusement in the American press: the Japanese believed what they had read about this remarkable figure, failing to comprehend the workings of the mysterious occidental mind.

The hoax perpetrated by the media and the intellectual community is of some interest for Hume's paradox about submission to authority. State capitalist democracy has a certain tension with regard to the locus of power; in principle, the people rule, but effective power resides largely in private hands, with large-scale effects throughout the social order. One way to reduce the tension is to remove the public from the scene, except in form. The Reagan phenomenon offered a new way to achieve this fundamental goal of capitalist democracy. The United States functioned through the 1980s without a chief executive. The office was, in effect, eliminated in favor of a symbolic figure constructed by the public relations industry. It is as if there was an election every few years to choose a Queen to perform certain ritual tasks: to appear on ceremonial occasions, to greet visitors, to read aloud the government pronouncements and programs, and so on. This is a major advance in the marginalization of the public. As the most sophisticated of the state capitalist democracies, the United States has often led the way in devising means to control the domestic enemy, and the latest inspiration will doubtless be mimicked elsewhere, with the usual lag.

Even when issues arise in the political system, the concentration of effective power limits the threat. The question is largely academic in the United States because of the subordination of the political and ideological system to business interests, but in democracies to the south, where conflicting ideas and approaches reach the political arena, the situation is different. As is again familiar, government policies that private power finds unwelcome will lead to capital flight, disinvestment, and social decline until business confidence is restored with the abandonment of the threat to privilege; these facts of life exert a decisive influence on the political system (with military force in reserve if matters get out of hand, supported by the ruler of the hemisphere). To put the basic point crassly, unless the rich and powerful are satisfied, everyone will suffer, because they control the basic social levers, determining what will be produced and consumed, and what crumbs will filter down to their subjects. For the homeless in the streets, then, the primary objective is to ensure that the rich live happily in their mansions. This crucial factor, along with simple control over resources, severely limits the force on the side of the governed and diminishes Hume's paradox in a well-functioning capitalist democracy in which the general public is scattered and marginalized.

Still the problem remains. Hume is right to stress that control over thought is a major factor in suppressing the natural beliefs of common sense and thereby ensuring submission to power. The general public is not supposed to understand this; that would undermine the goals. But elites have long been well aware that when obedience cannot be secured by the bludgeon, democracy must be subverted by other means. It is revealing to see how these concerns have been articulated over the years.

During the seventeenth-century English revolution, libertarian groups "represented the first "great outburst of democratic thought in history."[9] This awakening of the general populace raised the problem of how to contain the threat. The libertarian ideas of the radical democrats were considered outrageous by respectable people. They favored universal education, guaranteed health care, and democratization of the law, which one described as a fox, with poor men the geese: "he pulls off their feathers and feeds upon them." They developed a kind of "liberation theology" which, as one critic ominously observed, preached "seditious doctrine to the people" and aimed "to raise the rascal multitude . . . against all men of best quality in the kingdom, to draw them into associations and combinations with one another . . . against all lords, gentry, ministers, lawyers, rich and peaceable men" (historian Clement Walker). The rabble did not want to be ruled by king or parliament but "by countrymen like ourselves, that know our wants." Their pamphlets explained further that "it will never be a good world while knights and gentlemen make us laws, that are chosen for fear and do but oppress us, and do not know the people's sores."

These ideas naturally appalled the men of best quality. They were willing to grant the people rights but within reason and on the principle that "when we mention the people, we do not mean the confused promiscuous body of the people." Particularly frightening were the itinerant workers and preachers calling for freedom and democracy, the agitators stirring up the rascal multitude, and the printers putting out pamphlets questioning authority and its mysteries. "There can be no form of government without its proper mysteries," Walker warned, mysteries that must be "concealed" from the common folk: "Ignorance, and admiration arising from ignorance, are the parents of civil devotion and obedience," a thought echoed by Dostoevsky's Grand Inquisitor. The radical democrats had "cast all the mysteries and secrets of government . . . before the vulgar (like pearls before swine)," he continued, and have "made the people thereby so curious and so arrogant that they will never find humility enough to submit to a civil rule." It is dangerous, another commentator ominously observed, to "have a people know their own strength." After the democrats had been defeated, John Locke commented that "day-labourers and tradesmen, the spinsters and dairymaids" must be told what to believe; "The greatest part cannot know and therefore they must believe."[10]

These ideas have ample resonance until the present day. Like John Milton and other civil libertarians of the period, Locke held a sharply limited conception of freedom of expression. His Fundamental Constitution of Carolina barred those who "speak anything in their religious assembly irreverently or seditiously of the government or governors, or of state matters." The constitution guaranteed freedom for "speculative opinions in religion," but not for political opinions. "Locke would not even have permitted people to discuss public affairs," Leonard Levy observes. The constitution provided further that "all manner of comments and expositions on any part of these constitutions, or on any part of the common or statute laws of Carolines, are absolutely prohibited." In drafting reasons for Parliament to terminate censorship in 1694, Locke offered no defense of freedom of expression or thought, but only considerations of expediency and harm to commercial interests.[11]

With the threat of democracy overcome and the libertarian rabble dispersed, censorship was permitted to lapse in England, because the "opinion-formers . . . censored themselves. Nothing got into print which frightened the men of property," Christopher Hill comments. In a well-functioning state capitalist democracy like the United States, what might frighten the men of property is generally kept far from the public eye—sometimes, with quite astonishing success.

The concerns aroused by the seventeenth-century radical democrats were not new. As far back as Herodotus we can read how people who had struggled to gain their freedom "became once more subject to autocratic government" through the acts of able and ambitious leaders who "introduced for the first time the ceremonial of royalty," creating a legend that the leader "was a being of a different order from mere men" who must be shrouded in mystery and leaving the secrets of government, which are not the affair of the vulgar, to those entitled to manage them.

In the 1650s, supporters of Parliament and the army against the people easily proved that the rabble could not be trusted. This was shown by their lingering monarchist sentiments and their reluctance to place their affairs in the hands of the gentry and the army, who were "truly the people," though the people in their foolishness did not agree. The mass of the people are a "giddy multitude," "beasts in men's shapes." It is proper to suppress them, just as it is proper "to save the life of a lunatique or distracted person even against his will." If the people are so "depraved and corrupt" as to "confer places of power and trust upon wicked and undeserving men, they forfeit their power in this behalf unto those that are good, though but a few."[12] The good and few may be the gentry or industrialists or the vanguard Party and the Central Committee or the intellectuals who qualify as "experts" because they articulate the consensus of the powerful (to paraphrase one of Henry Kissinger's insights).[13]

They manage the business empires, ideological institutions, and political structures or serve them at various levels. Their task is to shepherd the bewildered herd and keep the giddy multitude in a state of implicit submission, and, thus, to bar the dread prospect of freedom and self-determination.

Similar ideas had been forged as the Spanish explorers set about what Tzvetan Todorov calls "the greatest genocide in human history" after they "discovered America" five hundred years ago. They justified their acts of terror and oppression on the grounds that the natives are not "capable of governing themselves any more than madmen or even wild beasts and animals, seeing that their food is not any more agreeable and scarcely better than that of wild beasts" and their stupidity "is much greater than that of children and madmen in other countries" (professor and theologian Francisco de Vitoria, "one of the pinnacles of Spanish humanism in the sixteenth century"). Therefore, intervention is legitimate "in order to exercise the rights of guardianship," Todorov comments, summarizing de Vitoria's basic thought.[14]

When English savages took over the task a few years later, they naturally adopted the same pose while taming the wolves in the guise of men, as George Washington described the objects that stood in the way of the advance of civilization and had to be eliminated for their own good. The English colonists had already handled the Celtic "wild men" the same way, for example, when Lord Cumberland, known as "the butcher," laid waste to the Scottish highlands before moving on to pursue his craft in North America.[15]

One hundred and fifty years later, their descendants had purged North America of this native blight, reducing the lunatics from ten million to two hundred thousand according to some recent estimates, and they turned their eyes elsewhere, to civilize the wild beasts in the Philippines. The Indian fighters to whom President McKinley assigned the task of "Christianizing" and "uplifting" these unfortunate creatures rid the liberated islands of hundreds of thousands of them, accelerating their ascent to heaven. They too were rescuing "misguided creatures" from their depravity by "slaughtering the natives in English fashion," as the New York press described their painful responsibility, adding that we must take "what muddy glory lies in the wholesale killing til they have learned to respect our arms," then moving on to "the more difficult task of getting them to respect our intentions."[16] This is pretty much the course of history, as the plague of European civilization devastated much of the world.

On the home front, the continuing problem was formulated plainly by the seventeenth-century political thinker Marchamont Nedham. The proposals of the radical democrats, he wrote, would result in "ignorant Persons, neither of Learning nor Fortune, being put in Authority." Given their freedom, the "self-opinionated multitude" would elect "*the lowest of the People*" who would occupy themselves with "Milking and Gelding the Purses of the Rich," taking "the ready Road to all licentiousness, mischief, mere Anarchy and Confusion."[17]

Apart from thc rhetorical flourishes, the sentiments are the standard features of modern political and intellectual discourse, increasingly so as popular struggles did succeed, over the centuries, in realizing the proposals of the radical democrats, so that ever more sophisticated means had to be devised to reduce their substantive content and introduce new mechanisms of subjugation to authority.

Such problems regularly arise in periods of turmoil and social conflict. After the American Revolution, rebellious and independent farmers had to be taught by force that the ideals expressed in the pamphlets of 1776 were not to be taken seriously. The common people were not to be represented by countrymen like themselves, that know the people's sores, but by gentry, merchants, lawyers, and others who hold or serve private power. The reigning doctrine expressed by the Founding Fathers is that "the people who own the country ought to govern it" (John Jay). The rise of corporations in the nineteenth century and the legal structures devised to grant them dominance over private and public life established the victory of the federalist opponents of popular democracy in a new and powerful form.

Quite regularly, revolutionary struggles pit aspirants to power against one another, though united in opposition to radical democratic tendencies among the common people. Lenin and Trotsky, shortly after seizing state power in 1917, moved to dismantle organs of popular control, including factory councils and soviets, thus proceeding to deter and overcome socialist tendencies. An orthodox Marxist, Lenin did not regard socialism as a viable option in this backward and underdeveloped country; until his last days, it remained for him an "elementary truth of Marxism, that the victory of socialism requires the joint efforts of workers in a number of advanced countries," Germany in particular.[18] In what has always seemed to me his greatest work, George Orwell described a similar process in Spain, where the fascists, communists, and liberal democracies were united in opposition to the libertarian revolution that swept over much of the country, turning to the conflict over the spoils only when popular forces were safely suppressed. There are many examples, often influenced by great power violence.

This is particularly true in the Third World. A persistent concern of Western elites is that popular organizations might lay the basis for meaningful democracy and social reform, threatening the prerogatives of the privileged. Those who seek "to raise the rascal multitude" and "draw them into associations and combinations with one another" against "the men of best quality" must, therefore, be repressed or eliminated. It comes as no surprise that Archbishop Romero should be assassinated shortly after urging President Carter to withhold military aid from the governing junta, which, he warned, will use it to "sharpen injustice and repression against the people's organizations" struggling "for respect for their most basic human rights," or that the media and intellectual opinion in the West should disregard the atrocity and conceal the complicity of the armed forces and the civilian government established by the US as a cover for their necessary work in carrying out the task that the Archbishop described.

Worse still, "the rot may spread," in the terminology of political elites; there may be a demonstration effect of independent development in a form that attends to the people's sores. Internal governing planning documents and even the public record reveal that a driving concern of US planners has been the fear that the "virus" might spread, "infecting" regions beyond. Examples include the first major postwar counterinsurgency operation in Greece in the late 1940s, the undermining of the labor movement in Europe at the same time, the US invasion of South Vietnam, the overthrow of the democratic governments of Guatemala and Chile, the attack against Nicaragua and the popular movements elsewhere in Central America, and many other examples.

Similar fears were expressed by European statesmen with regard to the American Revolution. This might "lend new strength to the apostles of sedition" (Metternich) and might spread "the contagion and the invasion of vicious principles," such as "the pernicious doctrines of republicanism and popular self-rule," one of the Czar's diplomats warned. A century later, the cast of characters was reversed. Woodrow Wilson's secretary of state Robert Lansing feared that if the Bolshevik disease were to spread, it would leave the "ignorant and incapable mass of humanity dominant in the earth"; the Bolsheviks, he continued, were appealing "to the proletariat of all countries, to the ignorant and mentally deficient, who by their numbers are urged to become masters . . . a very real danger in view of the process of social unrest throughout the world." Again, it is democracy that is the awesome threat. When soldiers and workers councils made a brief appearance in Germany, Wilson feared that they would inspire dangerous thoughts among "the American negro [soldiers] returning from abroad." Already, he had heard, Negro laundresses were demanding more than the going wage, saying that "money is as much mine as it is yours." Businessmen might have to adjust to having workers on their boards of directors, he feared, among other disasters, if the Bolshevik virus were not exterminated.

With these dire consequences in mind, the Western invasion of the Soviet Union was justified on defensive grounds, against "the Revolution's challenge . . . to the very survival of the capitalist order," according to John Lewis Gaddis, a highly regarded contemporary diplomatic historian. And it was also necessary to defend the civilized order against the popular enemy at home. Secretary of State Lansing explained that force must be used to prevent "the leaders of Bolshevism and anarchy" from proceeding to "organize or preach against government in the United States." The repression launched by the Wilson administration successfully undermined democratic politics, unions, freedom of the press, and independent thought in the interests of corporate power and the state authorities who represented its interests, all with the general approval of the media and elites generally, all in self-defense against the ignorant rabble. Much the same story was reenacted after World War II, again under the pretext of a Soviet threat, but, in reality, to restore submission to the rulers.[19]

When political life and independent thought revived in the 1960s, the problem arose again, and the reaction was the same. The Trilateral Commission, bringing together liberal elites from Europe, Japan, and the United States, warned of an impending "crisis of democracy" as segments of the public sought to enter the political arena. This "excess of democracy" was posing a threat to the unhampered rule of privileged elites—what is called "democracy" in political theology. The problem was the usual one: the rabble were trying to arrange their own affairs, gaining control over their communities and pressing their political demands. There were organizing efforts among young people, ethnic minorities, women, social activists, and others, encouraged by the struggles of benighted masses elsewhere for freedom and independence. More "moderation in democracy" would be required, the commission concluded, perhaps a return to the days when "Truman had been able to govern the country with the cooperation of a relatively small number of Wall Street lawyers and bankers," as the American rapporteur commented,[20] with more than a trace of nostalgia.

At another point on the political spectrum, the conservative contempt for democracy is succinctly articulated by Sir Lewis Namier, who writes that "there is no free will in the thinking and actions of the masses, any more than in the revolution of planets, in the migration of birds, and in the plunging of hordes of lemmings into the sea." Only disaster would ensue if the masses were permitted to enter the arena of decision-making, in a meaningful way. The leading neoconservative intellectual Irving Kristol adds that "insignificant nations, like insignificant people, can quickly experience delusions of significance." These delusions must be driven from their tiny minds by force: "In truth, the days of 'gunboat diplomacy' are never over. . . . Gunboats are as necessary for international order as police cars are for domestic order."[21]

These ideas bring us to the Reagan administration, which established a state propaganda agency that was by far the most extensive in American history, much to the delight of the advocates of a powerful and interventionist state who are called "conservatives" in one of the current Orwellian perversions of political discourse. The Office of Public Diplomacy, as it was called, was largely dedicated to mobilizing support for US terror states in Central America and to "demonizing the Sandinistas," as one administration official put it. When the program was exposed, another high official described it as the kind of operation carried out in "enemy territory"—an apt phrase, expressing standard elite attitudes towards the public: an enemy who must be subdued.

In this case, the enemy was not completely subdued. Popular movements deepened their roots and spread into new sectors of the population in the 1960s and were able to drive the state underground to clandestine terror instead of the more efficient forms of overt violence that Presidents Kennedy and Johnson could undertake before the public had been aroused.

As elites pondered the rising threat of democracy at home in the post-Vietnam period, they also had to deal with the spread of rot and cancers abroad. The mechanisms of thought control at home, and the real reasons for subversion and state terror abroad, are brought out with great clarity in one of the most spectacular achievements of the Reagan administration propaganda operation—which was, incidentally, strictly illegal, as Congress irrelevantly determined. Virtually as a reflex, the propaganda system concocted the charge that the current enemy, in this case Nicaragua, was planning to conquer the hemisphere. But it went on to provide actual proof: the evil communists had openly declared a "Revolution without Borders." This charge—which aroused no ridicule among the disciplined educated classes—was based on a speech by

Sandinista leader Tomás Borge, in which he explained that Nicaragua cannot "export our revolution" but can only "export our example while the people themselves of these countries . . . must make their revolutions"; in this sense, he said, the Nicaraguan Revolution "transcends national boundaries." The hoax was exposed at once, even noted marginally in the press. But it was too useful to abandon, and it was eagerly accepted by Congress, the media and political commentators. The phrase is used as the title for a major State Department propaganda document, and it was brilliantly exploited by Reagan's speechwriters to stampede Congress into providing $100 million of aid to the contras in response to the World Court judgment calling upon the United States to terminate its "unlawful use of force" and illegal embargo against Nicaragua.

The crucial point is that lying behind the hoax there is a valid insight, which explains its wide appeal among the educated classes. Early Sandinista success in instituting social reforms and production for domestic needs set the alarm bells ringing in Washington and New York. These successes aroused the same fears that agitate Metternich and the Czar, the people of the best quality since the seventeenth century, all those who expect to dominate by right: the rot might spread, the virus might infect others, and the foundations of privilege might crumble.

Despite all efforts to contain them, the rabble continues to fight for their rights, and, over time, libertarian ideals have been partially realized or have even become common coin. Many of the outrageous ideas of the seventeenth-century radical democrats, for example, seem tame enough today, though other early insights remain beyond our current moral and intellectual reach.

The struggle for freedom of speech is an interesting case, and a crucial one, since it lies at the heart of a whole array of freedoms and rights.[22] The central question is when, if ever, the state may act to interdict the content of communications.

One critical element is seditious libel, the idea that the state can be criminally assaulted by speech, "the hallmark of closed societies throughout the world," legal historian Harry Kalven observes. A society that tolerates laws against seditious libel is not free, whatever its other characteristics. In late seventeenth-century England, men were castrated, disemboweled, quartered, and beheaded for the crime. Through the eighteenth century, there was a general consensus that established authority could be maintained only by silencing subversive discussion, and "any threat, whether real or imagined, to the good reputation of the government" must be barred by force (Leonard Levy). "Private men are not judges of their superiors. . . . This wou'd confound all government," one editor wrote. Truth was no defense: true charges are even more criminal than false ones, because they tend even more to bring authority into disrepute.[23]

Treatment of dissident opinion, incidentally, follows a similar model in our more libertarian era. False and ridiculous charges are no real problem; it is the unconscionable critics who reveal unwanted truths from whom society must be protected.

The doctrine of seditious libel was also upheld in the American colonies. The intolerance of dissent during the revolutionary period is notorious. The leading American libertarian, Thomas Jefferson, agreed that punishment was proper for "a traitor in thought, but not in deed," and authorized internment of political suspects. He and the other Founders agreed that "traitorous or disrespectful words" against the authority of the national state or any of its component states was criminal. "During the Revolution," Leonard Levy observes, "Jefferson, like Washington, the Adamses, and Paine, believed that there could be no toleration for serious differences of political opinion on the issue of independence, no acceptable alternative to complete submission to the patriot cause. Everywhere there was unlimited liberty to praise it, none to criticize it." At the outset of the Revolution, the Continental Congress urged the states to enact legislation to prevent the people from being "deceived and drawn into erroneous opinion." It was not until the Jeffersonians were themselves subjected to repressive measures in the late 1790s that they developed a body of more libertarian thought for self-protection—reversing course, however, when they gained power themselves.[24]

Until World War I, there was only a slender basis for freedom of speech in the United States, and it was not until 1964 that the law of seditious libel was struck down by the Supreme Court. In 1969, the Court finally protected speech apart from "incitement to imminent lawless action." Two centuries after the Revolution, the Court at last adopted the position that had been advocated in 1776 by Jeremy Bentham, who argued that a free government must permit "malcontents" to "communicate their sentiments, concert their plans, and practice every mode of opposition short of actual revolt, before the executive power can be legally justified in disturbing them." The 1969 Supreme Court decision formulated a libertarian standard which, I believe, is unique in the world. In Canada, for example, people are still imprisoned for promulgating "false news," recognized as a crime in 1275 to protect the king.[25]

In Europe, the situation is still more primitive. France is a striking case, because of the dramatic contrast between the self-congratulatory rhetoric and repressive practice so common as to pass unnoticed. England has only limited protection for freedom of speech, and even tolerates such a disgrace as a law of blasphemy. The reaction to the Salman Rushdie affair, most dramatically on the part of self-styled "conservatives," was particularly noteworthy.[26] Doubtless many would agree with Conor Cruise O'Brien, who, when Minister for Posts and Telegraphs in Ireland, amended the Broadcasting Authority Act to permit the Authority to refuse to broadcast any matter that, in the judgment of the minister, "would tend to undermine the authority of the state."[27]

We should also bear in mind that the right to freedom of speech in the United States was not established by the First Amendment to the Constitution but only through dedicated efforts over a long period by the labor movement, the civil rights and anti-war movements of the 1960s, and other popular forces. James Madison pointed out that a "parchment barrier" will never suffice to prevent tyranny. Rights are not established by words but won and sustained by struggle.

It is also worth recalling that victories for freedom of speech are often won in defense of the most depraved and horrendous views. The 1969 Supreme Court decision was in defense of the Ku Klux Klan from prosecution after a meeting with hooded figures, guns, and a burning cross, calling for "burying the nigger" and "sending the Jews back to Israel." With regard to freedom of expression there are basically two positions: you defend it vigorously for views you hate, or you reject it in favor of Stalinist/Fascist standards.[28]

The fears expressed by the men of best quality in the seventeenth century have become a major theme of intellectual discourse, corporate practice, and the academic social sciences. They were expressed by the influential moralist and foreign affairs adviser Reinhold Niebuhr, who was revered by George Kennan, the Kennedy intellectuals, and many others. He wrote that "rationality belongs to the cool observers," while the common person follows not reason but faith. The cool observers, he explained, must recognize "the stupidity of the average man," and must provide the "necessary illusion" and the "emotionally potent oversimplifications" that will keep the naive simpletons on course. As in 1650, it remains necessary to protect the "lunatic or distracted person," the ignorant rabble, from their own "depraved and corrupt" judgments, just as one does not allow a child to cross the street without supervision.[29]

In accordance with the prevailing conceptions, there is no infringement of democracy if a few corporations control the information system; in fact, that is the essence of democracy.

In the *Annals of the American Academy of Political and Social Science*, the leading figure of the public relations industry, Edward Bernays, explained that "the very essence of the democratic process" is "the freedom to persuade and suggest," what he calls "the engineering of consent." If the freedom to persuade happens to be concentrated in a few hands, we must recognize that such is the nature of a free society. From the early twentieth century, the public relations industry has devoted huge resources to "educating the American people about the economic facts of life" to ensure a favorable climate for business. Its task is to control "the public mind," which is "the only serious danger confronting the company," an AT&T executive observed eighty years ago. And today, the *Wall Street Journal* describes with enthusiasm the "concerted efforts" of corporate America "to change the attitudes and values of workers" on a vast scale with "New Age workshops" and other contemporary devices of indoctrination and stupefaction designed to convert "worker apathy into corporate allegiance."[30] The agents of Reverend Moon and Christian evangelicals employ similar devices to bar the threat of peasant organizing and to undermine a church that serves the poor in Latin America—with the help of the Vatican, unfortunately. They are amply funded for these activities by the intelligence agencies of the US and its clients and the closely linked international organizations of the ultraright.

Bernays expressed the basic point in a public relations manual of 1928: "The conscious and intelligent manipulation of the organized habits and opinions of the masses is an important element in democratic society. . . . It is the intelligent minorities which need to make use of propaganda continuously and systematically." Given its enormous and decisive power, the highly class-conscious business community of the United States has been able to put these lessons to effective use. Bernays's advocacy of propaganda is cited by Thomas McCann, head of public relations for the United Fruit Company, for which Bernays provided signal service in preparing the ground for the overthrow of Guatemalan democracy in 1954, a major triumph of business propaganda with the willing compliance of the media.[31]

The intelligent minorities have understood this to be their function. The dean of US journalism, Walter Lippmann, described a "revolution" in "the practice of democracy" as "the manufacture of consent" that has become "a self-conscious art and a regular organ of popular government." This is a natural development when "the common interests very largely elude public opinion entirely, and can be managed only by a specialized class whose personal interests reach beyond the locality," and the "men of best quality," who are capable of social and economic management.

These doctrines of sociology and psychology having been established by the device of authoritative pronouncement, it follows that two political roles must be clearly distinguished, Lippmann goes on to explain. First, there is the role assigned to the specialized class, the "insiders," the "responsible men," who have access to information and understanding. Ideally, they should have a special education for public office and should master the criteria for solving the problems of society; "In the degree to which these criteria can be made exact and objective, political decision," which is their domain, "is actually brought into relation with the interests of men." The "public men" are, furthermore, to "lead opinion" and take the responsibility for "the formation of a sound public opinion." Tacitly assumed is that the specialized class serve the public interest—what is called "the national interest" in the webs of mystification spun by the academic social sciences and political commentary.

The second role is "the task of the public," which is much more limited. It is not for the public, Lippmann observes, to "pass judgment on the intrinsic merits" of an issue or to offer analysis or solutions, but merely, on occasion, to place "its force at the disposal" of one or another group of "responsible men." The public "does not reason, investigate, invent, persuade, bargain or settle." Rather, "the public acts only by aligning itself as the partisan of someone in a position to act executively," once he has given the matter at hand sober and disinterested thought. "The public must be put in its place" so that we "may live free of the trampling and the roar of a bewildered herd." The herd "has its function": to be "the interested spectators of action," not the participants; that is the duty of "the responsible man."[32]

These ideas, regarded as a progressive "political philosophy for liberal democracy," have an unmistakable resemblance to the Leninist concept of a vanguard party that leads the stupid masses to a better life that they cannot conceive or construct on their own. In fact, the transition from one position to the other, from Leninist enthusiasm to "celebration of America," has proven quite an easy one over the years. This is not surprising, since the doctrines are similar at their root, the difference lying primarily in an assessment of the prospects for power: through exploitation of mass popular struggle or service to the current masters.

There is, clearly enough, an unspoken assumption behind the proposals of Lippmann and others: the specialized class are offered the opportunity to manage public affairs by virtue of their subservience to those with real power—in our societies, dominant business interests—a crucial fact that is ignored in the self-praise of the elect.

Lippmann's thinking on these matters dates from shortly after World War I, when the liberal intellectual community was much impressed with its success in serving as "the faithful and helpful interpreters of what seems to be one of the greatest enterprises ever undertaken by an American president" (*New Republic*). The enterprise was Woodrow Wilson's interpretation of his electoral mandate for "peace without victory" as the occasion for pursuing victory without peace, with the assistance of the liberal intellectuals, who later praised themselves for having "impose[d] their will upon a reluctant or indifferent majority," with the aid of propaganda fabrications about Hun atrocities and other such devices. They were serving, often unwittingly, as instruments of the British Ministry of Information, which secretly defined its task as "to direct the thought of most of the world."[33] Fifteen years later, the influential political scientist Harold Lasswell explained in the *Encyclopaedia of the Social Sciences* that we should not succumb to "democratic dogmatisms about men being the best judges of their own interests." They are not; the best judges are the elite, who must, therefore, be ensured the means to impose their will, for the common good. When social arrangements deny them the requisite force to compel obedience, it is necessary to turn to "a whole new technique of control, largely through propaganda," because of the "ignorance and superstition (of) the masses." Others have developed similar ideas and put them into practice in the ideological institutions: the schools, the universities, the popular media, the elite journals, and so on.

Such doctrines are entirely natural in any society in which power is narrowly concentrated but formal mechanisms exist by which ordinary people may, in theory, play some role in shaping their own affairs—a threat that plainly must be barred.

The techniques of manufacture of consent are most finely honed in the United States, a more advanced business-run society than its allies and one that is in important ways more free than elsewhere, so the ignorant and stupid masses are potentially more dangerous. But the same concerns remain standard in Europe, as in the past. In August 1943, South African Prime Minister Jan Christian Smuts warned his friend Winston Churchill that "with politics let loose among those people, we may have a wave disorder and wholesale Communism set going all over those parts of Europe." Churchill's conception was that "the government of the world" should be in the hands of "rich men dwelling at peace within their habitations," who had "no reason to seek for anything more" and, thus, would keep the peace, excluding those who were "hungry" and" ambitious." The same precepts apply at home. Smuts was referring specifically to southern Europe, though the concerns were far broader. With conservative elites discredited by their association with fascism and radical democratic ideas in the air, it was necessary to pursue a worldwide program to crush the anti-fascist resistance and its popular base and restore the traditional order, to ensure that politics would not be let loose among those peoples; this campaign, conducted from Korea to Western Europe, would the first topic of the first chapter of any serious work on post–World War II history.[34]

The same problems arise today. In Europe, they are heightened by the fact that, unlike the United States, its variety has not yet largely eliminated labor unions and restricted politics to factions of the business party, so that some impediments remain to rule by people of the best quality. These persistent concerns help explain the ambivalence of European elites towards détente, which brings with it the loss of a technique of social control through fear of the great enemy.

The basic problem, recognized throughout, is that as the state loses the capacity to control the population by force, privileged sectors must find other methods to ensure that the rascal multitude is removed from the public arena. And the insignificant nations must be subjected to the same practices as the insignificant people. The dilemma was explained by Robert Pastor, Latin American specialist of the Carter administration, at the extreme liberal and dovish end of the political spectrum. Defending US policy over many years, he writes that "the United States did not want to control Nicaragua or other nations in the region, but it also did not want to allow developments to get out of control. It wanted Nicaraguans to act independently, *except* when doing so would affect US interests adversely."[35] In short, Nicaragua and other countries should be free—free to do what we want them to do—and should choose their course independently, as long as their choice conforms to our interests. If they use the freedom we accord them unwisely then, naturally, we are entitled to respond in self-defense.

The ideas expressed are a close counterpart to the prevailing liberal conception of democracy at home as a form of population control. At the other extreme of the spectrum, we find the "conservatives" with their preference for quick resort to Kristol's methods: gunboats and police cars.

A properly functioning system of indoctrination has a variety of tasks, some rather delicate. One of its targets is the stupid and ignorant masses. They must be kept that way, diverted with emotionally potent oversimplifications, marginalized, and isolated. Ideally, each person should be alone in front of the TV screen watching sports, soap operas, or comedies, deprived of organizational structures that permit individuals lacking resources to discover what they think and believe in interaction with others, to formulate their own concerns and programs, and to act to realize them. They can then be permitted, even encouraged, to ratify the decisions of their betters in periodic elections. The rascal multitude are the proper targets of the mass media and a public education system geared to obedience and training in needed skills, including the skill of repeating patriotic slogans on timely occasions.

The problem of indoctrination is a bit different for those expected to take part in serious decision-making and control: the business, state, and cultural managers and the articulate sectors generally. They must internalize the values of the system and share the necessary illusions that permit it to function in the interests of concentrated power and privilege—or at least be cynical enough to pretend that they do, an art that not many can master. But they must also have a certain grasp of the realities of the world, or they will be unable to perform their tasks effectively. The elite media and educational systems must steer a course through these dilemmas; not an easy task.

It is intriguing to see in detail how it is done, but that is beyond the scope of these remarks.

I would like to end by stressing again one crucial point. The instinct for freedom can be dulled, and often is, but has yet to be killed. The courage and dedication of people struggling for freedom, their willingness to confront extreme state terror and violence, is often amazing. There has been a slow growth of consciousness over many years and goals have been achieved that were considered utopian or scarcely contemplated in earlier eras. An inveterate optimist can point to this record and express the hope that with a new decade, and soon a new century, humanity may be able to overcome some of its dire social maladies; others might draw a different lesson from recent history. It is hard to see rational grounds for affirming one or the other perspective. As in the case of many of the natural beliefs that guide our lives, we can do no better than to choose a kind of Pascal's wager: by denying the instinct for freedom, we will only prove that humans are a lethal mutation, an evolutionary dead end: by nurturing it, if it is real, we may find ways to deal with dreadful human tragedies and problems that are awesome in scale.

Notes

1 Noam Chomsky's contribution to the event drew upon material that would appear in subsequent papers: "Mental Constructions and Social Reality," Conference on Knowledge and Language, Groningen, May 1989; "The Culture of Terrorism: The Third World and the Global Order," Conference on Parliamentary Democracy and State Terrorism after 1945, Hamburg, May 19, 1990.

2 George E. Davie, *The Democratic Intellect: Scotland and Her Universities in the Nineteenth Century* (Edinburgh: University of Edinburgh, 1961), 274ff.

3 Marchamont Nedham (1650), cited in Edmund S. Morgan, *Inventing the People: The Rise of Popular Sovereignty in England and America* (New York: Norton, 1988), 79; Hume, 1, cited with the qualification just noted.

4 Diego Ribadeneira, "Panama Plans Murder Charge for Noriega," *Boston Globe*, January 1, 1990.

5 Eduardo Galeano, *Days and Nights of Love and War* (New York: Monthly Review Press, 1983).

6 For fuller discussion, see the memorial lectures for Russell delivered by Chomsky at Trinity College, Cambridge; Noam Chomsky, *Problems of Knowledge and Freedom: The Russell Lectures* (New York: Pantheon Books, 1971).

7 James Harris, Ralph Cudworth; see Noam Chomsky, *Cartesian Linguistics: A Chapter in the History of Rationalist Thought* (New York: Harper & Row, 1966); for further discussion, see Noam Chomsky "Language and Freedom," in Noam Chomsky, *The Chomsky Reader*, ed. James Peck (New York: Pantheon Books, 1987); Noam Chomsky, *For Reasons of State* (London: Penguin Books, 2003).

8 See Noam Chomsky, *Turning the Tide: US Intervention in Central America and the Struggle for Peace* (Boston: South End Press, 1985), chapter 5; Thomas Ferguson and Joel Rogers, *Right Turn: The Decline of the Democrats and the Future of American Politics* (New York: Hill & Wang, 1986); Michael Benhoff, "Letters," *Z Magazine*, March 1989; Rob Ferguson, *Socialist Review* 19, no. 4 (1989).

9 Margaret Judson, cited in Leonard W. Levy, *Emergence of a Free Press* (Oxford: Oxford University Press, 1985), 91.

10 Christopher Hill, *The World Turned Upside Down* (London: Penguin Books, 1975); with regard to Locke, Hill adds, "at least Locke did not intend that priests should do the telling; that was for God himself."

11 Levy, *Emergence of a Free Press*, 98–100. On the "massive intolerance" of Milton's *Areopagitica*, commonly regarded as a groundbreaking libertarian appeal, see John Illo, "Areopagiticas Mythic and Real," *Prose Studies* 11, no. 1 (May 1988). Milton himself explained that the purpose of the tract was "so that the determination of true and false, of what should be published and what should be suppressed, might not be under control of... unlearned men of mediocre judgment," but only "an appointed officer" of the right persuasion, who will have the authority to ban work he finds to be "mischievous or libellous," "erroneous and scandalous," "impious or evil absolutely against faith or manners," as well as "popery" and "open superstition."

12 Morgan, *Inventing the People*, 75–76.

13 See "Common Sense and Freedom," pages 135–40, this volume.

14 Tzvetan Todorov, *The Conquest of America: The Question of the Other* (New York: Harper & Row, 1983), 5, 150.

15 Francis Jennings, *Empire of Fortune: Crowns, Colonies, and Tribes in the Seven Years War in America* (New York: Norton, 1988), chapter 1. Indians have "nothing human except the shape," Washington wrote: "... the gradual extension of our settlements will as certainly cause the savage, as the wolf, to retire; both being beasts of prey, tho' they differ in shape"; ibid., 62; Richard Drinnon, *Facing West: The*

Metaphysics of Indian-Hating and Empire-Building (Norman, OK: University of Oklahoma Press, 1980), 65, citing a Washington letter of 1783.

16 See Chomsky, *Turning the Tide*, 162–63.

17 Morgan, *Inventing the People*, 75–76.

18 Lenin, 1922, cited in Moshe Lewin, *Lenin's Last Struggle* (New York: Pantheon Books, 1968). Lewin's interpretation of Lenin's goals and efforts is far from what I have indicated here, however.

19 For references here and below, where not otherwise cited, see Chomsky, *Turning the Tide*; Noam Chomsky, *Necessary Illusions: Thought Control in Democratic Societies* (Boston: South End Press, 1989); for more on Robert Lansing and Woodrow Wilson, see Lloyd C. Gardner, *Safe for Democracy: Anglo-American Response to Revolution, 1913–23* (Oxford: Oxford University Press, 1984), 157, 161, 261, 242.

20 Samuel P. Huntington, in Michael Crozier, Samuel P. Huntington, and Joji Watanuki, *The Crisis of Democracy: Report on the Governability of Democracies to the Trilateral Commission* (New York: Trilateral Commission, 1975), 9n1.

21 Irving Kristol, "Where Have All the Gunboats Gone," *Wall Street Journal*, December 13, 1973.

22 For further discussion and references, see Chomsky, *Necessary Illusions*, appendix V, sec. 8.

23 Levy, *Emergence of a Free Press*, xvii, 9, 102, 41, 130.

24 Ibid., 6, 167.

25 Ibid.

26 For a few of the many examples that might be cited in the case of France, see Chomsky, *Necessary Illusions*, 344. On the Rushdie affair, see Christopher Frew, "Craven Evasion on the Threat to Freedom," *Scotsman*, August 3, 1989, referring to the shameful behavior of Paul Johnson and Hugh Trevor-Roper—who were not alone. Rushdie was charged with seditious libel and blasphemy in the courts, but the High Court ruled that the law of blasphemy extended only to Christianity, not to Islam, and that only verbal attack "against Her Majesty or Her Majesty's Government or some other institution of the state" counts as seditious libel; "Bid to Prosecute Rushdie Is Rejected," *New York Times*, April 10, 1990. Thus, the Court upheld the basic doctrines of the Ayatollah Khomeini, Stalin, Goebbels, and other opponents of freedom, while recognizing that English law, like that of its counterparts, protects only domestic power from criticism.

27 Conor Cruise O'Brien, cited in *British Journalism Review* 1, no. 2 (Winter 1990).

28 Levy, *Emergence of a Free Press*, 226–27; Harry Kalven, *A Worthy Tradition: Freedom of Speech in America* (New York: Harper & Row,

1988), 63, 227f., 121f. No such brief commentary on freedom of speech can pretend to be adequate. As noted, more complex questions arise when we pass from expression of views to expression that borders on incitement to action (say, ordering a killer with a gun to shoot), and when we consider the right to a private space and other matters.

29 See Noam Chomsky, "Reinhold Niebuhr," *Grand Street* 6, no. 2 (Winter 1987).

30 Cited in Herbert Schiller, *Culture Inc.: The Corporate Takeover of Public Expression* (New York: Oxford University Press, 1989).

31 Thomas P. McCann, *An American Company: The Tragedy of United Fruit* (New York: Crown Publishers, 1976), 45. On the ludicrous performance of the media, also see Chomsky, *Turning the Tide*, 164f; William Preston and Ellen Ray, "Disinformation and Mass Deception: Democracy as a Cover Story," in Richard O. Curry, ed., *Freedom at Risk: Secrecy, Censorship, and Repression in the 1980s* (Philadelphia: Temple University Press, 1988).

32 Clinton Rossiter and James Lare, *The Essential Lippmann: A Political Philosophy* (Cambridge, MA: Harvard University Press, 1982).

33 Cited from secret documents in Randal Marlin, "Propaganda and the Ethics of Persuasion," *International Journal of Moral and Social Studies* 4, no. 1 (Spring 1989). For more on these matters, see "Intellectuals and the State."

34 For some details, see Noam Chomsky, "Democracy in the Industrial Societies," *Z Magazine*, January 1989, and sources cited.

35 Robert Pastor, *Condemned to Repetition: The United States and Nicaragua* (Princeton, NJ: Princeton University Press, 1987), 32; emphasis in the original.

Introducing Day Two*

James Kelman

Leading on from my introduction yesterday morning and to the origin of this two-day conference, I mentioned how for my own part it began from an essay I was doing derived from a reading of Noam Chomsky's work. My intention was to give a broad idea of what was going on, so that a general readership could gain some understanding. It seemed to me that there was a way into the work which might open up areas that are normally sealed off to those without specialized knowledge.

If I have any specialized knowledge myself, it is probably literature, prose fiction. The way our education system operates these days we are taught to look at the world as a series of boxes; inside each is an area of study. The teacher opens the box for you and lets you have a look inside, and then when you finish school the box gets locked up again and the key vanishes. My own experience is of some folk knowing about Professor Chomsky's work in linguistics, some about the politics, others who know about the general philosophical side, others yet again who know about his contribution to the study of mind.

So in my essay the objective was to draw some things together: the term I'm looking for is "generalist." I was trying

* This is a revised version of the talk I prepared to introduce Day Two. At the event, I had to cut it short and improvise on some of it, as I spoke without notes. Derek Rodger, editor of *Scottish Child* magazine had begun the session with basic "housekeeping" information.

to give a generalist account, in what used to be the Scottish way in the sense that Scottish education leant towards a generalist approach. The name of George Davie here immediately arises. His work on the Scottish tradition is fundamental to my own understanding. The crucial value of this generalist approach is how it provides the conditions of entry into any specialist box you like. And once you grasp the point you no longer have quite the same worries about being "presumptuous"; that's only for those who believe that technical matters should be trusted to the "experts."

The role of ordinary person as "watchdog" on society's "experts" is crucial to Professor Chomsky's political writings. In general terms, if his work is about anything it is about the primacy of the individual, the essential and fundamental common sense of each and every human being, the facility of thinking and judging for ourselves.

And from a different vantage point, every attempt to disseminate technical information for the public at large becomes an act of political significance.

When I began work on the essay—for *Edinburgh Review*—I had no real appreciation of the extent of the controversy surrounding him, not simply in reference to the politics but to his work in linguistics and the study of mind generally. If his politics are libertarian socialist his philosophical stance is rationalist; he takes the view that freedom is the fundamental right of every individual, and that certain faculties are innate in human beings—an intellectual position which has been fairly controversial, not to say pretty much of a philosophical nonstarter, at least in Anglo-American terms, for the past 250 years.

My reading for the essay was diverted by articles being published by *Edinburgh Review* on Scottish philosophy, in particular the "Common Sense" tradition. Most of what I have now gleaned on the subject is due to the work of George Davie. During my own period at University, David Hume was the only Scottish philosopher I recall being asked to examine. It is worth noting that the "distinctive Scottish tradition" can be said to have arisen in direct opposition to Hume's skepticism, yet his is the only side of the argument to be studied seriously. His main rival of the day was Thomas Reid, Professor of Moral Philosophy at Glasgow University. What struck me about Reid's advocacy of natural judgment was how it seemed to me to offer the possibility for a philosophy of Common Sense without having to rely on innate ideas—and my use of "without having to rely on innate ideas" is no doubt a straight reflection of the prejudiced viewpoint of the mainstream Anglo-American position on the subject.

I was also interested in what seemed to be a chain of thought extending from Reid, by way of major Scottish thinkers like William Hamilton, Clerk Maxwell, Robert Brown, J.F. Ferrier and also the poet and novelist James Hogg which tied in with a line of thought apparent in the work of the great Russian tradition, writers like Gogol and on from there, and in Germany there was Goethe (whom Hogg translated), and a view of the "existential voice" in literature I had discussed and picked up on from the many conversations I've had with Tom Leonard over the past few years.

It was intriguing too about this notion of "Common Sense" or natural judgment that this period in time "coincided" with a more general spread of learning; an exchange and dissemination of knowledge, and a rise in creativity among working-class people with a bit of time to spare, in particular the weavers. And, inevitably, it was a time of social unrest, something of which I had been familiar, having researched the period for a play based on the lives of two of the three weavers murdered by due process of the British State back in 1820.

Eventually, I sent a copy of George Davie's *The Democratic Intellect* to Noam Chomsky, and included some his uncollected articles, which Peter Kravitz of *Edinburgh Review* had loaned me.

I had made contact with Noam Chomsky before then. In the summer of last year, his English publishers were organizing a public lecture by him in Battersea Town Hall. I wrote to ask if he had the time might he consider travelling north to give another public lecture, this time in Scotland. And, if he agreed, we would work out the finer details later on; I'm referring here to friends involved in the Free University group. His diary was full. But he said he would keep my letter on file. A couple of months later, he made contact; due to a cancellation, he would be able to make the trip in a year's time (Chomsky operates his diary two years in advance).

Then I discovered he had received another invitation to travel north, once again from a non-academic source.

Now I should say that after the publication of my last novel, *A Disaffection*, I was interviewed by the *Scottish Child* magazine and later photographed for it by someone I had never known before; this was the magazine's editor, Derek Rodger. In the manner of all such extraordinary flukes, once we got talking I found that Derek was the other person in Scotland who had issued Chomsky the invitation.

After much discussion within the Free University and the *Scottish Child*, we agreed it was best to combine our efforts. In fact, in hindsight, I don't know how much of a choice we had, given Noam Chomsky had already made his own position clear, that we might work together. It so happens that the *Scottish Child* initiative countered and balanced our own by being less oriented towards the philosophical and perhaps political context.

From here on it became a tale of organization, but organization without official funding other than Arts Council sponsoring of contributing writers for doing readings, and I mean by that poets and prose-fiction writers.*

* I later met a man from the Arts Council who said to me, off the record: "Come, come James, Noam Chomsky a writer!" I responded, "Look at the number of books he's published!" In the end, they did grant us the basic contributor's fee.

As you know, the level of interest in the event has been great. It has succeeded because of the determination and enthusiasm of those involved in the organizing, the different levels of support we've had, and the many people involved throughout the two days in the different workshops and discussion groups.

Govan's Pearce Institute proved the place best suited for our purposes. That applies not only to the fine facilities it can offer but to the actual history of the location, both recent and ancient. At a personal level, the Govan connection appealed strongly to me. My great aunt lived much of her life surrounded by a large troop of cats in a dilapidated house along from here, Copland Road. More to the point, my granny lived sixty years in Uist Street. She and my grandpa worked at Fairfield Shipyard, a couple of hundred yards along the road from here. That's where they met. After his retiral my grandpa played dominoes right here, at the Pearce Institute. So there ye are!

First on this morning is Professor Chomsky and our second speaker, George Davie, will be giving a reply to Professor Chomsky's keynote address of yesterday.

Common Sense and Freedom

Noam Chomsky

I am torn between two conflicting impulses. A sense of duty leads me to want to speak about the topic I've been asked to address. But I also feel a good deal of empathy with sentiments expressed at the plenary session by many people who felt that there is something quite unsatisfying about general and abstract discussion of questions of deep human significance—such as self-determination & power—unless it is brought to bear *quote* directly upon concrete and substantive problems of daily life: what we should do about specific circumstances of injustice and oppression.*

If we pursue the second course, we have to be serious about it. However much insight we might hope to develop in general terms about self-determination, freedom, and justice, it would still leave us far from the task of designing a specific course of action in particular conditions and situations, historical or personal. We might draw a lesson from the history of the sciences. It was not until the nineteenth century that practical engineering work could expect to draw

* Noam Chomsky had been asked to speak on the topic "Common Sense and Freedom." The previous day he had attended a couple of workshops where general issues had arisen. This was encouraged by the organizers. The conference was marked by the widely differing experiences and perspectives of participants. In a different workshop, Chomsky might have encountered different priorities.

much from fundamental science, and we need hardly stress that in the domains that we are concerned with today, we are very far from even much more primitive stages of scientific understanding.

To be serious about real historical situations, we have to come to understand their particularities and to apply judgments that are by no means firmly based. Take the question of national self-determination, which has arisen several times. If we want to say something sensible about particular cases—say, Northern Ireland, the Ibos and Kurds, the Israeli-Palestinian conflict—then we have to understand these situations. General precepts may be helpful, but only in a limited way, and the human problems are too important for glib proposals to be warranted or even tolerable.

The same is true with regard to other questions that arose in the plenary session, such as educational policy or political democracy under state capitalism or democratization of the media.

So it seems that I have two choices: to keep to the general issues of freedom and common sense (as dictated by a sense of duty); or to discuss specific questions of power, justice, and human rights. If I were to take the latter course, I'd have to keep to questions to which I've given some thought and study. Thus, in the case of national self-determination, I would feel able to discuss the question of Israel-Palestine but not that of Northern Ireland. In the former case, what I have to say might be right or wrong, smart or stupid, but at least it would be based on inquiry and thought.

At a conference like this one, the second course seems to me the appropriate one for group sessions or for the general discussion that will follow. For the introductory comments such as these, the general issues seem a more proper choice. So I'll follow the sense of duty and keep to some general remarks about these—but limited ones, so that we can turn the discussion of more concrete and urgent matters without undue delay.

On the matter of common sense and freedom, there is a rich tradition that develops the idea that people have intrinsic rights. Accordingly, any authority that infringes upon these rights is illegitimate. These are natural rights, rooted in human nature, which is part of the natural world, so we should be able to learn about it by rational inquiry. But social theory and action cannot be held in abeyance while science takes, for example, its halting steps towards establishing truths about human nature, and philosophy seeks to explain the connection, which we all sense exists, between human nature and rights deriving from it. We, therefore, are compelled to take an intuitive leap, to make a posit as to what is essential to human nature, and on this basis to derive, however inadequately, a conception of a legitimate social order. Any judgment about social action (or inaction) relies upon reasoning of this sort. A person of any integrity will select a course of action on grounds that the likely consequence will accord with human rights and needs and will explore the validity of these grounds as well as one can.

According to one traditional idea, it is of fundamental human need—and hence a fundamental human right—to inquire and to create, free of external compulsion. This is a basic doctrine of classical liberalism in its original eighteenth-century version, for example, in the work of Wilhelm von Humboldt, who inspired Mill. Obviously, consequences were immediately drawn. One is that whatever does not spring from free choice but only from compulsion or instruction or guidance remains alien to our true nature. If a worker labors under the threat of force or of need or a student produces on demand, we may admire what they do, but we despise what they are. Institutional structures are legitimate insofar as they enhance the opportunity to freely inquire and create out of inner need; otherwise, they are not.

For people with any faith in the worth and dignity of human beings, this is an attractive vision. We can proceed to draw from it a whole range of conclusions about legitimate institutions and social action.

This picture contrasts with a conflicting one that has dominated much intellectual discourse: the view that people are empty organisms, malleable, products of their training and cultural environment, their minds a blank slate, on which experiences writes what it will. Human nature is, then, a historical and cultural product, with no essential properties beyond the weak and general organizing principles with which the largely vacuous system may be endowed. If so, there are few moral barriers to compulsion, shaping of behavior, or manufacture of consent. From these assumptions, we derive a different conception of a legitimate social order, one that is familiar in our daily lives. This too is an attractive view—from the standpoint of those who claim the right to exercise authority and control.

Looked at in this way, the empty organism view is conservative, in that it tends to legitimate structures of hierarchy and domination. At least in its Humboldtian version, the classical liberal view, with its strong innatist roots, is radical in that, consistently pursued, it challenges the legitimacy of established coercive institutions. Such institutions face a heavy burden of proof: it must be shown that under existing conditions, perhaps because of some overriding consideration of deprivation or threat, some form of authority, hierarchy, and domination is justified, despite the prima facie case against it—a burden that can rarely be met. One can understand why there is such a persistent attack on Enlightenment ideals, with their fundamentally subversive content.

I should add that this is far from the usual way of framing the issues, but I think it is defensible and proper.

Apart from preferences and hopes, which of these conceptions, or which alternatives to them, leads us towards the truth about human nature? To answer such questions, one must refine and elaborate the framework of ideas. That has been done to a limited extent, and when it is, we can raise questions of truth and falsity. It is, I think, a fair conclusion that in any domain where we know anything, the empty organism thesis, or any of its variants, is demonstrably false. It is therefore tenable only beyond the reach of our current understanding, a conclusion that is certainly suggestive.

Nevertheless, the thesis that lacks empirical support has always been widely accepted. Why should this be the case? One speculation derives from the question: who benefits? We have already seen a plausible answer: the beneficiaries are those whose calling is to manage and control, who face no serious moral barrier to their pursuits if empty organism doctrines are correct. The beneficiaries are a certain category of intellectuals, who can offer a service to systems of power and domination. But on average, it is this group that will attain reward and respectability, hence be recognized for their intellectual contributions. Pursuing this logic, we can see at least one reason why ideas about the mutability and essential vacuity of human nature should gain status and become entrenched, however slightly their merit.

In a few domains, it has been possible to pose the questions of fact in a serious way, and inquiry has borne some fruit. In these domains, it has been possible seriously to face the question of what we "innately know," a question raised in the announcement of this meeting. It has been possible to gain some understanding of those parts of our knowledge that come from the original hand of nature, in Hume's terms—from genetic endowment, in the modern version. We quickly learn that these components of our knowledge and understanding are far beyond anything that Hume envisioned. His predecessors appear to have been far closer to the mark: Lord Herbert of Cherbury and the Cambridge Platonists of the seventeenth century and the continental rationalists of the same era.

The more we investigate, the more we discover that basic elements of thought and language derive from an invariant intellectual endowment, a structure of concepts and principles that provides the framework for experience, interpretation, judgment and understanding. The more we learn about these matters, the more it seems that training is an irrelevance and learning an artefact, except at the margins. It seems that mental processes grow in the mind along their natural, intrinsically determined path, triggered by experience and partially modified by it, but apparently only in fairly superficial ways. This should not be a surprising conclusion. If true, it means that mental organs are like bodily organs—or, more accurately, like *other* bodily organs, for these are organs of the body as well. Despite conventional empiricist and behavioral dogma, we should not be startled to discover that the mind and brain are like everything else in the natural world, and that it is a highly specific initial endowment that permits the mind to develop rich and articulated systems of knowledge, understanding, and judgment, largely shared with others, vastly beyond the reach of any determining experience.

Where does this leave us with respect to social theory and action? Still pretty far away, I am afraid. There is a large gap between what we must establish to ground the choice of action and what we grasp with any confidence and understanding. Whether the gap can be filled is not clear. No one knows how to do it now, and we are left with the unavoidable necessity to act on the basis of intuition and hope. Mine is that something like the classical liberal doctrine is correct, and that there is no legitimacy to the commissar, the corporate or cultural manager, or any of those who claim the right to manipulate and control us, typically on specious grounds.

A Response to Noam Chomsky

George E. Davie

Yesterday there was a reference to a local boy, David Hume. I had an Indian colleague at Edinburgh University who was very amused to find that the students in Indian universities would all know of at least the names of the famous Indian philosophers, if nothing else about them, but he had tested his students in Edinburgh, and the names of the local philosophers, David Hume, etc., meant nothing to them—Adam Smith they had vaguely heard of. But still, traditions can be a dead weight, and it's maybe an advantage in Scotland that they hadn't bothered about traditions, that they had to start afresh—although this often meant they did the same thing again and again.

I don't want to bother you too much with that sort of thing, but to start off with what Professor Chomsky said, quoting from Hume, that politics was based, to some extent, on opinion. The government had, so to speak, in order to keep its position, to persuade the majority to accept their rule, to accept that they were right. And Hume does then raise this as a kind of puzzle, how amazing it is that governments can manage to do this; the few persuading the many.

Now, the point can best be brought out by reference to something I heard in the early sixties at the School of African Studies in Edinburgh when during a discussion—Nkrumah had published a philosophy book, and they had a discussion about it—one of the Africans there, speaking about the

Organisation for African Unity in its early days, said that it was very much influenced by the fact that the educational systems in the emergent African countries tended to be either influenced or based on the British model or the French model. And he said that when you got finally down to the question of principles, then those with the French basis would keep talking about Greek philosophy, and those with the British basis would keep speaking about down-to-earth statistics.

Now, this particular thing is relevant because Hume—though he was a great statistician and his best-seller was a popular book on economics—would have sided with the French rather than the British. We had to follow up the statistics with the Greek philosophy, or else something like it. The thing was that Hume was irritated. He thought that we could do more in Britain to go back to the subject of first principles, and not just stick to statistics. On the whole he didn't make much impression on the British, and the French view that was just emerging was more to his taste. Incidentally, in that connection—if I can allude to a subject that seems liable to raise considerable storms given some of the comments from the floor yesterday—it was at that particular point that Hume made his contribution to Feminism. He said that one advantage of the French system of widening the thing was that at least in polite society the women didn't retire after dinner to let the gentlemen drink their coffee and brandy. They joined in the conversation about politics, philosophy, and life in general.

Now that's just by way of, basically, a kind of long introduction to what I wanted to say, about one or two things on the Scottish philosophers. Not so much about Thomas Reid as about Hume, and Adam Smith who was on the whole quite the greatest of Scottish philosophers. Smith was quite a chap. When Smith was a Professor in Glasgow people in Europe eventually got to hear that there was a professor in the West of Scotland with something new to say, and they came to listen to him from all over the place—much like Professor Chomsky today.

To get more to the background of this, and to make a point which is to some extent a query for Professor Chomsky: he was right in saying that what Hume said about politics being based on opinion was to do more with developed than with primitive society, and Hume was very definite about that. The foundations of primitive society didn't really have to do with opinion. People didn't decide that getting together would be a good thing and then get together. They were together from the start. And human life is social from the start, Hume said.

The important point was then his definition of "social." He took the distinguishing feature of the social bond to be the division of labor. George Berkeley had said that it was labor. But Hume (and Francis Hutcheson and so on) said it was the division of labor—exchanges and so forth, something like the market. This was, of course, on a very small scale and they distinguished between—as we still do—a face-to-face society and an extended society where people are not aware of what's going on, where things take place behind people's backs. And it's in this extended society that government arises.

The classical philosophers, like Hume or Smith, wouldn't have thought that there was anything but a plurality of societies which could come into conflict with one another. With reference to the urban society Hume says the mother(s) of cities are camps, and the limit for power and so forth is the temporary appointment of leaders, in particular kinds of circumstances, when these communities are defending themselves. And this is a basic feature of society; it tends to be missed out when speaking about society in general; but there it is, the plurality, world governments being unworkable.

Another point—particularly with reference to Hume—is that societies develop in different directions, especially because of this useful concept of "the division of labor." It's carried less far in some societies, less developed societies, where people learn to be "jacks-of-all-trades." And then, of course, in more advanced societies people are more specialized.

In that connection Hume and the others didn't think it was going to be easy to get any kind of elimination of specialization, or of any "evening-out."

And this brings me to what Professor Chomsky said about those who consider human nature to be structured and those who consider human nature as being plastic; —whether it's a matter of abilities or not. Hume made the distinction, in general, between what he said was a society where the division of labor was advanced—something like the market society—and other societies where the division of labor was not so advanced, where you have something like the "command economy," as we would call it. In this particular case, he was thinking of the great continental monarchies who were all protective and interventionist, although nothing much came of their interventionism. It wasn't, according to Hume and Smith, going to be easy to get rid of this opposition between the market economy (with specialization and very considerable material wealth) and the other kind of economy—monarchist or whatever—which was very tightly organized. And Hume had said that they might have to live together and learn what they could from one another. (Things like dramatic performances and so on were very often better done in the monolithic, centralized and monarchical societies; as well as politeness, a touch of deference and so forth.)

Of course, we see, or seem to see at the moment, that this is dissolving; the end of history so to speak—that the market economy is going to spread right through the rest of Europe. But this might not be an advantage for us at all, because this goes beyond deference and lies beyond borders. There are the Ayatollahs for instance and there are the Chinese, and they may develop in other ways. So we will still be requiring, of course, a certain amount of military defense, much like the Cold War, as oppositions arise.

This leads, once again, to the question: could you not get a fair government, an egalitarian government, which would eliminate the necessity for armed forces, the police, prisons, etc. And, of course, there is the study of the victory of egalitarianism in the various egalitarian revolutions; the great one being the French, but to some extent there is the English one, and there is also the Russian one. And, of course, the very interesting point that comes out here. The attainment of power by an egalitarian government contains one curious and very disturbing consequence, according to experience, and this is the Terror. What is the Terror directed against? It's not so much against the people, with their various views; the Terror is directed by the Committee of Public Safety, or the Politburo, against its own members. They have to remain together, they dread the business of dividing, because unity is strength. Therefore, even in the extreme case of the victory of an honestly egalitarian government, you can't get rid of this concept of Terror. There it is in the case of the French and the Russians; and there was something of that no doubt within the Revolution in England, the 1640s, when Cromwell took power. There are points Professor Chomsky—who is of course well aware of them—tended to leave in the background.

Secondly, one point to do with the business of philosophical politics, and where philosophy and these things come in. Somebody was saying that people carried out the action and other people, the thinkers, took the credit. This is maybe so, but action is as likely to go wrong as to go right; so thinkers, insofar as they take the credit, are also the people who get the blame. You know, when the French Revolution is discussed in a popular kind of way, the famous phrase: "Is the fault Voltaire's, or is the fault Rousseau's." And the point is that this intellectual thing is not by any means valueless. And one can refer to Professor Chomsky's own work.

I can take, for example, a point that Chomsky has spoken about in one of his books and has also been looked at by Harry Bracken. It concerns the question of racism, with particular reference to color and intelligent behavior. Is there a connection or not? Hume took this up, but orthodox science, following him, had one way of settling that, and that was a great many behavioristic studies about defining what intelligent behavior would be, creative behavior, in this part of the world or that part of the world, people of this color or that color. And with immense labor you arrive at some kind of generalization.

This is the orthodox way and Harry Bracken (following Chomsky) made the point that it is a good example of how science can be misplaced and go off the rails. Because if you look into Aurel Kolnar's *War against the West*, a very good analysis of the intellectual background to the rise of Nazism: it was due to German Wissehnschaft being interpreted as a rather crude behaviorist scientific theory. As soon as you get into this business of deciding by means of behavioristic analysis the connection of color, or the bodily structure, to intelligent behavior, you're onto the business of measuring skulls; and the most absurd and horrible racist things can be kept alive.

Now what Harry Bracken was saying, and what Chomsky ascribed to him, was that this was, of course, a misplacement of science. It was not the way to discuss this question at all. It's what would be called a conceptual question. And simply to use common sense and reason, it is evident that the color of an object or person has no connection with behavior or intelligence. That it doesn't seems to me fairly clear; you can call this common sense, you can call it what you like. Science has clearly gone dangerously wrong on this point.

This point can be extended further if we go back again to our business of the variety of communities; advanced communities with the division of labor and all the rest of it, wealth etc. and market economies; and the more backward economies with a poorer division of labor. Now, one of the most interesting features that comes from Rousseau—but was elaborated by the Scottish philosophers Adam Ferguson and Adam Smith, eloquently and clearly—was that there was another side to the thing. There is an old notion that wealth corrupts, and on analysis this is not entirely false. An over-extended division of labor that doesn't teach people how to keep in touch with one another can lead to the general demoralization of society. Countries of course have ways of defending themselves against that, but you can see that the advanced countries sometimes seem to be in danger of moronization. The poorer countries don't have that danger because they tend to be "jacks-of-all-trades."

Or putting it in another way, it's interesting to contrast agriculture with factory production; the agricultural worker at that time had to do all the various jobs, had to be a "generalist;" and the factory worker, of course, was much more specialized. And the fact was that this unspecialized agricultural laborer was the vehicle of good sense (this has gone in countries like America because of the specialization of agriculture). Nevertheless, the poorer countries, more backward ones, are not absolutely without resources against the richer countries. This is not exactly self-determination, it's the way things are, where backwardness has redeeming features.

We have seen a lot of these things in Scotland for various reasons. One was the '45 rebellion. That was a terrifically dramatic event. In the South of Scotland, they thought of themselves—thirty years after the Union—as the improved part of the country, and the Highlands were the unimproved. Yet when the rebellion broke out they found themselves absolutely incapable of defending themselves against this "unimproved" part of the country. Their great-grandfathers would've taken the pikes down from the wall and faced up to the Highlanders. But the post-Union people just couldn't do it at all. They just opened the gates of Edinburgh and hoped for the best. And they finally got the English in to break the power of the Clans, as Adam Smith points out.

Nevertheless, they kept—for whatever reason, and many other countries have a memory of this—a tribalized people's distrust of experts, as pointed out by the amusing philosopher Gellner. Of course we had been a tribalized people. Not as of late, in the literal sense, though some have tried to compare

Glasgow in the late nineteenth century with some of the great African cities. The tribalization has gone on in various ways but it is still the official doctrine of this country that they distrust specialization.

That's what has to be said. Science is the great thing, but there is considerable criticism of it, the dangers of science, and of it going astray. And the great book on that of course is Husserl's *Crisis of the European Sciences*. He was a mathematician originally and the main point of it is that, of course mathematics unveils the world and gives us more power, but as soon as you get a new and more powerful form of mathematics you forget the old one that's buried in it, and forget the reason of the old one. So that, in a way, the more power we have over the world through mathematics—as we do—the less we understand it, the more mysterious it is to people.

This is—put again—the stultification that can exist in relation to the division of labor, and science.

One further point about "common sense," the Scots' use of the term (in Thomas Reid's case to mean an irresistible and natural belief), the important point is that common sense, we have to remember, was a technical term introduced by Aristotle, and it has to do with the interlacing of the senses. Hence, we don't know anything about our brains except the end-organs, ear, eyes etc.—we know a bit about them. And it is from controlling these end-organs that the child learns to determine the size of things at a distance, or to measure time by watching the movement of shadows.

And you can see that there are great difficulties about the point, which both Chomsky and Harry Bracken have raised about common sense, the rational things that we are supposed to be able to do. But there is a good deal in the works of some of the Scottish philosophers that tries to wrestle with these problems. I'll just leave it there and hope that Professor Chomsky and yourselves will be stimulated to think about some of the questions I've touched on.

Interview with Noam Chomsky, January 11, 1990*

Professor Gus John

Gus John: Professor Chomsky, you have been addressing a conference on Self-Determination & Power here in Glasgow, and one of the themes you've elaborated upon is that of the process of oppression by nation-states, dictatorial or otherwise; of their peoples and the patterns of resistance to oppression that have persisted throughout human history. We have seen in recent times quite systematic and successful attempts at resistance to oppression in the struggle for freedom, most notable of which, in the last month or so, have been in Eastern Europe. There have also been the struggles in Southern Africa, particularly since Soweto in 1976, and the struggles of the people in the "front-line" states—Angola, Mozambique, and so on. Taking all of those things together, what would you say are the prospects for the struggle for freedom and liberation movements in other parts of the world, particularly in relation to those smaller states that don't have as high a profile.

Noam Chomsky: I think we want to begin by making a distinction between two of the points you mentioned. One of them is between a population and its own government. Typically, every state in history has regarded its own population as an enemy. The state represents some form of internal power, and it has to control its domestic population. Over [the course of]

* Recorded for the BBC World Service.

history, there has been constant popular revolt against forms of oppression, sometimes embodied in the state system and sometimes embodied in the power structure that the state system represents. That's one thing.

The other, which the rest of your comment mostly had to do with, was the resistance to foreign oppression. So in the case of the European satellites, the governments were essentially artificial constructs imposed by foreign forces, and when the foreign force was withdrawn, they very quickly collapsed. They were tyrannical but very fragile; they had very little support in the way of a popular domestic power base.

In the case of Africa, it's a matter of slowly disentangling the continent from centuries of murderous and barbaric European rule and oppression, which virtually destroyed it. And that's still very much in process.

Elsewhere in the world there's the same process of what's called "decolonization"—efforts by formerly colonized people to escape somehow the controls imposed by the European conquest of the world, which had devastating consequences wherever it went. In Latin America and Central America, the struggles continue.

What's dramatically different about the Eastern European case—in fact, it perhaps has no historical precedent—is that the tyrannies actually collapsed, virtually without a struggle. Romania aside, there was virtually no bloodshed, and Romania is the one place that was not very firmly under Soviet control.

What happened is that for internal reasons inside the Soviet Union changes took place—they are associated with Gorbachev, but they are much deeper—which led to the withdrawal of Soviet power from the satellite states. And then popular governments were able to overthrow the governmental structures, which basically collapsed virtually without resistance. That's almost unheard of.

Gus John: But what I find fascinating about that is that it has all been very much welcomed by the United States, Britain, and the Western world. That popular uprising, as you say, without bloodshed, is seen as a rather positive thing which gives hope for the future. And yet in terms of what is happening, let's say in relation to Southern Africa, and South Africa in particular, those same countries—Britain, France, and the United States—give tacit and quite active support to that murderous regime there...

Noam Chomsky: That's perfectly consistent. In fact, an even more dramatic contrast in many ways is with the uprising in Eastern Europe and the struggles for freedom and democracy in Central Africa. That's the closest counterpart to Eastern Europe in the US domain. And every effort to resist tyranny and oppression, to resist the traditional rule of the oligarchy and the military in the US domain: every such effort has been met with murderous violence and repression.

The comparison between, say, El Salvador, Guatemala, and Nicaragua, on the one hand, and Eastern Europe, on the other, is very dramatic. The US will not tolerate—and its European allies will not tolerate—freedom, independence, democracy, and social reform in the regions that remain under their control. If they do go through decolonization, they will try very hard to institute a system which will still be subordinate to foreign capital and foreign interests. And that is completely consistent with their attitude towards Easter Europe.

The reasons why the popular uprisings in Eastern Europe are welcome, partially, with some ambivalence, is that there is a hope in Western Europe and the US that these regions can be turned into another form of Third World—that they themselves can be colonized.

I don't want to overgeneralize—Hungary is different from Poland, and they're both different from Romania—but at a rather general level. Western Germany in particular, carrying Europe along with it, is reestablishing rather traditional quasi-colonial relationships with the East. At least that's what they are looking forward to. The model for Poland is something like

Mexico or Brazil; a country with an internal formal democracy but governed by IMF rules, subordinate to foreign capital, an area which will; be able to provide resources, cheap, easily exploitable labor, to serve as a market for excess production; ultimately it will be a place where you can export pollution. In fact, the Western model for, say, Poland is roughly the same as the US model for Mexico.

Gus John: But doesn't that rather presuppose that the people of Eastern Europe, with their newly found freedoms, would actually be themselves amenable to those sorts of developments and would not, in a sense, want to challenge what they consider to be the unacceptable faces of capitalism?

Noam Chomsky: That's right. And don't forget that the West will not accept capitalism for itself. Capitalism is something you impose on the Third World, because that makes the Third World more easily exploitable. So the IMF model (that really is capitalist), the US and Europe do insist that the Third World and now Poland accept the IMF model and that makes them easily exploitable, as I say. But internally, in the Western powers, they are state capitalist, which is something quite different.

In terms of history, the US and Europe developed quite differently from the model they are imposing on the Third World. Germany developed through state-directed industrial development and much the same was true of the US. Why does the US have a steel industry (or had a steel industry, until it collapsed)? The reason was that in the late nineteenth century the US instituted really high tariffs to prevent cheap British steel from flooding the market and establishing a British steel industry which would have undercut any American competition. And during the period of railroad building and industrialization it was possible to build a domestic steel industry by protectionist measures.

The US has always been highly protectionist; it remains so today. The Reagan administration, while talking about free enterprise, introduced more export restrictions and protectionist measures than the last six presidents combined. It's no different in Europe. Germany and Japan, they are even more so. But take the US, which at least has this rhetoric about free enterprise, the sectors of the US economy which are competitive internationally are those that are state-subsidized and state-coordinated. High-tech industry is subsidized by the public through the "Pentagon system." Capital-intensive agriculture, which is the other major export, is enormously subsidized by the state. So capitalism is fine. But we're not going to accept that for ourselves. The same businessman who gives a rousing speech about free enterprise takes the next plane to Washington to make sure that the subsidy is coming.

Gus John: Okay, but I'm interested in your theory of the potential market that Eastern Europe would provide for West Germany, Britain, or whoever. But that won't be possible really without the organization of labor in very precise ways to serve that market.

Noam Chomsky: That's right.

Gus John: What do you see as the prospect for organizing that successfully, given the particular organization that the Eastern European workers have been used to?

Noam Chomsky: That's an important question. And it's essentially the same question that arises everywhere in the Third World, the colonized world. Of course, people will resist the kind of structure that is going to subordinate them to foreign power. But whether they'll resist it successfully or not is another question.

Now, each place does it in terms of their own historical particularity. In Eastern Europe, we will have to become more differentiated, because the countries are different. Poland is a striking place at the moment because the West is trying, I presume as an experiment, to impose almost classical Third World conditions, and it's an open question whether the Polish working class will accept it. The way in which Poland is to develop, in the Western sense that is, integrated as a subordinate part of the of the Western-dominated system, is by imposing the burden on the poor and the working class. And Europe will sooner or later be using Poland probably as a source of cheap labor and as a market, and for the rest of Europe—the Eastern bloc—as a source of resources.

I presume Japan will eventually be doing the same in the Siberian region. There are factors blocking Japan at the moment, like the Kuril Islands and so on, but, with Japan having masses of excess capital and Siberia offering resources that can be developed, it's kind of natural to expect that they'll get together and that there will be free-trade zones in Vladivostok, and that Japan will try to integrate Siberia into its Eastern system.

These things don't, of course, happen mechanically. People resist, and they pursue their own plans too. To come back to Southern Africa, it doesn't simply absorb itself into the Western European system, it's resisted and they try to achieve a measure of independence. It's extremely difficult; countries that try, like Mozambique and Angola, are going to suffer for it.

Gus John: Yes, but in the same way as there is that international organization of capital, there is also the international organization of labor. And one would have thought that the paradox facing the West is that those people whom they would wish to use as cheap labor would, no doubt, very soon want to make alliances with the organized trade union movements within the West itself—through whose activity an enormous number of economic gains have been made for the working classes. How do you see that unfolding?

Noam Chomsky: Well, first of all, solidarity of labor is far harder to gain and obtain than solidarity of capital, for all sorts of obvious reasons. Secondly, the labor movement in the West is under very severe attack. In the US, it's been virtually eliminatcd. By now, I think, little over 15 percent of the workforce is unionized, and labor basically isn't a force in the US. Western

Europe is a little behind the US in this respect but going in the same direction. England is a case in point, and continental Europe will go the same way.

Business is extremely class-conscious, highly class-conscious. In fact, when you read the business literature it has a kind of vulgar Marxist tone to it. Business is always fighting a class war, rather consciously. And in more sophisticated countries like the US it is quite conscious.

For labor to defend itself, it's not easy. Take, say, the US, the US has a very violent labor history, very violent. There was a long struggle extending over decades to achieve a forty-hour working week and other labor gains. It's interesting that that is almost completely eroded. There is no forty-hour week any more. Workers work a lot more than that, typically, and you have to have two workers in the family to survive. Real wages have been declining since 1973. There isn't any sense of solidarity about strikes any more. The media cooperate in this; for example, there was a miners' strike in Siberia recently which got a lot of coverage in the press, lots of laudatory coverage for workers fighting for their rights. At the same time, there was a major miners' strike at Pittston, in West Virginia, a very significant strike. It involved sit-ins in the mines for the first time since the 1930s; it had substantial public support. There was lots of repression, violent repression, and that was barely reported. In fact, almost no one in the US barely knew about it.

This is just one aspect of a traditional procedure. There has been an intensive battle by business, the corporate media, the government, all interlinked, since the late 1930s, to undermine the achievements of labor—and the labor movement has essentially collapsed under that attack, or come close to collapsing, with the cooperation of labor bureaucrats and others.

So my point is, for the Third World—and that's going to include Eastern Europe—to develop a sense of solidarity with Western labor, that first requires that Western labor exists. And at the moment it's fighting for its life.

Gus John: I want to raise now another important aspect of your life's work, and that is scrutinizing and challenging US global policy. I'd like to concentrate, before we return to Western Europe, on Latin America and the Caribbean.

One of the things that fascinate me as a native of Grenada is that, as I understand it, over 90 percent of the US population hadn't a clue where Grenada was on the map, and yet the US state department managed to convince them that a) Grenada was a threat to US internal interests and b) that it was justified to both invade Grenada and lose American lives there. Obviously, that happens in relation to all sorts of other people, in Latin America and so forth. Can you tell me, how does the US continue to do that, repeating mistake after mistake and feeling obviously quite unchallengeable?

Noam Chomsky: I wouldn't call these things mistakes. They're not mistakes; they're successes.

Gus John: I'm not suggesting that as far as the US interpretation of it is concerned, the Grenada invasion was a mistake. Quite clearly it was a success, but...

Noam Chomsky: How do you convince the population?

Gus John: Yes, how does the US continue to legitimize such foreign exploits and explain them acceptably to the American people?

Noam Chomsky: There is a formula which the government and its propagandists, which includes the media, that they move to instantaneously, by a reflex. Two things: first of all, you associate the target of your attack with the Soviet Union; secondly—if you can even manufacture a fabricated case—you talk about saving American lives. The case of Grenada was classic. There was a fabricated pretext of the need to save the lives of the students at the Medical School, which is a complete fabrication. But the media covered it up. They presented it as if it were true; they concealed the facts and they are still concealing the facts. Secondly, ludicrous as it may sound, Grenada was presented as an outpost of Soviet strength—part of a Russian effort to strangle the US. I still recall hearing the chairman of the Joint Chiefs of Staff on the radio intoning sober warnings about how if the Russians invaded Western Europe, Grenada would interdict the Caribbean sea lanes and prevent the oil going to our beleaguered European allies and so on. It's hard to listen to this sort of stuff without laughing.

But since, as you say, people don't even know where Grenada is, or what it is, unless they happen to have taken a cruise ship there once, it is sort of credible. Once you've established a propaganda framework, and for years and years you have driven into people's heads that what John F. Kennedy called "the monolithic and ruthless conspiracy" is attempting to strangle us, and it's using outposts like Cuba and Grenada—and whoever else you feel like attacking—to do so, then the reflex works, briefly at least. As long as you can have a cheap war, you know you attack a completely defenseless target, then the population will rally round the flag, for a couple of days.

The Panama invasion is another recent case. That's the reflex. In fact, the Panama invasion is interesting in this respect, it's of historic interest, because this is the first time since World War II that the US propaganda system has not been able to conjure up a Russian threat. Even the imagination of the State Department and the editorial writers didn't reach that far in 1989.

Gus John: So did the American people totally buy the drugs explanation?

Noam Chomsky: Well, it's interesting what happened in the case of Panama. It was pretty obvious two or three years ago, at least to everyone in power, that it was going to be pretty difficult to play the usual record the next time the US wanted to invade a country. The Russians simply could not be portrayed as menacing during the Gorbachev years, much as they tried.

In the mid-1980s there was an attempt to conjure up an image of crazed Arab terrorists taking over the world, and that worked for a while, sufficing to justify the bombing of Libya.

In the case of Panama, the US was backing Noriega until about 1985–1986, when their policy changed—in 1987. Clearly, then the media took the cure and began the process of demonizing Noriega. Noriega who happens to be a sort of minor thug, was turned into the worst villain since Atilla the Hun. In fact, bad as he may be, in comparison with the people the US supports, say in El Salvador, Guatemala, and even Honduras, he looks pretty good. If you look at the human rights record in Panama, it's bad, but it doesn't come close to that of the US clients. As far as drug-running is concerned, he was a minor figure before and remained so afterwards. But the media understood what they had to do, and they turned Noriega into an absolute monster who was terrorizing the planet.

The "drug war," which is largely fraudulent, largely designed for population control, not for ending drugs, reached its peak through a White House media blitz campaign in September [1989] that helped lay the background.

The timing of the invasion was important; January 1, 1990, a large part of the administration of the Canal went over to Panamanian hands, and it was necessary to ensure that a compliant obedient government be in place in Panama based on US friends, bankers, and oligarchs, the traditional base for US support prior to that event. They turned against Noriega, not because he was more of a criminal than he had been before, but because he was becoming independent. The media went along ,and they did create the basis for this, and it was quite astonishing to see. I'll give you just one example...

Gus John: Before you do, can I follow that and ask: Is there any evidence that people in the US who are themselves oppressed—albeit not by any foreign domination—are sufficiently conscious of what is actually going on in other countries so that they want to question what it is their own government is attempting to do in relation to those other peoples?

Noam Chomsky: First of all, it's important to bear in mind that most of the population in the US has no relationship to policy. So the population is typically quite opposed to policy, very strongly opposed. For example, during the Reagan years, the population was overwhelmingly opposed by large margins to just about every Reagan program. In the case of the attack against Nicaragua, the population has consistently been two to one opposed to it. In the case of Panama, it's very hard to judge, but if you look at, say, letters to the editor in newspapers—which is just one measure of something—they are very hostile to the invasion, also very informed; they have a lot of information that doesn't appear in the media and so on. So there are certainly sectors of the population, and I wouldn't be surprised if there are substantial sectors, which are very opposed. Most of the population just doesn't know.

This comes back to your initial point about self-determination. As governments over the years, over the centuries, in fact, have lost the capacity to control their own population by force, they have turned to other measures to ensure obedience. Propaganda is the chief one, and this, again, is quite conscious.

By now, there is a very elaborate propaganda system in the US, involving everything, from the public relations industry and advertising to the corporate media, which simply marginalizes a large part of the population. They technically are allowed to participate by pushing buttons every few years, but they have essentially no role in formulating policy. They can ratify decisions made by others.

Now, there's a small sector of the population—maybe 20 percent or so, sometimes called the political class, the managers basically—and they have to have some sense of what's going on, but they're heavily indoctrinated too. The result is that you have the democratic forms but the substance is quite limited.

Gus John: Okay, let us take you back to Eastern Europe and talk about the propaganda machine. It's been typically active in relation to the Soviet Union and the ever-present threat placed before the American people. The extent to which that is no longer possible because Gorbachev has virtually ended the demonology of the Soviet Union means that it would be more difficult now for that propaganda machine to continue to project the Soviet Union and the Soviet bloc in quite those ways. Now, do you see that entering into the general consciousness of the American people to such an extent that they would want to demand that their government spends much less on the military and turn their attention to the sort of social policies that would end homelessness, unemployment, and so on?

Noam Chomsky: Well, a major task for the propaganda system—and I stress that includes the media, the intellectuals, and so on—is to prevent that from happening. Yes, it could happen in the natural course of events. As it becomes more and more difficult to portray the Soviet Union as a menace, one major technique of population control is being lost. The same is true in Western Europe. Therefore, other techniques will have to be devised, and it's not going to be easy.

There is popular pressure to turn military spending towards social needs. But there had always been such pressure. For example, right through the Reagan years—the years of the big military buildup—the population was overwhelmingly in favor of more spending on social needs and less spending on military needs...

Gus John: Yes, but at least Reagan could continue to invoke the Soviet Union in his debates with Senate.

Noam Chomsky: That's right. Now it will be harder to do that. But they will still have to do it. The reason is that the military spending is functional. It basically serves two functions. One is that it does provide intervention forces—the US is a global power and it does have to regularly intervene. And you have to have an intimidating posture if you are going to intervene; you have to prevent anyone getting in the way.

But an even more significant function is that the military system is essentially the state-industrial-management-industry. That is the way in which the state imposes a public cost, forces the public to subsidize high-technology industry.

This isn't simply a matter of weapons. Take the computer industry, which is the core of modern industrial society. It is the costs of research and development which are not profitable. They are typically borne by the public, by the taxpayer, through the military system. The state provides the guaranteed market for excess production from the electronics industry through the military. It has been possible to bulldoze the population into accepting this, which is essentially a subsidy from the poor to the rich, by invoking the Soviet threat. And now other means are going to be required to do the same thing. Because US business, which basically runs the government and determines social policy, is not going to lightly abandon a major public subsidy which provides it with its profitability and competitive edge. Other means will have to be devised to do what so-called "military Keynesianism" has done in the past.

It is striking to see how this works. There were, for example, some rumors a few months ago—probably not true—that the government might be backing away from a Pentagon-based consortium for semiconductors—and there was a huge protest from liberal congressmen, incidentally. They know—they may talk to their constituents about social spending—but they know perfectly well that their job is to keep industry happy, and that can't be done through private enterprise. Everybody understands that, and nobody believes in capitalism. It has to be done through public assistance. In the US system, that means, basically, through the Pentagon system.

For a while the Kennedy Administration tried some alternatives; they tried NASA, the space system; they tried to get people excited about men on the moon and that sort of business. It worked for a while, but it doesn't have the lasting appeal of a major enemy.

Gus John: What do you see all that meaning for the US relationship with NATO, particularly in the context of possible German reunification?

Noam Chomsky: The US would like to maintain the bloc system in Europe. It's happy to have the erosion of Soviet control over the satellites but it does want to maintain the Warsaw Pact and NATO. In fact, on James Baker's last visit to Berlin he did talk about the reunification of Germany as a desirable goal but, he added, within NATO. Now everyone knows that that's the one thing the Russians are extremely unlikely to accept. A unified Germany within a hostile military alliance is extremely frightening from the point of view of the Soviet Union, for perfectly obvious historical and strategic reasons. So when Baker and the US insist that a unified Germany remains within NATO they are saying that we don't want a unified Germany.

Why, then, is the US so eager to maintain NATO? Well, that's one of the ways of maintaining US influence over Europe. The US regards Europe as a very serious rival. The traditional view, for the last thirty years, has been—and that has been quite openly stated—that Europe should keep to "regional concerns," as Kissinger put it. It should pursue its regional interests within the overall framework of power maintained by the US.

That's becoming much more difficult. The US does not have the power, relative to Japan and Europe, that it had at one time; and one of the ways in which the US hopes to maintain its—at least residual—influence over Europe is to keep it down, basically, through integrating it into the NATO system. Within the military system the US does have the major power.

European elites have essentially the same interests, because they are worried about their own populations. If the Cold War really declines on their side, if the bloc-system declines, then that eliminates an element of population control, and it means that domestic politics may increase. Europe still does have labor unions and labor parties and a partially independent press and so on. All of these popular democratic forces may be galvanized if the military conflict declines, and that's a reason why European elites too are not so happy about the decline of NATO and the moves towards detente. They'd like the opportunities to exploit the East, but they have another problem domestically with their own populations.

Gus John: So if you were to crystal gaze for a moment, where do you think we might be in the year 2000?

Noam Chomsky: I think for about twenty years or so it's been plain that the world is drifting towards three major power blocs. One is a yen-based Japan bloc, with Japan and its satellites, another is a US-based dollar bloc, and a third is essentially a German-based European bloc.

As the Soviet system of power erodes and probably will collapse in one form or another, I suspect that there will at least be an effort to integrate that whole region—the rest of Eurasia—into the European and Japanese systems, as a kind of Third World, which to a great or less extent will probably work.

The US is carrying out a defensive reaction. The free trade arrangement with Canada was essentially a way of incorporating Canada into the US bloc as a quasi-colony. Northern Mexico is already basically integrated as a colony of the US. The Caribbean Basin Initiative didn't get very far, but its logic was to try to turn the Caribbean countries and Central America into a US version of Japan's East Asia, a place where you can get cheap labor for assembly plants and specialized agricultural production and so on. There will be efforts to pursue that, but it's not going to be so simple. Europe and Japan have their own interests.

In earlier periods this is the kind of development that led to global war. It's not going to do so in this case, presumably, for two reasons: one, because interpenetration of capital is much higher, so the relationship between private capital and the state is a much looser relationship than it was in the past, because of the international flow of capital; and the other reason is that war is just inconceivable, since if there is a war, that is just the end. Some other arrangement, presumably, would have to be worked out.

But it's a situation rife with potential conflict, and for the Third World it means just new forms of exploitation.

Gus John: Hopefully, there will also be new forms of resistance of such exploitation. What's your view of that?

Noam Chomsky: The resistance in Third World countries is really astonishing. Let's, say, just compare Eastern Europe and Central America. It's been very dramatic and exciting to see how popular movements in Eastern Europe have mobilized and succeeded in achieving a degree of freedom, but we have to remember that they are facing nothing like what the Central American movements are facing. They are not facing death squads, mass murder by the state, and massive torture backed by the regional superpower.

What's amazing to me, constantly, is the ability of oppressed people and their willingness to continue to struggle. Whether it's in Southern Africa or Central America or South East Asia or at home, say, in the civil rights movement, the courage of oppressed people to struggle in the face of severe oppression and extraordinary violence is inspiring, and extremely hard for secure people, like me, at least, to understand. But it's a dramatic and exciting fact, and it undoubtedly will continue as it has through history.

Gus John: I want to ask, in the light of recent events in Eastern Europe, what forms of democracy do you see emerging in the coming years?

Noam Chomsky: I think that's hard to predict. You can see what the West will try to influence. What they will try to create is a kind of Brazilian model, a system with a formal democracy—with elections and so on—but two-tiered societies: a wealthy entrepreneurial class linked to Western interests and serving them, and a general mass of the population which is largely marginalized; passive observers and consumers rather than participants.

Of course, the Eastern Europeans have their own ideas, and they'll struggle to develop something different. It will again vary from country to country—internal power will often be opposed—but there will be an effort on the part of many to impose a reasonable social contract; that means some kind of social democratic system with welfare and labor rights which the West will be strongly opposed to—as Western elites are in their own countries. Whatever remains from the Communist Party system will try to secure its own power; that will probably fail as it's too artificial...

Gus John: Which is presumably what students in Romania have been protesting about...

Noam Chomsky: Right now, it's too early to see what they're protesting about because what they are doing is overthrowing a murderous tyranny. It's yet too early to see what they're striving for; it's obvious what they're fighting against.

I don't think we can generalize in Eastern Europe. The countries are quite different. In East Germany, for example, the opposition has included, been spearheaded by, a social democratic or socialist element. In Poland, the opposition was spearheaded by a labor union at one point, but, though the labor union still exists in name, it does not have anything like the popular base that it had ten years ago. I suspect in the coming period we may find rather serious struggle between the remnants of the Solidarność leadership and much of the workforce. Hungary and Czechoslovakia are quite different, and Romania is different. As the Soviet Union itself begins to collapse, as is likely, we will find some more things there.

There's another problem in Eastern Europe, and that is the nationality problem. Nationalities are going to seek independence, but independence and democracy are very different things. Nationalist movements have often sought independence and become violent and vicious tyrannies. There's lots of mutual hatred. There is no reason to suspect that automatically a nationalist movement is going to lead to a free society. It could lead to a very ugly society. The Russian Empire, ugly as it was, did subdue, to some extent, nationalist and ethnic tensions, rather in the way the Ottoman Empire suppressed ethnic and nationalist tensions inside its domain. As the empires collapse, these tensions and conflicts arise, and they can be extremely ugly.

Gus John: And I suspect these are among Gorbachev's greatest fears in relation to the national question.

Noam Chomsky: They should be anybody's fears.

Gus John: Professor Chomsky, thank you.

Terrorizing the Neighborhood: American Foreign Policy in the Post–Cold War Era

Noam Chomsky

This essay is based on a lecture delivered by Noam Chomsky in January 1990 at Edinburgh University, shortly after the US invasion of Panama. It has been rewritten by the author, with the addition of footnotes and sources.[1] *The lecture was followed by a session of questions and answers, reproduced here as they occurred, with editing solely for reasons of style.*

When I was invited to speak on Central America a few weeks ago, I thought I would discuss the likely evolution of US policy toward the region in what many see as a post–Cold War era. But before I had a chance to address the question, I was upstaged by the Bush administration, which announced the answer I was intending to give, loud and clear: more of the same.

But not precisely the same. Some adjustments are needed in the propaganda framework. The US invasion of Panama in December is a historic event in one respect. It is the first US act of international violence in the post–World War II era that was not justified by the pretext of a Soviet threat. When the United States invaded Grenada six years earlier, it was still possible to portray the act as a defensive reaction to the machinations of the Russian bear, seeking to strangle us in pursuit of its global designs. John Vessey, Jr., chairman of the Joint Chiefs of Staff, could intone solemnly that in the event of a Soviet attack on Western Europe, Grenada might interdict the Caribbean sea lanes and prevent the United States from providing oil to its beleaguered allies. Through the 1980s, the attack against Nicaragua was justified by the danger that if we didn't stop the Russians there, they would be pouring across the border at Harlingen, Texas, two days' drive away. There are more sophisticated (and equally weighty) variants for the educated classes. But in the case of Panama, not even the imagination of the State Department and the editorial writers extended that far.

Fortunately, the problem had been foreseen. When the White House decided a few years ago that its friend Noriega was getting too big for his britches and had to go, the media took their cue and launched a campaign to convert Noriega, who remained a minor thug, exactly as when he was on the CIA payroll, into the most nefarious demon since Attila the Hun. The effort was enhanced by the "war on drugs," a government-media hoax launched a few months earlier in an effort to mobilize the population in fear, now that it is becoming impossible to invoke John F. Kennedy's "monolithic and ruthless conspiracy," the "Evil Empire" of Ronald Reagan's speechwriters. It was a smashing success. With fringe exceptions, after the operation had been completed, the media rallied around the flag with due piety and enthusiasm, funneling the most absurd White House claims to the public while scrupulously refraining from asking the obvious questions or seeing the most obvious facts.

Naturally, the Bush administration was delighted. A State Department official observed that "the Republican conservatives are happy because we were willing to show some muscle, and the Democratic liberals can't criticize because it's being so widely seen as a success."[2] The State Department followed the standard newspeak conventions in contrasting "conservatives," who advocate a powerful and violent state, to "liberals," who sometimes disagree with the "conservatives" on tactical grounds. These salutary developments "can't help but give us more clout," the same official continued.

As for the general population, many were also doubtless enthusiastic about the opportunity to "kick a little ass" in Panama—to borrow some of the rhetoric designed by George Bush's handlers as part of their comical effort to shape an effete New England WASP into a Texas redneck. But it is interesting to read the letters to the editor in major newspapers, which tend to express hostility to the aggression, along with much shame and distress, and often provide analysis of American foreign policy in the post–Cold War era and insights that the professionals have been careful to avoid.

A not untypical professional reaction was given by the respected *Washington Post* correspondent David Broder. He notes that there has been some carping at "the prudence of Bush's action" from "the left" (meaning, some centrist liberals, anything else being far beyond his horizons, as is the idea that there might be criticism on grounds other than prudence). But he dismisses "this static on the left" with scorn: "what nonsense." Rather, the invasion of Panama helped clarify the "new national consensus" on "the circumstances in which military intervention makes sense." The "best single definition" of the new consensus was given by Reagan's defense secretary Caspar Weinberger, who outlined six criteria that are "well-considered and well-phrased." Four of them state that intervention should be designed to succeed. The other two add that the action should be "vital to our national interest" and a "last resort" to achieve it.[3] Oddly, Broder neglected to add the obvious remark about these impressive criteria: they could readily have been invoked by Hitler.

Continuing to explore the consensus, Broder believes: "Democratic nominee Michael Dukakis, after floundering around on the question of military interventions, came up with a set of standards strikingly similar to Weinberger's" during the 1988 presidential campaign. These standards, as outlined by his senior foreign policy adviser, were that US force could be used "to deter aggression against its territory, to protect American citizens, to honor our treaty obligations and take action against terrorists" after peaceful means had failed. "The Panama invasion met all of those tests," Broder concluded. One can appreciate the joyful mood among State Department propagandists. Even they did not dare to claim to be deterring Panamanian aggression or taking action against terrorists. While there had been the ritual gesture toward international law, it was neither intended seriously nor taken seriously. Even traditional jingoists would go no further than to say that the "legalities are murky" (editors of the *Wall Street Journal*).[4] In fact, it is transparently impossible to reconcile the invasion with the supreme law of the land, as codified in the UN Charter, the Organization of American States (OAS) Treaty, and the Panama Canal Treaty. Hardly less ludicrous is the claim, to which we return, that the invasion aimed to protect American citizens.

Broder is pleased that "we have achieved a good deal of clarity in the nation on this question—the right of intervention—which divided us so badly during and after the Vietnam War," and this "important achievement . . . should not be obscured by a few dissident voices on the left," with their qualms about the prudence of the action. Despite the abysmal intellectual and moral level of the performance, Broder may well be right about the consensus. His evaluation recalls a comment by one of the most significant figures in twentieth-century America, the radical pacifist A.J. Muste: "The problem after a war is with the victor. He thinks he has just proved that war and violence pay. Who will now teach him a lesson?"

Ever since the latter days of the Indochina wars, elite groups have been concerned over the erosion of popular support for force and subversion—what is termed the "Vietnam syndrome." Intensive efforts have been made to cure the malady but, so far, in vain. The Reaganites assumed that it had been overcome by the propaganda triumphs over postwar Indochina, Afghanistan, and Iran. They learned differently when they tried to return to the traditional pattern of intervention in Central America and were forced to retreat to clandestine and indirect measures to terrorize and intimidate popular forces seeking democracy and reform. Through the 1980s, hopes have been voiced that we have finally overcome "the sickly inhibitions against the use of military force" (Norman Podhoretz, referring to the glorious triumph in Grenada). In the more nuanced tones of the liberal commentator, Broder too is expressing the hope that finally the population has been restored to health and will end its childish obsession with the rule of law and human rights. His "new consensus," however, is largely illusory, restricted to the sectors that have always recognized that the global designs of US power require the freedom to resort to state violence, terror, and subversion. The new consensus is more properly described as a heightened self-confidence on the part of those who shared the old consensus.

This renewed self-confidence on the part of proponents of intervention, including liberals of the Broder variety, may well reduce some of the internal constraints on the resort to violence and subversion, but there are conflicting factors that limit these options. It is understood across the spectrum that it would be "imprudent" to attack anyone capable of fighting back. It's one thing to strike manly poses and exult in heroic exploits after attacking Panama, already under virtual US military occupation; or Grenada, defended by a handful of militia and Cuban construction workers with no military training; or Libya, defenseless against bombardment.[5] But those who revel in the new jingoism are surely aware that the consensus is fragile and will vanish if violence faces resistance, while much of the population remains infected by the Vietnam syndrome despite all efforts to overcome it. Intervention is still further constrained by the relative decline in US power, accelerated by the economic mismanagement of the Reaganites. The "new clarity" on the right of forceful intervention is likely to have limited consequences. Let's put Panama aside for the moment and turn to more general questions. Note first that there are several reasons why it makes sense to expect the post–Cold War era to be much like what came before, apart from matters of tactics and propaganda.

The Cold War has regularly been portrayed as a superpower conflict, and it was, but that is only a fraction of the truth. Reality protrudes when we look at the typical events and practices of the Cold War.

On Moscow's side, the Cold War is illustrated by tanks in East Berlin, Budapest, Prague, and more recently the invasion of Afghanistan, the one case of Soviet military intervention well outside the historic invasion route from the West. Domestically, the Cold War served to entrench the power of the military-bureaucratic elite whose power derives from the Bolshevik coup of 1917.

For the US, the Cold War has primarily been a history of worldwide subversion, aggression, and state-run international terrorism, with examples too numerous to mention. Second, it has served to maintain US influence over industrial allies and to suppress independent politics and popular activism, an interest shared by local elites. The domestic counterpart within the United States has been to entrench the military-industrial complex that elicited Eisenhower's farewell warning—in essence, a smoothly functioning welfare state for the rich, with a national security ideology for population control. The major institutional mechanism is a system of state industrial management to sustain high-tech industry, relying on the taxpayer to fund research and development and provide a state-guaranteed market for waste production. This crucial gift to the corporate manager has been the domestic function of the Pentagon system (including NASA and the Department of Energy, which controls nuclear weapons production); benefits also extend to the computer and electronics industries and other sectors of the advanced industrial economy. The

Cold War provided a large part of the underpinnings for the system of public subsidy and private profit that is proudly called "free enterprise."

We may take note of the broad if tacit understanding that the capitalist model has limited application; business leaders have long recognized that it will not do for them. The successful industrial societies depart radically from this model, as has generally been true in the past—that is one reason why they are successful industrial societies. In the United States, the sectors of the economy that remain competitive internationally are those that feed from the public trough: high-tech industry, capital-intensive agriculture, pharmaceuticals, and others. The glories of free enterprise provide a useful weapon against government policies that might benefit the mass of the population. Of course, capitalism will do just fine for the former colonies—now including, it is hoped, the former Soviet empire, as it collapses and is subjected to Western needs. For the regions that are to provide such benefits as cheap labor, resources, markets, tax-free havens, and opportunities to export pollution, the model is highly recommended; it facilitates their exploitation. But these doctrines must be restricted to the proper targets. The rich and powerful at home have long appreciated the need to protect themselves from the destructive forces of free market capitalism, which may provide suitable themes for rousing oratory, but only so long as the public handout is secure, the regulatory apparatus is in place, and state power is on hand to ensure proper obedience on the part of the lower orders.

Putting it schematically, for the Soviet Union, the Cold War has primarily been a war against its satellites; and, for the United States, it has been a war against the Third World, with ancillary benefits with regard to domination of the other industrial societies. For both superpowers, the Cold War has served to entrench a certain system of domestic privilege and coercion. Naturally, the policies pursued within the Cold War framework have been unattractive to the general population, which accepts them only under duress. Throughout history, the standard device to mobilize a reluctant population has been the fear of an evil enemy dedicated to our destruction. The superpower conflict served the purpose admirably. The Cold War has had a functional utility for the superpowers, which is one reason that it has persisted.

These central features of the Cold War system help explain its typical events and practices, as well as the ideological constructs that have accompanied it. In the West, it is regularly conceded well after the fact (the fact being some exercise of subversion or aggression in the Third World or renewed benefits through the Pentagon system at home) that the threat of Soviet aggression was exaggerated, the problems misconstrued, and the idealism that guided the actions misplaced, but the requisite beliefs remain prominently displayed on the shelf. However fanciful, they can be served up to the public when needed—often with perfect sincerity, in accord with the familiar process by which useful beliefs arise from perceived interests.

Recent history provides many examples. In the post–Vietnam War period, the elites understood that it would be necessary to take stern measures to restore US power and corporate profits. That required an interventionist policy abroad and a determined class war at home. As a virtual reflex, the policies were justified by rampaging Soviet power. In fact, as the CIA now quietly concedes, Soviet military spending, which had surged after the dramatic demonstration of Soviet weakness during the Cuban missile crisis, began to level off in the mid-1970s, exactly the opposite of what was claimed in the West to justify the Carter-Reagan military buildup and the attack on social programs.

The breakup of the Portuguese Empire and the failure of the US effort to maintain Western control over Indochina were interpreted as evidence that the Soviet Union was marching on from strength to strength, even establishing its domination of such international powerhouses as Grenada, South Yemen, and Nicaragua. The fact of the matter is that Soviet power worldwide had been declining since its peak (which was not very high, in comparison to the United States) since about 1960. More generally, both superpowers had been declining in their power to coerce and control since about that time—a relative decline, of course; in absolute terms, the power to destroy always advances.

No matter how exotic the claims and the intellectual constructs, it was always fair to assume that they would be taken seriously by the docile intelligentsia. The more critical might say, as usual, that the threat was exaggerated, but the basic assumptions of the propaganda framework were very rarely challenged. The services of the left should, incidentally, not be underestimated. Now one side has called off the game, at least temporarily. It is not true that the Cold War has ended. Rather, it has perhaps half ended. For the United States, which remains a player as before, the change in the rules requires new forms of propaganda and some tactical adjustments—a problem, but there is a compensating gain. The withdrawal of the limited Soviet deterrent frees the United States to be more unconstrained in the exercise of violence. Thus, Washington has "more clout." Recognition of these welcome possibilities has been explicit in public discourse from the early stages of Soviet initiatives toward detente, as I have discussed elsewhere. Expressing his pleasure over the invasion of Panama, Elliott Abrams observed that "Bush probably is going to be increasingly willing to use force." The use of force is more feasible than before, he explained, now that "developments in Moscow have lessened the prospect for a small operation to escalate into a superpower conflict."[6]

Similarly, the test of Gorbachev's "New Thinking" is regularly taken to be his willingness to withdraw support from those whom the United States is trying to destroy; only if he allows us to have our way will we know that he is serious about detente. This interpretation is entirely natural in a lawless, terrorist political culture and, therefore, elicits little comment or even notice.

Notice that the Russian moves have helped to dispel some conventional mystification. The official story has always been that we contain the Russians, deterring them and thwarting their global designs, but the reality, as has been evident from the start, is that the fear of potential superpower conflict has repeatedly served to contain and deter the United States. What is termed "Soviet aggression" in the Third World has typically consisted of moves by the Kremlin to protect and sustain targets of US attack. Now that the Soviet Union is limiting, perhaps terminating, these efforts, the United States is freer to pursue its global designs by force and violence, and the rhetorical clouds begin to lift. To summarize, one reason to expect that US policy toward Central America will be "more of the same" after the Cold War has ended is that the crucial event hasn't taken place. As I said earlier, viewed realistically, the Cold War has at most half ended. Its apparent termination is an ideological construct more than a historical fact, based on an interpretation that masks some of its essential functions. For the United States, much of the basic framework of the Cold War remains intact, apart from the modalities of population control. The latter problem—a central problem facing any state or other system of power—still remains and will have to be addressed in new and more imaginative ways as traditional Cold War doctrine loses its efficacy.

There is also a deeper reason why US policy in Central America and elsewhere is likely to pursue essentially the same course as before, with adjustments in tactics and propaganda. Within a narrow range of variation, policies express institutional needs. US policies have been stable over a long period, because the dominant institutions are stable and subject to very little internal challenge. Politics and ideology are largely bounded by the consensus of the business community. On critical issues, there is tactical debate within the mainstream, but questions of principle rarely arise. To recall a striking case, during the Indochina wars and since, the framework of "defense of South Vietnam" was unchallenged among the political elites and educated classes. They could easily perceive that the Soviet Union invaded Afghanistan and that the pretense to be defending it was an absurdity, but claims of similar character and validity by the US propaganda system passed without challenge. The trivial fact that the United States had invaded South Vietnam and virtually destroyed it was unthinkable and remains so.

Extraordinary historical circumstances have also safeguarded US institutions from any serious external challenge. After World War II, the United States was in a position of relative power, wealth, and security without historical parallel. The conventional description of the Cold War system as bipolar is rather misleading; the Soviet Union was always a junior partner in world management and was never even close to being an economic rival. Other challenges to US dominance have arisen over the years; these have influenced tactical decisions and may continue to do so significantly as they continue to mount.

The basis of policy is outlined with considerable clarity in the internal record of planning during and after World War II.[7] The Third World is to "fulfill its main function as a source of raw materials and a market" for the industrial societies, which were to be reconstituted within a global order subordinated to the needs of the United States (meaning, the dominant elites within it). In Latin America, as elsewhere, "the protection of our resources" must be a major concern, the influential State Department planner George Kennan explained. Since the main threat to "our resources" and our interests generally is indigenous, we must realize, Kennan continued, that "the final answer might be an unpleasant one," namely, "police repression by the local government." "Harsh government measures of repression" should cause us no qualms as long as "the results are on balance favorable to our purposes." In general, "it is better to have a strong regime in power than a liberal government if it is indulgent and relaxed and penetrated by Communists." The term *Communist* is used here in the technical sense it has assumed in American political discourse, referring to labor leaders, peasant organizers, priests organizing self-help groups, and anyone who has the wrong priorities and thus gets in our way.

The right priorities are explained in the highest-level top secret documents. The major threats to US interests are persistently identified as "nationalist regimes" that are responsive to popular pressures for "immediate improvement in the low living standards of the masses" and diversification of the economies for domestic needs. This dangerous tendency conflicts not only with the need to "protect our resources" but also our concern to encourage "a climate conducive to private investment" and "in the case of foreign capital to repatriate a reasonable return." The Kennedy administration identified the roots of US interest in Latin America as in part military (the Panama Canal, strategic raw materials, etc.), but perhaps still more "the economic root whose central fiber is the $9 billion of private US investment in the area" and extensive trade relations. The need "to protect and promote American investment and trade" is threatened by nationalism, sometimes called "ultranationalism," that is, efforts to follow an independent course, interfering with the functions that the region is to fulfill. The preference is for agro-export models serving the interests of US-based agribusiness, chemical, and energy corporations (pesticides and fertilizers, in particular) and, in later years, cheap labor for assembly plants, unsupervised banking, and other useful services.

These policies also tend to be unpopular in the targeted countries, but, for their populations, no subtle measures of control are necessary. Under an Agency for International Development (AID) cover, "public safety missions" trained local police forces. The principle, as outlined by the State Department, was that the police "first detect discontent among people" and "should serve as one of the major means by which the government assures itself of acceptance by the majority." An effective police force can often abort unwanted developments that might otherwise require "major *surgery*" to "redress these threats" with "considerable force." But police violence may not suffice. Accordingly, US planners stressed the need to gain control over the Latin American military, described as "the least anti-American of any political group." Converting the mission of the military from "hemispheric defense" to "internal security," the Kennedy liberals and their successors were able to overcome the problem of "ultranationalism" by establishing and backing National Security States on a neo-Nazi model, with consequences that are well-known. These measures also overcame the concerns expressed in the internal record over the excessive liberalism of the Latin American governments, the protection of rights afforded by their legal systems, and the completely unacceptable free flow of ideas, which undercut US efforts at indoctrination and ideological control. Where the police and military cannot be controlled directly, as in post-Somoza Nicaragua or Panama, it is necessary to overthrow the government and install a more compliant regime.

These policies are givens; they are subject to no challenge and no debate. It would be misleading to say that there is near unanimity on these matters in Congress, the media, and the intellectual community. More accurately, the basic doctrines are out of sight, out of mind, like the air we breathe, beyond the possibility of recognition, let alone discussion. Within the framework established by these invariant principles, debate is legitimate, indeed encouraged, not only because there are tactical differences among elites that should be aired and clarified for their benefit, but also because lively controversy (crucially, within proper bounds) provides the sense that the formal freedoms actually function, an essential means of population control when appeal to force is not a viable option.

These invariant conditions have certain consequences. One is the striking correlation between US aid and human rights abuses. Lars Schoultz, the leading US academic specialist on human rights and US foreign policy in Latin America, found that US aid "has tended to flow disproportionately to Latin American governments which torture their citizens . . . to the hemisphere's relatively egregious violators of fundamental human rights." The correlation is strong, includes military aid, is unrelated to need, and persists through the Carter human rights administration. Reaganite support for mass slaughter and terror makes it superfluous to raise the question for this grim era. Other studies have found the same phenomenon worldwide. The reason is not that US policymakers like torture. Rather, it is an irrelevance. What matters is to bar independent development and the wrong priorities, and, for this purpose, it is often necessary (regrettably) to murder priests, torture union leaders, "disappear" peasants, and otherwise intimidate the general population. Governments with the right priorities will therefore be led to adopt such measures. Since the right priorities are associated with US aid, we find the secondary correlation between US aid and human rights violations.

A second consequence is the general US opposition to social reform, unless it can be carried out in conformity to overriding US interests (meaning, again, the interests of the privileged classes). While this is occasionally possible in the Third World, such circumstances are rare. Even where social reform could be pursued along with subordination to US interests (Costa Rica is the obvious example), Washington has reacted with considerable ambivalence.[8]

A third consequence is the extreme hostility of the US government toward democracy. The reason is obvious: a functioning democracy will be responsive to appeals from the masses of the population and will likely succumb to excessive nationalism.

Democratic forms are, of course, acceptable, even praiseworthy, if only for purposes of population control at home. But they are acceptable only when they function within the prescribed bounds. Honduras is a case in point. Its November 1989 elections received scanty but generally favorable coverage in the US media, which described them as "a milestone for the United States, which has used Honduras as evidence that the democratically elected governments it supports in Central America are taking hold."[9]

A closer look shows just how they are taking hold. The November elections were effectively restricted to the two traditional parties. One candidate was from a family of wealthy industrialists, the other from a family of large landowners. Their top advisers "acknowledge that there is little substantive difference between the two and the policies they would follow as president," the press reports.[10] Both parties represent large landowners and industrialists and have close ties with the military, the effective rulers, who are independent of civilian authority under the Honduras constitution but heavily dependent on the United States, as is the economy. The Guatemalan *Central America Report* adds that "in the absence of substantial debate, both candidates rely on insults and accusations to entertain the crowds at campaign rallies and political functions." Popular participation was limited to ritual voting. The legal opposition parties (Christian Democratic and Social Democratic) charged massive electoral fraud.

Human rights abuses by the security forces escalated as the election approached. In the weeks before the election, there were attacks with bombs and rifle fire against independent political figures, journalists, and union leaders. In preceding the months, the armed forces launched a campaign of political violence, including assassination of union leaders and other extrajudicial executions, leaving tortured and mutilated bodies by roadsides for the first time. The human rights organization CODEH reports that at least seventy-eight people were killed by the security forces between January and July, while reported cases of torture and beatings more than tripled over the preceding year. But torture and death squad operations remained at a low enough level so as not to disturb elite opinion.

Starvation and general misery are rampant, the extreme concentration of wealth has increased during the decade of "democracy," and 70 percent of the population is malnourished. Despite substantial US aid and no guerrilla threat, the economy is collapsing, with capital flight and a sharp drop in foreign investment and almost half of export earnings devoted to debt service. All of this is also completely irrelevant for the masters, as long as there is no major threat to order and profits flow.[11]

In short, Honduras is quite an acceptable democracy, and there has been no concern over the "level playing field" for the elections, unlike Nicaragua.

Even El Salvador and Guatemala, murderous gangster states run by the US-backed military are considered democracies—sometimes "fledgling democracies." Elite opinion expresses considerable pride in having established and maintained these charnel houses, with "free elections" permitted after "the playing field had been levelled" by Pol Pot–style terror, including mass slaughter, torture, disappearance, mutilation, and other effective devices. Physical destruction of the independent media and murder of editors and journalists who do not toe the line passed virtually without comment—often literally without report—among their Western colleagues.

Colombia is also described as a democracy, though a democracy under threat from narco-traffickers. By congressional and media standards, however, democracy is not under threat, because the two parties that share political power are "two horses (with) the same owner" (former President Alfonso

López Michelsen)—rather as in the United States. Nor is "democratic normalcy" threatened by a system with such features as these: death squads have killed about one thousand members of Unión Patriótica, the one party not owned by the oligarchy, since its founding in 1985, leaving the unions and popular organizations with no meaningful political representation: disappearance and execution of labor, Indian, and community leaders is a regular part of daily life, while "many Colombians insist that army troops often act as though they were an occupation force in enemy territory" (Americas Watch); these death squads dedicated to extermination of "subversives" are in league with the security forces (Amnesty International); the death squads sow "an atmosphere of terror, uncertainty and despair," and "all families in which even one member is somehow involved in activities directed towards social justice" are under constant threat of disappearance and torture, conducted with "impunity" by the military and their allies (Pax Cristi), including "cocaine gangs" and the owner of the two horses. All of this leaves the playing field level and poses no threat to "democratic institutions," no challenge to "America's historic purpose of advancing the cause of freedom in the world," to quote a leading US scholar.

Occasionally, one hears an honest comment. For example, Joachim Maître of Boston University, one of the leading academic supporters of Reagan administration policies in Central America, observes candidly that the United States has "installed democracies of the style of Hitler Germany" in El Salvador and Guatemala, but such praiseworthy willingness to face the facts is far from the norm.

Although democracy is acceptable when pursued in the manner of US terror states, strong measures must be taken to prevent it when popular organizations are allowed to function, threatening the monopoly of the political system by the business-landowner elite. Signs of such deviation, as in El Salvador and Guatemala a decade ago, require that death squads be unleashed to administer a dose of reality and to "level the playing field" so that "democracy" can be restored. Similarly, alarm bells ring when a government comes to power "that cares for its people," in the words of José Figueres, the founder of Costa Rican democracy, referring to the Sandinistas, who brought Nicaragua the first such government in its history and should be allowed "to finish what they started in peace; they deserve it." For expressing such improper sentiments, this leading figure of Central American democracy has been censored from the free press in the United States.[12]

Such transgressions plainly require stern discipline. Accordingly, hostility to the Sandinistas has been uniform in elite circles. This is no exaggeration. Surveys of opinion pieces in the national press at peak periods of debate over policy toward Nicaragua reveal close to 100 percent conformity to this requirement—that is, conformity at the level of a well-run totalitarian state. No less interesting are the topics excluded from discussion. There is no mention of the fact that unlike the US clients, the Sandinistas, whatever their sins, did not slaughter their own populations. The equally uncontroversial fact that they attempted social reforms and directed resources to the needs of the poor majority receives passing mention in about 2 percent of commentary surveyed. The figures reflect the significance accorded to mass slaughter and the suffering of the poor within US political culture, relative to more important matters that guide policy.

The media included tactical debate over the best way to restore Nicaragua to "the Central American mode" and impose "regional standards"—those of the US client states. That fact is often put forth as proof of the independence and even adversarial nature of the media. But it is hardly surprising, given that, by 1986, some 80 percent of leadership elements (corporation executives, etc.) were opposed to the Contra option, recognizing that there are more cost-effective ways to strangle and destroy a weak and small country completely dependent on its relations with the US for survival. Even if the media were solely serving as a propaganda instrument for the nexus of state-private power, they would permit, indeed encourage, such discussion.

In Congress as well, debate kept to the question of how best to rid ourselves of the Sandinistas. Should we use violence and terror, as the Reaganites demanded, or should we find other ways to ensure that the government "festers in its own juices," as the leading Democratic dove senator, Alan Cranston, preferred: embargo, blocking foreign aid, etc.? As distinct from Honduras and the two outright terror states where everything is in order, Nicaraguan elections are a matter of deep concern, and from the outset of the electoral campaign the US interfered massively to gain victory for its candidates. Some attention has been given to the enormous financial aid to the US-backed candidates, amounting to about half the combined monthly wage of every person in Nicaragua, but this is the least part of the effort to undermine free elections. Far more significant, but considered quite uncontroversial, are such actions as the White House statement of November 1989 promising "to lift the trade embargo and assist in Nicaragua's reconstruction" if the US candidate, Violeta Chamorro, were to win the election, issued as she opened her campaign at a meeting in Washington with President Bush. In brief, Bush informed Nicaraguan voters that they had a free choice: vote for our candidate or watch your children starve. That is how we "level the playing field." For deeply committed totalitarians, elections conducted under such conditions are "free and fair."

A second and perhaps still more extreme form of US intervention to bar the threat of free elections, considered not only uncontroversial but meritorious, was the "peace process" scam conducted with the cooperation of Costa Rican president Oscar Arias since 1987. Here the record is very clear, though brilliantly concealed by the loyal media in the United States and Europe. A series of agreements were made, each intended by the United States and its clients to be observed by Nicaragua but to be violated by every other participant. Each successive step left the US allies free to pursue their programs of violence and repression and maintained the Contra threat in violation of the agreements, while Nicaragua was subjected to microscopic examination. Any minor deviation from the increasingly narrow strictures led to impassioned denunciation by Arias and other cynics, who remained silent, or even approved (as in the case of Arias) when the US clients carried out far worse abuses. This was a highly successful procedure, continued right through the electoral campaign, to ensure that the US candidate would be able to offer a credible promise that the Contra terror would be ended, while the Sandinistas could offer only more suffering. The US-Arias diplomacy is a perfect example of Stalinist-style "salami" tactics, regarded as quite praiseworthy by Western opinion. We learn a good deal about Western culture and its profound contempt for democracy by observing this charade over the past several years.[13]

In this context, we may return briefly to the Panama invasion. After offering a series of pretexts, the White House settled on the need to "protect American lives." The White House announced that there had been "literally hundreds of cases of harassment and abuse of Americans" in recent months by Noriega's forces—though, curiously, they issued no warning to Americans to stay away, up until the day of the invasion. A US soldier was killed under disputed circumstances, but what tipped the scales was the threat to the wife of an officer who was arrested and beaten. Bush "often has difficulty in emotionally charged situations," the *New York Times* reported, "but his deep feelings clearly came through" when he spoke of this incident, proclaiming in his best Ollie North rendition that "this president" is not going to stand by while American womanhood is threatened.[14] The press did not explain why "this president" refused to even issue a protest a few weeks earlier when an American nun, Diana Ortiz, had been kidnapped, tortured, and sexually abused by the Guatemalan police—or why the media did not find the story worth reporting when it appeared on the wires on November 6 and have ignored repeated calls for an investigation by religious leaders and congressional representatives. Nor were Bush's "deep feelings" contrasted with the response of "this president" to the treatment of American women and other religious and humanitarian workers in El Salvador a few weeks later, a small footnote to the brutal government actions praised by Secretary of State James Baker at a November 29 press conference as "absolutely appropriate"—a comment that was suppressed, perhaps regarded as not too useful in the midst of the furor about the murder of the Jesuit priests.[15]

Another pretext for the invasion was our commitment to democracy, deeply offended when Noriega stole the 1989 election that had been won by the US-backed candidate Guillermo Endara, now placed in office by the invasion. An obvious test comes to mind: What happened in the preceding election in 1984, when Noriega was still *our* thug? The answer is that Noriega stole the election with more violence than in 1989, barring the victory of Arnulfo Arias and installing Nicolás Ardito Barletta, since known in Panama as "fraudito." Washington opposed Arias, who was considered a dangerous nationalist, preferring Ardito Barletta, whose campaign was financed with US government funds through the National Endowment for Democracy, according to US Ambassador Everett Briggs. George Shultz was sent down to legitimatize the fraud, praising "Panamanian democracy" at the inauguration. The media thoughtfully looked the other way.

Our 1989 favorite, Guillermo Endara, was close to Arias and remained his spokesman in Panama until the latter's death in 1988 in self-imposed exile. The *Washington Post* now reports that Endara was chosen to run in 1989 "largely because of his close ties to the late legendary Panamanian politician Arnulfo Arias, who was ousted from the presidency by the military three times since the 1940s"—accurate but crucially selective. The media once again looked the other way when, during the invasion, Endara denounced the "fraud of 1984," and they do not ask why our fabled "yearning for democracy" was mysteriously awakened only when Noriega had become a nuisance to Washington rather than an asset.[16] Other pretexts were equally weighty but need not detain us.

The reasons for the invasion were plain enough but largely avoided in media commentary. As is well-known, Manuel Noriega had been working happily with US intelligence since the 1950s, right through the tenure of George Bush as CIA director and later drug czar for the Reagan administration. By the mid-1980s, however, the United States was beginning to reassess his role and decided to remove him. A largely middle- and upper-class civic opposition developed, leading to street protests that were brutally suppressed by the Panamanian military under the command of Colonel Eduardo Herrera Hassan. Hassan's troops "most energetically shot, gassed, beat and tortured civilian protesters during the wave of demonstrations against General Noriega that erupted here in the summer of 1987," the *New York Times* observes, while reporting without comment that Colonel Hassan, "a favorite of the American and diplomatic establishment here," is to be placed in command of the military with their new "human rights" orientation after the liberation of Panama by the United States—the ability to tolerate cognitive dissonance is a wondrous trait and a prerequisite to success in the ideological professions. A program of economic warfare was designed to erode Noriega's support among the poor and black population who were his natural constituency, while minimizing the impact on the US business community, a General Accounting Office (GAO) official testified before Congress.[17]

One black mark against Noriega was his support for the Contadora peace process for Central America, to which the United States was strongly opposed, as usual preferring the arena of violence in which it reigns supreme to that of diplomacy, where it is much weaker. His commitment to the war against Nicaragua was in question, and when the Iran-Contra affair broke, his usefulness was plainly at an end. A more general problem was his nationalist and populist gestures, a carryover from the Torrijos period when the traditional white oligarchy was displaced. On New Year's Day 1990, administration of the Panama Canal was to pass largely into Panamanian hands, and a few years later the rest was to follow. A major oil pipeline is 60 percent owned by Panama. Clearly, traditional US clients had to be restored to power, and there was not much time to spare.

Further gains from the invasion were to tighten the stranglehold around Nicaragua and Cuba, which, the government and media complained, had been making use of the free and open Panamanian economy to evade the US trade sanctions and embargo (declared illegal by the World Court, but no matter). These intentions were signaled symbolically by the contemptuous violations of diplomatic immunity, including the break-in at the Nicaraguan Embassy ("by error," for those who believe in Santa Claus) and repeated detention of Cuban Embassy personnel—all grossly illegal, but that arouses no concern at home, apart from the fear of a precedent from which the US might suffer. And there were domestic political gains, as already discussed. Even the vulgar display outside the Vatican Embassy, with rock music blaring and other childish antics, was generally considered good clean fun—and, by the military, an imaginative exercise in psychological warfare. The press adhered to the canons of its fabled objectivity, for example, when TV crews in a hotel overlooking the Vatican Embassy displayed a pineapple cut in half outside their room, or when National Public Radio amused its elite intellectual audience with an interview with a fruit and vegetable dealer who was asked whether Noriega's pockmarked face really did look like a pineapple.[18]

All in all, a very successful operation. The United States can now proceed to foster democracy and successful economic development, as it has done with such success in the Caribbean and Central American region for many years. The prospect is seriously put forth, as if history and the obvious reasons for its regular course did not exist, another testimony to the stability of the reigning intellectual culture and its remarkable capacity to tolerate absurdity as long as it is serviceable.

Let's finally turn to the general background against which US foreign policy toward Central America will evolve. There are, of course, significant changes underway in the world order. In 1992, Europe will take another step toward integration into a German-dominated confederation. The Soviet Union has not only relaxed its grip on its satellites but is actually encouraging steps toward freedom and democracy. The rapid collapse of the fragile tyrannies that had been installed by the Soviet army, virtually without bloodshed in most cases, is a remarkable event lacking any close historical precedent.

The Soviet Union has received faint praise in the United States for its restraint. There is little thought, however, that the United States should reciprocate or encourage its satellites to do the same. On the contrary, as already discussed, the reaction is to exploit the decline of the Soviet deterrent and to resort more freely to the use of force and other forms of intervention and subversion to bar the way to independent nationalism and desperately needed social change within the traditional US domains. Front-page headlines report Soviet apologies for their invasion of Afghanistan and Czechoslovakia, while commentators sagely discuss the possibility that, finally, the Russians may join the community of civilized nations. It is hardly likely that the United States might apologize for the invasion of South Vietnam and the Dominican Republic, the devastation of Cambodia and Laos, the overthrow of the democratic governments of Guatemala and Chile, the dedicated support for near-genocide in Timor, a campaign of international terrorism against Cuba that has no precedent or analogue, a decade of murderous destruction in Central America, and numerous other crimes. In fact, it would take a diligent search to find a voice calling on the United States or its European allies to rise to the moral level of the Kremlin in this regard.

As noted, Soviet military expenditures began to level off in the mid-1970s and are declining in the course of Gorbachev's attempts to rescue the stagnant command economy. While the militancy of the Reagan administration may have slowed these developments, they did not stop them, and, by the mid-1980s, Washington was compelled to reduce its aggressiveness, hysterical rhetoric, and military growth, as the costs of Reaganite economic mismanagement became unacceptable. Fortuitously, both superpowers, for independent reasons, are on a path away from confrontation.

The dramatic changes in Eastern and Central Europe are a further and quite significant step in the erosion of the bipolar system that emerged from World War II, though it is worthwhile to stress again that the United States was always by far the dominant power, with its Soviet rival a distant second. It has been evident since the late stages of the Indochina wars at least that a new global order has been taking shape, with three major blocs: US-based, Japan-based, and a German-based European system. Europe is reconstructing traditional quasi-colonial relations with the East, and Japan is beginning to follow suit. If the United States were to lag in exploiting this entry into the Western-dominated Third World, it would be left a second-class power, an island off the coast of Eurasia. Not surprisingly, the prospect arouses concern.

Though the reasons have changed over the years, the United States has always had a certain ambivalence about the unification of Europe. In the circumstances of the postwar world, it was feared that the Russians had the advantage in the political "game," as it was called, so that the game had to be cancelled, with West Germany "walled off from Soviet influence," in George Kennan's phrase.[19] Meanwhile, labor and other popular forces were to be undermined and the traditional order largely restored, as elsewhere. The British Foreign Office favored the partition of Germany to bar Soviet influences, viewing "economic and ideological infiltration" from the East as "something very like aggression." Eisenhower also regarded "Soviet political aggression" as the real danger and saw NATO as a barrier against this threat.

Stalin's 1952 proposal to unify Germany with free elections was flatly rejected because of the condition that a reunited Germany not join a hostile US-run military alliance, a sine qua non for any Soviet leadership. Had this and later initiatives been pursued, there might have been no Berlin Wall and no invasions of East Berlin, Budapest, and Prague.

In the early postwar period, the United States gave substantial support to integration of Western Europe, on the plausible assumption, largely fulfilled, that US-based corporations would gain rich opportunities for investment and profit. As European recovery proceeded, the prospects became less favorable. Currently, the United States looks askance on moves toward European integration that might strengthen its major rivals on the world scene, while undermining the US influence that results from East-West confrontation and the pact system. Its spokesmen call for retaining the NATO and Warsaw Pacts to enhance "stability"—meaning US influence. European elites have a mixed reaction; exploitation of the East is a tempting prize, but they have their own reasons to be concerned about the loss of a powerful device of population control.

The United States has been undertaking a defensive reaction to the rise of its German- and Japan-based competitors. Since the latter days of the Indochina war, US elites have engaged in intensive efforts to increase corporate profits, weaken unions and the welfare system, temper the "crisis of democracy" by restoring public apathy, and strengthen state-corporate linkages. They have also sought to solidify the US-controlled bloc. The recent free trade agreement with Canada draws it more closely into the US sphere, and a similar relation with Mexico is not unlikely. The ineffectual Caribbean Basin Initiative, which may be revived, was an attempt to incorporate that region still more tightly within the US-dominated bloc, along with such parts of Latin America as may be economically viable. The United States is also concerned with maintaining its dominance over the world's major energy resources in the Middle East, one reason why it continues to bar the way to a diplomatic settlement of the Arab-Israeli conflict, a matter too complex to pursue here. These efforts are likely to have only limited success, with Japan and Europe increasingly pursuing their own conflicting interests.

With regard to Central America, the US need to control it and repress freedom and democracy there is, if anything, increasing. The capacity to achieve these ends is growing in one respect: the withdrawal of Soviet support for targets of US attack in accord with Gorbachev's "New Thinking" gives the United States more latitude to impose its will by force and other means, as Elliott Abrams and others rightly conclude.

But the capacity to achieve the traditional ends is declining in other respects. The crucial factor is that indigenous popular forces that are the targets of subversion and violence continue to resist, with remarkable courage and tenacity. A second factor, already noted, is the diversification in the global system, as Europe and Japan pursue their own independent paths. From the point of view of the people of the Third World, this prospect offers some advantages: it is better to have three robbers with their hands in your pocket than only one. Their squabbles over the loot may offer some room for maneuver, and European solidarity movements might, in principle, play a larger part by influencing their governments and through their own efforts. Domestic dissidence is not a factor to be taken lightly. Within the United States, though largely outside of established structures, it was strong enough to drive the government underground to clandestine terror instead of the more efficient use of overt force through the 1980s and continues to impose limits on the exercise of direct violence and other means of coercion, thus allowing some scope for the unending struggle for freedom and justice.

Questions and Answers

Could you give us an idea of the long-term aim of all this benevolence, because it looks like the Japanese are getting a greater market share?

Japanese investment in Mexico has been increasing very fast. There's a degree of intervention in Central America, and quite a lot in South America (in fact, there's a big Japanese community in Brazil). To give an indication of the relative weakness of the United States over the years, Japan is now actually involved in two exploratory efforts to seek an alternative to the Panama Canal in Nicaragua—one a government initiative, one a corporate conglomerate. That's the kind of thing a couple of decades ago that no one would even mention; the United States would have driven them out. It would have been completely unacceptable, but at this point the United States can't do much about it. So little, in fact, that these Japanese initiatives are not even discussed in the United States; I don't think they've even been reported. So yeah, Japan will try to get in there, and so will Europe.

Parts of this region, South America in particular, are traditional European areas of influence and control, for Britain in particular. During World War II, the United States used the weakness of Britain under attack as a way of driving them out of their traditional Latin American markets. That was one of the reasons why if you look at the Lend-Lease Bill you discover that there were conditions in it saying that Lend-Lease aid could not go to England if British reserves went above a certain level. Part of the reason for that was so that the United States could take over traditional British markets in Latin America. In some of these documents where they talk about after the war and the need to take over the Latin American military, its more pointed than that. What they say is we have to displace the British and the French from their control of the Latin American military, so that we can take control of it. Undoubtedly, Europe will try to get back into the act as it gets stronger, more confident, and more willing to confront the United States. These are the kinds of problems that in past years led to global wars.

They are not going to do it this time for a number of reasons. One of them being the inter-penetration of capital; the other being exactly what stopped wars in Europe in 1945. I mean, the history of Europe is a history of mindless savagery and barbarism, and it terminated in 1945, because the next step would have been the end. The same is true of global war. It's a pretty safe prediction, because if you're wrong, nobody's going to know about it.

Can I ask you about President Nixon's overtures to the Chinese?
Well, it wasn't President Nixon, it was the whole American business community and the American government. The Tiananmen Square massacre was a bit of a problem. The United States had no objection to it in principle. I mean, the Tiananmen Square massacre, for example, was not worse than the Gwangju massacre in 1980 in South Korea. Probably fewer people were killed than in the Gwangju massacre, which was extremely barbaric. In fact, Korea used troops that had been under American command, and nobody cared. It was barely reported; Jimmy Carter, the president at the time, made some statements about how South Korea wasn't yet ready for democracy and that sort of thing. Tiananmen Square was pretty horrible, but it was the same kind of thing. Basically, nobody cared.

There was a problem with Tiananmen Square. The problem was that the press was all over the place. Gorbachev had just been there; the whole international press corps was there, television cameras were focusing on it, and it was just a stupid mistake to carry out a massacre under the glare of television lights. That's not the way you do it. You wait until people are looking the other way.

Furthermore, there's a kind of contradiction in the way the United States deals with China. On the one hand, it's a reflex in the press that when an "official enemy" carries out some atrocity you go berserk because of your deep feelings for human rights—which are somehow suppressed when "our side" is responsible for similar, or worse, atrocities. On the other hand, China's an ally. It's been an ally since the 1970s. It's kind of an enemy, because it's an official communist power, but it's also an ally. You're kind of stuck. So they reported the Tiananmen Square massacre, and everyone shed the proper tears, but it was well understood that this was for show, and for what propaganda gains could be had from it. Shortly after the massacre, *Business Week*, which is the expression of liberal business opinion, was saying, "Look, we can't let this get out of hand, because the commercial interests in China are too important, and we have to re-establish them."

We now know that within a month of the massacre, National Security Adviser Brent Scowcroft was sent to China (the official story was that he was sent to China to tell them about our deep feelings for human rights, but the actual story will come out in thirty years, when the documents are released) to assure the Chinese leaders that we don't mean any of this stuff. In fact, just a couple of days after the Tiananmen Square massacre, George Bush's brother went to China to firm up a contract that he had arranged in Shanghai, for a golf course or something like that. It was clear—you've got to put this in perspective—China's an important ally and good business partner. When the government announced they were selling $300 million worth of communications and other high-tech equipment to China, the White House spokesman said, "Look, this is $300 million worth of business for American firms." It's kind of interesting. Some commentators in the United States noticed that there was something funny about invading Panama to save human rights while we on the same day announce that we're sending $300 million worth of high-tech equipment to China, to leaders whose human rights record was a thousand times worse. So a couple of people said, "Gee, this seems kind of inconsistent, what's going on?" Nobody would point out the obvious—that it's not the least bit inconsistent, it's completely consistent. In both cases it's good for business, and that's the consistent feature. It's not Nixon.

Nixon, whatever you think about him, is a kind of statesman. He has a grasp of world affairs and says what he thinks; he makes some sense. The same thinking was going on for everyone else. China was an important market and place for cheap labor, where you can pay much less and get them to work much harder than you can in Hong Kong these days.

What's the American role in the Iran-Iraq War?

We can only speculate about that because there's no real documentary record, but it looks as though the US role was to keep it going, as it was for most of the world—the Soviet Union, Western Europe, etc. The best thing was to have them kill each other, because both Iraq and Iran were problems. They were both nationalist regimes with independent interests (brutal and so on, but nobody much cares about that). They were a nationalist threat, and they could have been a spreading threat. So as long as they're killing each other, it's not too much of a problem.

The idea was to supply both sides, and the United States and its allies did, in fact, supply both sides. Toward the end, Iran's preponderant power was beginning to show, and it looked as if they were going to win, and that's no good, so the United States intervened to support Iraq and prevent that. The move to send American warships into the Gulf which was called "freedom of shipping" or something—that was actually to block Iran.

Freedom of shipping in the Gulf was actually threatened by Iraq, not by Iran, for a very simple reason. Iraq had pipelines for its oil, and Iran didn't. In fact, even when an American ship was attacked by Iraqi forces, they still went after Iran, because the idea was to shift the balance so that it would be a standoff. Since then the United States has been rebuilding its relations with Iraq—they've just announced again, right in the middle of the Panama invasion, that they're relaxing loan sanctions—and they're trying to restore connections with Iran too, to bring them into the American sphere.

Are you at all optimistic that in the future the US domestic population might be able to exert more influence on the administration in these global aspirations, given the fact that the perception of the "evil enemy" Russia has dissipated somewhat?
That's going to be interesting to see. Panama is the first real test of the need to invade another country without the pretext of the Russians, and it worked neatly. How long you can go along with that I don't know. The Russians were a very convincing threat. They're violent, they've got missiles, they're brutal, they do all sorts of horrible things, and they're big and powerful, and so on; that's a real threat. People like Gaddafi and Noriega, you can turn them into short-term threats, but it's pretty hard to carry off for a long period.

I think the same's true for the "war on drugs." You can get people terrified of narco-traffickers, but how long is it going to be before they see that the problem is not in Colombia and in the slums, the problem is "social policy," basically. If you're worried about substance abuse, you can't only be concerned with the maybe five thousand deaths a year from illicit drugs; you're also you're going to be concerned with the three hundred thousand deaths a year from tobacco, two hundred thousand deaths a year from alcohol . . . so many questions have got to be asked. The United States, incidentally, is one of the major narcotraffickers in the world, forcing Asian countries to take tobacco under the threat of trade sanctions. I don't suspect the anti-drug hysteria will last long. It's going to be interesting to see what kind of threat can be conjured up to keep the domestic population under control.

I wouldn't assume that it can't be done. There's eighty years of experience on the part of a very sophisticated public relations industry and a very well-disciplined intellectual class that has long been committed to this. There are a lot of things you can think of that might work, but it's not going to be as simple as one might think.

I'd like your comments on American policy in relation to the Palestinian problem.

The Palestinians are one of the nationalist forces that are just in the way, and since 1967—shortly after the 1967 war—the United States has been very impressed with Israel's capacity to use force. That's always impressed them. When Israel won the war so handily in 1967, US support for Israel shot way up. Since then, Israel's been what's regarded as a strategic asset.

This is not particularly new. We now know that as far back as 1948, with Britain withdrawing from the region, the Joint Chiefs of Staff identified Israel as a strategic asset, as a base for the exercise of American power in the region. Through the 1950s, that increased; in 1967, the alliance was set. To keep Israel as a strategic asset—meaning a base for the use, or at least threat, of American power in the region, to keep down independent nationalism, and also, by this point, as a mercenary state that can be called upon to carry out ugly actions around the world, for example, providing arms to Noriega, when the United States was still supporting him—you really have to keep Israel embattled.

A political settlement would take the lid off, as it would elsewhere—it would mean Israel would become integrated into the region, domestic regional politics would begin to develop, etc. The United States has been opposed to settlement there since about 1970 and is the main barrier to a political settlement. There could possibly be at least a political settlement to the Arab-Israeli conflict, and the whole world knows what it is. There's enormous international consensus behind one or another variety of the "two-state" solution. It's certainly been feasible since the mid-1970s, when the United States first vetoed it at the UN when it was introduced by the Arab states and the PLO, and it remains feasible, but it won't happen, because the United States will block it.

In fact, it's kind of intriguing to watch the way the press in the United States deals with this issue. The *New York Times* has, in fact, conceded—there's a line that you can find somewhere embedded in a story—that the United States is the only country in the world that is supporting what is called the "Shamir plan" (which is actually the "Baker-Peres-Shamir plan"). That's a plan that bars the possibility of any political settlement. Its basic premise is that there can be no additional Palestinian state (meaning in addition to Jordan—already considered a "Palestinian" state), and there can be no change in the status of Judea, Sumer, or Gaza, except according to the guidelines of the Israeli government, which rules out any Palestinian self-determination—that's the "Baker-Peres-Shamir plan."

Notes

1 Unfortunately, the notes and sources are incomplete. It is no longer possible to find the relevant information. Thirty years have elapsed since the lecture was delivered. It was considered better to stay with what we have rather than do without.

2 Stephen Kurkjian and Adam Perlman, *Boston Globe*, January 5, 1990.

3 David Broder, "When US Intervention Makes Sense," *Washington Post Weekly*, January 22, 1990.

4 Frederick Kempe and Jose de Cordoba, "Dictator's Dodge: Legalities Are Murky, but Panama Cheers Noriega's Downfall," *Wall Street Journal*, December 26, 1989.

5 or a recent review of the military fiasco in Grenada, see *Wall Street Journal*, January 15, 1990. On the role of the media in suppressing the crucial facts about the invasion, see Noam Chomsky, *Necessary Illusions: Thought Control in Democratic Societies* (Boston: South End

Press, 1989). On the government-media fraud concerning the Libya bombardment, see Noam Chomsky, *Pirates and Emperors Old and New: International Terrorism in the Real World* (Boston: South End Press, 2002).

6 Kurkjian and Pertman, *op. cit.*; the latter quote is the interviewer's paraphrase.

7 For details and references, see Noam Chomsky, *Turning the Tide: US Intervention in Central America and the Struggle for Peace* (Boston: South End Press,1985); Noam Chomsky, *On Power and Ideolog: The Managua Lectures* (Boston: South End Press, 1987); also see Gabriel Kolko, *Confronting the Third World: United States Foreign Policy 1945–1980* (New York: Pantheon Books, 1988).

8 For a review of the declassified record and other relevant material, see Chomsky, *Necessary Illusions.*

9 Wilson Ring, *Boston Globe,* November 24, 1989. Also *New York Times,* November 24. For further references, here and below, see Noam Chomsky, "Tasks Ahead IV: Post–Cold War Cold War," *Z Magazine,* March 1990.

10 Ring, *op. cit.*

11 *Central America Bulletin* (CARIN), August 1989; Council on Hemispheric Affairs, *News and Analysis,* November 24; *Washington Report on the Hemisphere,* November 22; *Central America Report* (Guatemala), November 17, 24; *Latin America Press* (Peru), August 24, 1989.

12 See Chomsky, *Necessary Illusions* and sources cited therein.

13 For extensive details, see Chomsky, *Necessary Illusions.*

14 Marlin Fitzwater, *Boston Globe,* December 20, 1989; Andrew Rosenthal, *New York Times,* December 22, 1989.

15 Associated Press, November 6, December 2, 1989; January 6, 1980; Associated Press, *Miami Herald,* November 7, 1989; Patti McSherry, *In These Times,* December 20, 1989; Baker, Rita Beamish, Associated Press, November 29, 1989.

16 Julia Preston, *Washington Post Weekly,* December 25, 1989; Associated Press, December 20; Boston Globe, December 21, 1989. On the 1984 elections, see, among other sources, Seymour Hersh, *New York Times,* June 22, 1986; John Weeks, "Panama: The Roots of Current Political Instability," *Third World Quarterly,* July 1987; Alfonso Chardy, *Miami Herald,* March 3, 1988; Ken Silverstein, *Columbia Journalism Review,* May–June 1988.

17 Larry Rohter, NIT, January 2, 1990; Paul Blustein and Steven Mufson, *Washington Post Weekly,* December 25, 1989.

18 Diego Ribadeneira, *Boston Globe,* December 30, 1989; National Public Radio, reported by Blase Bonpane.

19 For sources, see Noam Chomsky, "Democracy in the Industrial Societies," Z *Magazine,* January 1988.

Correspondence Three

January 16, 1990

Dear Mark,

Just returned from a trip to Scotland, my first travel since the operation. Went fine, so I guess I'm back on the road. The Scotland affair might be of some interest to you. It was quite different from the usual, and it was filmed by people who seem to be fairly professional (independent movement activist types but evidently knowing their business). The affair was a two-day conference in Govan, a run-down suburb of Glasgow that used to be a ship-building area but is now the usual mixture of slum and high rise, mostly slum. It was held in a community hall that was donated by some magnate about a century ago for the locals, and is used for community groups (aged, homeless, etc.). The participants were basically local activists, artists, etc., pretty far out of the mainstream; about one-third unemployed, in fact. There was enormous interest, and they had to turn away hundreds of applicants. The Labor Party was much annoyed by the whole thing: first, because they couldn't control it; and second, because they can't stand the libertarian tone of these riffraff. They actually cancelled a talk they'd invited me to give on Central America, because I refused to dissociate myself from the conference (ended up giving it at the university in Edinburgh—the sequence of events was quite educational for all concerned, including Labor Party and Central America activists). There was lots of national and local press coverage—also interviews on BBC, press, the usual outside the US borders. Press conferences were held in the pub across the street (filmed, I think). The only institutional sponsor was another pub, kind of bohemian hangout for local artists and writers. If any of this sounds interesting, I can put you in touch. Would be different, anyway. I turned down all the academic invitations, which seemed to ruffle the expected feathers. Interesting couple of days, actually.

January 29, 1990

Dear Jim,

I'm still on a high from that great week in Scotland. I really wished my wife had come along. She'd have loved it. It was an exhilarating experience for me—far more satisfying than the usual routine on these myriad speaking tours. Are there any plans for follow-up activities? It would be a shame to let all that energy go to waste. Hope we can keep in touch and find another opportunity to enter the fray together one of these days. Thanks very much for the book, which looks fascinating, and a great source for marvelous quotes. Which reminds me: I haven't heard yet from the people who were doing the editing (forgot their names, I'm afraid). They were going to send me details about the format they wanted for my talks. I guess they want all three: the long one the first day, the Central America talk the night before, and the remarks the second day. Are there any further plans about publication?

Best.

February 2, 1990

Dear Noam,

In effect this opening paragraph is a postscript. I have been waiting to enclose the check, but so far do not have it to hand because of the astonishing ramifications of getting pounds transferred into dollars—inefficiency on their part (also a reluctance to acknowledge it), which is why you have yet to hear from me. Your letter arrived an hour ago, and I am delighted by your response to the visit. The people in charge of the book (and those involved with the film) are people I trust; they want to do the best by it, and I'll be in constant contact with them. We shall communicate with you on it directly when there is something to report. I want to keep the rest of the letter as I wrote over a week ago on the assumption I would be writing and enclosing the check—what the bank did, in fact, was send the dollars money order to my home address but under the name of the account which I opened for the event, and since no one called Self-Determination Event lives up this block of flats, the Post office will have it back, and then return to sender, the bank, who will then have to telephone myself, and so on. It's nonsense, and I apologize for it. For myself, I suppose it means there's a lack of freshness about the following, but I won't tamper with it:

January 24, 1990

Your visit has been something that will stay with us here for a very long time. These things are personal though. Part of my method as a writer is to steer clear of analysis and allow the discovery to take place on the page. It carries over into other aspects, I suppose, of the way I live—and occasionally gets me in hot water, privately as well as publicly, I'm afraid. When people here ask me how the event was, there is no reply available, though as an organizer I can say: it has happened and, therefore, has had to have been a success. The power of the tense. . . If there was an intention it was to get certain issues raised into public discourse. I'm aware that certain points I may have said from the platform on the Thursday (eventually, I had no time to prepare anything written for it) were open to criticism, both from yourself and others; I had hoped they would spark off a debate and was always ready to be wrong. It's good to have the process on occasion, rather than just consolidating a position; maybe it is a bit precious to talk in these terms, but there is such a lack of general criticism around that I see nothing wrong in throwing something into the arena. Maybe that's just an excuse.

At the airport you asked, I hope ironically, if I was going to do anything more in terms of straight philosophy. On the car journey home, of course, I thought of the correct response, as presumptuous as you could predict, yes, I shall embark on something but perhaps only if you write some short stories—but maybe you have already. . . . The problem with philosophy for myself is that it takes me so damn long to discover anything—it wasn't until midway through the last draft of the essay I did on your work that I suddenly appreciated how crucial is the argument surrounding theory of knowledge, I also suddenly appreciated the enormity of what Descartes was attempting, not to say the beauty of Berkeley's position on existence, and so on.

Incidentally, an appalling attack was launched on George Davie in one of our "quality" daily newspapers the other week by a "socialist" academic who attended the event: "a passionate philosopher of the Scottish nationalist right" was about the most mild of his several abuses. It was ironic to see that one of the attacks was the sort of thing you will have experienced many times from the orthodox left position, in opposition to "human nature." Chris Frew, our acting press-officer, should have sent you a copy of it by now; I sent a reply to the letters' page, which I will send on soon.

As an aside, on the issue of tradition versus nationalism, I had meant to mention Mendele the Bookseller to you at some stage, I think one of the few writers you name in the interview with James Peck; I came onto him by stumbling on a novel of his in one of the secondhand bookshops here—which fortunately you had no time to get around otherwise you would have required another jumbo jet. It's rare to hear of anyone acquainted with his work, although I dare say within Jewish culture it isn't so rare—yet even amongst folk from a Jewish background that I know it is still rare—but there was never time to get onto the subject. Originally, I had wanted the idea of tradition-bearing/the affirmation of indigenous cultures (in opposition to nationalism) and so on to have had more of a role in the two-day event—inviting Chinweizu (his *Decolonization of African Literature* which in some respects is falling into the trap: existence in the face of [in spite of] tradition), but it wasn't to be. I've only lately come to Ivo Andric's work and at this time look to him re one of the cultures that constitute Yugoslavian culture, as I would to Sforim, Aleichem, Peretz re Yiddish; the truly interesting side of the problem, where the unhealthy aspect occurs in the likes of Isaac B. Singer (though so much of what he does is great I think); and in that line, here in Scotland, Sorley MacLean re Gaelic (about eighty thousand Gaelic speakers here, mainly in the Western Islands, the Hebrides) and the reaction against it—keep Gaeldom "pure"—the blood and earth extension—such as Whitman, Carlos Williams will be central to the line in USA English language, confronting folk like Eliot and the Great Tradition. An immense area which leads back into the arena of Herzen, Turgenev, Tolstoi, Dostoevsky, and the Slavophile movement et al.

Etc.!

Mark Achbar has phoned since writing the above. We shall be of whatever help to him that we can. The project he and the others in the "Necessary Illusions" team have embarked on sounds very worthwhile, exciting.

I hope there's been no reaction to your health since returning home; maybe the Glenlivet proved an elixir (the English translation of the Gaelic for whisky is "water of life"—the nearest phonetic transcription I can give is "ooiski vaa").

And back to February 2.

Just to repeat, I am very, very pleased that the trip proved a good one; I was with close friends last night—Tom Leonard, Alasdair Gray, Peter Kravitz and a chap by the name of Joe Hendry, and mentioned your response. They had all been at the event and in very different ways enjoyed it greatly. All had been up at my place on the informal get-together. Alasdair you met and spoke with, a major novelist and also a fine painter, the guy with the beard in his mid-fifties who can speak on anything at all; at present he is involved in a History of the Preface. Tom also attended the meal we had in the Indian restaurant. His latest book will be sent to you, *Radical Renfrew*, a collection of poetry from 1790 to 1914—tremendous scholarship—an excavation of the writings of marginalized writers, mainly working-class men and women; I quote from Tom's work in the essay you've read by myself. Peter Kravitz is editor of *Edinburgh Review*, of which you now have copies. he and one of his friends were instrumental in sparking old George Davie back into the fray; Peter has done a great deal here, reinvigorated the intellectual life to a surprising extent—somebody who does a great deal very quickly; now aged about thirty and has achieved it during about eight years. The last guy, Joe Hendry, booked you into the hotel you were at, he's the Chief Librarian of Renfrew District and totally transformed the area into the second highest spending (on books) library service in Britain (second only to the City of Westminster i.e. that wee place in London where the queen of britain dwells). Joe is a great wheeler-dealer. He introduced the policy here of no fine on overdue books, especially in council housing areas, his attitude was and is that if folk from a housing scheme want to lift a book by Kafka or James Joyce then great, and he would go and buy the library another.

An aside on Tom, he found it impossible to say hello to either yourself or George Davie on the first night at my house, and he ended up drinking too much, and when he woke up next morning he was so frustrated by his behavior that he emptied every drop of alcohol in the house right down the drain.

All the very best to you and your family.

October, 4 1990

Dear George,

Thanks for your good letter the other week. I'm glad the "foreword" to your three essays worked; I found it quite tricky to hit the correct note while hinting at some of the exciting matters being raised—not only of tremendous historical significance, but of great contemporary relevance. The tricky part lay in the constraints of space, getting the thing down to one page etc. Doing the essay on "Chomsky and the Scottish Common Sense tradition" was nothing short of liberation for myself: in realizing something of the major nature of Chomsky's achievement and in becoming aware of the "tradition" properly, I had read a little beforehand, but I had never really understood it—"sorting with a sure hand the incredible complexities" is a phrase of yours you will readily recognize; but, at the risk of irritating yourself, this is precisely what you have done. I don't know how many times I have read particular essays of yours; I always feel a bit thick anyway, a common experience in doing philosophy, but it takes me ages to work things out, the key (dynamic) lines of thought always just out of reach, you think you have them one day and they've evaporated the next, the underlying search for coherence etc. etc. But I must say this, that your work lies somewhere at the very core of my own understanding (for better or worse!), not simply of the Scottish tradition but generally, for in coming to terms with the Scottish line, for example, I had also to come to terms with the beauty of just what exactly Descartes was attempting. I suppose I had never quite grasped the fundamental relevance of theory of knowledge before either, of how everything seems to land back there: "How do we know?" Exciting stuff. Philosophy has always been exciting for me anyway, in a way similar to one of the strong points Tom Leonard makes in his introduction to *Radical Renfrew*—which you must read if you haven't already, his argument on democracy you'll find of great interest—the point in question about how literature is nothing less than a dialogue between writer and reader, a dialogue that spans time and space; in this sense for me philosophy as literature, Lucretius telling me about the "most mobile small invisible particles there are;" Kant's revelation or Hamann's excitement, Kierkegaard's irritation, Schopenhauer's pathos, Fichte's journey to knock on Kant's door etc. etc., these things have always been highly personal to me, absolutely vital.

But I need a rest from it; also in the writing, one has to stand back and say that's that, I now have to go to work. I'm looking forward to doing more reading though, John Millar and Stewart and that period; what will come of that, who knows—maybe a novel, with a bit of luck.

Give my regards to Elspeth. I hope she's getting ahead in any new work she's involved in. Perhaps if you both have a moment you should spend a couple of hundred quid and a bit of time in acquiring one of these beasts this letter is being composed on.* It is genuinely labor saving; it makes life so much easier.

* An Amstrad 9568 PC.

April 15, 1990

Dear Noam

I began writing to you at the end of February but never finished the letter, events were moving so fast. You should know that your contributions to the media here in Britain were important for many people. Along with a couple of others, like Edward Said, it provided something that wasn't forthcoming elsewhere—e.g., your *Guardian* article earlier this year was being passed around in a pub I go to occasionally.

I enclose the last Gulf war issue of the small newspaper some of us here have been bringing out for the past year or so; the local politics contained in it occasionally cause ructions—in one issue the "Gorbals Story" has resulted in resignations in the local Labour Party branch and had a couple of folk barred from their local Unemployed Workers Centre (because they were known to have been involved in supplying us with information). I've spent much of my time taking to do with local government issues, and it's been good and worthwhile to annoy so many officials—real old-fashioned Tammany Hall style politics are to the fore.

I also enclose a copy of my new story collection, which Farrar, Straus & Giroux have opted out of publishing in USA; maybe somebody else will pick it up there. Plus a small edition of four of George Davie's essays which we hope will provide an introduction to many, to the important work he has been concerned with for so long.

I enjoyed your last letter following on from my long stay in Newfoundland last year, which seems like an age ago now, and with the sun and blue sky here images of the village where we go, its natural deep harbor etc.—it would be good taking out a boat...

And I hope you get the chance of some of that soon.

Stay well.

May 28, 1990

Dear Jim and Derek,

Finally, with the pressures of the year winding down a bit, I got to the task of finishing up the papers for the Glasgow conference and sent them off to Ramsey. I am really sorry it took so long and hope that this hasn't caused too much of a delay in the publishing plans.

You (Jim) mentioned in your letter some time back that you would be sending copies of an ugly attack on George E. Davie and a response by Chris that was to appear, and also said that Tom Leonard's *Radical Renfrew* would be on the way. I don't think they arrived—though, maybe they got lost in the shuffle here. You can't imagine the disorder that accumulates.

I'd been invited to a conference in the Basque country that seemed to have much the character of ours in Glasgow but couldn't go. They asked me for a paper for their volume of essays anyway, and I said I'd send them the one for Glasgow, if that is OK with you. The editor is a guy named José Goñi.

I also said that he should write to you to ask permission formally. They seem to be good people. It was a great couple of days, a wonderful way for me to break my six-month long fast (of no travel), and a source of warm memories ever since. Hope to get to see you soon before too long. Keep in touch.

Best.

May 28, 1990

Dear José Goñi,

Enclosed is a copy of the paper I mentioned to you, for the Glasgow conference on Self-Determination & Power. It's quite long. If you feel it is appropriate for your volume, you might want to cut it down some. Also, it you'd like to go ahead, I think it would be proper to write a letter to James Kelman (address below), who is editing the Glasgow volume. He's a fine libertarian Scottish novelist. I'm sure they'll have no objections (I'm dropping him a note myself), but I think it would be a good idea.

Hope to make it to your corner of the world before too long. My daughter and her family will be out there in a few weeks. Maybe you'll run into them (Avi Chomsky, Jon Aske, Sandi Aritza (their year-old daughter).

June 1990

Dear Noam,

Many thanks for sending the papers you delivered to the January in Govan event; I've enjoyed reading them—being on the platform and I suppose the organizational neurosis meant I had difficulty in concentrating on things in general so I missed a lot. The book of the event is still in process, but it certainly advances. It isn't topical; the sooner the better, yes, but preferably to be done properly as opposed to quickly. The movie of the event is slightly more difficult through cash problems; eventually it will happen, but when I don't know. This coming Tuesday (first week July) myself and others will view it for the first time—the entire twelve hours' worth (or as much as we can stomach). So far no word from the fellow in the Basque country but obviously we'll be glad to oblige with copies of your papers and help in any other way we can. Apart from the establishment of two vegetarian restaurants (separate enterprises) by two couples who attended the self-determination event . . . there have been certain knock-ons, not specifically; but supportive of local campaigns—poll-tax of course, but also others relating to Glasgow in particular. Without question there has been an air of general criticism around. Myself and others have been described by city officials recently as "an embarrassment to the Cultural Workforce," by which they mean arts administrators and some politicians—the ones who have brought Pavarotti and Frank Sinatra (and paid him £500,000 [approximately $890,000] in advance) as part of the Glasgow European Culture Capital 1990 "celebrations." More of this anon. I also enclose two recent articles of my own which may interest you.

All the best to you and your family; I hope your health has continued to improve.

June 26, 1990

Dear James Kelman,

We are enclosing a copy of the last letter we have received from Noam Chomsky. As you may know, we (a popular magazine of the Basque Country) organized a congress on individual and collective rights (extermination). We invited Noam Chomsky, but he couldn't manage.

As you can see he has sent us the paper he presented in Glasgow thinking that it would be quite unsuitable for the volume we are going to publish. We have translated it into Basque and Spanish and before editing it we are asking for your permission to include it in our volume.

If your answer is affirmative—and I hope it will be—we will go ahead, and as soon as we finish it, we will send you a couple of copies of the volume.

Thank you very much for all your kindness and waiting for your reply.

Sincerely.

July 16, 1990

Dear Jim,

Thanks for the instructive material you sent. I was particularly glad to see the article on Rushdie. About Young, can't say I really understood what he was talking about. I think your decision to let it pass is wise.

I'm glad to hear that there was some follow-up (including backlash, always good to make one think one is doing something right) to the conference. More coming, I hope. Glad also to hear that the book and film are coming along. I've just been busy turning the paper I sent you for the conference into a large part of a chapter in a forthcoming book, probably Verso, tentatively titled *Deterring Democracy*. Slowed down just now by a (very pleasant) several-week visit from my daughter and year-old granddaughter. Grandparenthood has all the advertised features—lots of pleasures and the lingering ability to give the brat back to her mother when the going gets out of hand; not a luxury to enjoy the first time around.

Got a note from Tom Leonard saying that the book is on the way. Looking forward to seeing it. Keep in touch.

Best.

October 29, 1990

Dear Jim,

Hope your trip to Newfoundland went well. Sounds marvelous. Never passed a whale when we sail at Cape Cod (we have a nineteen-foot day sailer), but sometimes we've come upon dolphins. Sometimes, in fact, even sail right around them. My son, who is an avid windsurfer, has ambled about right among them. They seem to enjoy it. But jigging a squid? Don't know what it is, but I do know that I don't want to do it. Glad to see that the Canadian government is working hard on the things that really matter, like making sure that some poor slob doesn't pick up a bottle without taxes.

Down at the cape, there are the same kinds of problems for the fishermen. It is an increasingly hard life. The fishing grounds are depleted, income is so low that the equipment is deteriorating, young folk just go away, and apart from a few odd-balls who just like the life (which is tough, especially in winter), the crews get older and older.

I've had an invitation from St. John's for a couple of years, but haven't been able to work it out yet. If I do, maybe a side trip to the Burin Peninsula. Maybe we can time it right and run a joint seminar on Scottish Common Sense philosophy (maybe I'll know enough about it by then to participate). Think the locals would enjoy it as a change?

Much enjoyed seeing your article in *Edinburgh Review*. Hope that the last story breaks through—and that things are going well.

Best.

December 29, 1994

Dear Noam,

It's a couple of years now since I wrote to you, in the aftermath of the Self-Determination & Power event held in Glasgow, 1990.

A couple of hours ago, the postman brought me your AK Press CD entitled *The Clinton Vision* (and great seeing young Mister Kanaan continues the work so well from San Francisco).* This has spurred the communication.

I hope to be in the States towards the end of next month, doing a short sort of reading/promotional tour, taking in various cities, one of which seems to be Boston, though I don't yet have the itinerary. If I do get to Boston, I'll certainly try to make contact with you, at least for a quarter-of-an-hour chat—I hope accompanied by a good espresso coffee and a fair old malt whisky.

My latest novel was published by Norton in New York and it'll be interesting to see the review/critical response.† A Chicago-based, small satirical mag., *The Baffler*, is publishing a couple of extracts. So far, the *New York Times* has Savaged it, the reviewer taking her line from the prejudiced stance of a few UK hacks. In this she was able to do what a few media folk had their hands tied from doing over here, to attack on the grounds of the lack of Literary Merit. Apart from sort of middle-brow reviewers in this country my work is usually assumed to have literary merit. However, she had the benefit of reviewing in hindsight so to speak; the novel was awarded a top literary prize over here, and it caused an incredible outcry, national front-page news for two to three days, with my name becoming

---

* Ramsey Kanaan, founder of AK Press, had recently moved to Oakland, California.

† James Kelman, *How Late It Was, How Late* (London: Secker & Warburg, 1994).

synonymous for the term "fuck." I also had the temerity to give them a lecture from the pulpit on receipt of the prize.

You would have found it amusing obviously but there was also a good side to it, dragging certain questions to do with language and culture into the public domain; and of course seeing how quickly so many commentators were prepared to reveal and revel in their racism, cultural elitism, xenophobia and so on.

As I say it'll be interesting to see the wider response in the US. I haven't been in your country for thirty-odd years (Kennedy was shot the week after I arrived). My brother and his family have lived in Nassau County, Long Island, for more than twenty years, and I have only seen him twice in all that time. Marie, my wife, will be flying out for the last few days which we'll spend there with him.

I hope things are well with you and that your health is equal to the various and plentiful work projects you've no doubt undertaken. It would be good to see you, if you are around and in a position to snatch an hour off. I'll be in the States approximately three to four weeks from January 20th onwards.

All the best.

April 17, 1998

Dear Noam,

I enclose an invitation to you from the organizers of the Bloody Sunday Justice Campaign, to deliver their memorial lecture early next year. I was across in Derry a couple of weeks ago and offered to act as "middleman" in this connection. Given that I could simply have provided them with your address at MIT, this role gives me the excuse to be back in contact with you. I know some of the organizers of this campaign and they are good people. Mary Mortimer told me that your health hadn't been too good recently, which information I passed onto the organizers. I also advised them that your diary was overloaded, often working two years in advance. If it is not possible that you can accept their invitation, perhaps you might consider doing the memorial lecture on another occasion.

My own personal news is that I'll be based at the University of Texas at Austin for the coming year, from August onwards, on a visiting professorship—a rather grand title—giving the benefit of my own experience as a writer, on two courses, one for graduate students and one for undergraduate students. My wife Marie is giving up her own job and coming with me. It's a huge change for us but quite exciting. When all's said and done, in financial terms, it isn't very good, we'll be keeping on our own home here in Scotland, obviously, so in respect of living expenses... etc. etc. But really, we are looking forward to it and regard it as a year-long vacation—and getting Marie out of a job she has come to hate. I also like the idea of contact with the students. I was in Texas last year, and there's something quite exciting about it (maybe I'm over-compensating here).

My own financial situation doesn't alter much—always in debt! But only to my publishers. Just as I got used to having Random House UK Ltd. for the past six months, now they've been bought out by a mega German corporation. I have a new collection of short stories published this July, but I'm sure the new guard will be the same as the old, when it comes down to it all they actually want is another novel. And I've owed them one now for a couple of years. . . . Ah well.

I'll be in Hamburg a month from now for a solidarity event organized by the Freedom for Ismail Beşikçi campaign.

All the best.

November 4, 1998

Dear Noam,

Hullo from Austin, Texas. I meant to write earlier, having been here since August. I confess—and the term seems appropriate—that I am enjoying being here very much, and this extends to the campus at UT. I'm enjoying the students, they cheer me up if ever I need it. It is my first time as an academic. In my own country of course I cannot be employed in such a capacity, having failed to procure the necessary qualifications. Last May you sent me a brief letter with the names of a couple of writers/academics that you were acquainted with here, and I misplaced the letter and never got to familiarize myself with the names. But, was James Sledd one of them? I suspect it may have been. Anyway, I have been fortunate enough to make his acquaintance via other sources (also got hold of a collection of his essays); myself and Marie, my wife, will be going down to meet him and his wife sometime soon in what he describes as his "ramshackle old cottage" up in the Hill Country. He is eighty-four years of age and sharp as razor. He has quite a reputation down here, and continues to publish in a local radical journal.

I hope you are keeping well.

All the best to you.

February 4, 2002

Dear Noam,

A brief note to see if this email address still operates. I haven't been in touch with you for a long while, but I do see your name now and again. . .!

And I was pleased to hear about your trip to Turkey, where you met up with Şanar Yurdatapan.

A new collection of my essays appears this week, and I want to send you a copy. Can you confirm that this old postal address that I have also operates—c/o E39-219, Dept of Linguistics & Philosophy, MIT, Cambridge, Mass. 02139, USA.

I had a new novel out some months ago, entitled *Translated Accounts*; unfortunately, people seem to find it unreadable.

Ah well.

I hope you are keeping healthy and managing to avoid some of the calls on your time.

All the best,

Jim.

ps I shall also send this, in hope, by Air Mail.

April 2, 2002

Dear Jim,

Some things never change, like my e-mail address, mail address, and crazy life, getting crazier all the time. Turkey was fascinating, particularly the Southeast, where I was able to spend a day. Am supposed to write something about it but have been so utterly overwhelmed that I haven't been able to write about that or a thousand other things I'm supposed to do.

Glad to hear about what you're up to and look forward to seeing it in print—and I promise to understand.

Will you be in Texas next fall? I recall that you were going up and back. I'll be passing through Austin for a day or two on my endless rabble-rousing expeditions.

Noam

April 27 2002

Jim,

Your collection of essays just arrived, and I turned at once to the one on your visit to Istanbul. Wonderful, and evoked in me both poignant recent memories and feelings of guilt that I haven't been able to write anything about it. Mainly time: am so utterly involved in urgent demands, right now Israel-Palestine horrors, that there's scarcely a moment for anything that requires some thought. And this does. I envy you your remarkable ability to capture it all so evocatively and movingly.

Hope you don't mind that I gave your e-mail address to someone who is compiling a collection on persecution of publishers in Turkey. She asked me for some suggestions about people who might contribute.

We have our own variants here. Just heard one this morning, which is very ominous. One of the big banks has just seized assets of a distributor that apparently was behind in payments, which means the advances given them by small publishers, who barely survive at best; and the bank is now going after the publishers directly, demanding sums they can't even dream of. Don't understand how they can get away with it, but, knowing the history of law versus liberty, assume that they'll find a way, which will be a disaster. Worse than state repression in many ways.

Noam

In Conversation: James Kelman and Noam Chomsky, 2004*

James Kelman: As in the UK, there are many people in the United States ashamed and outraged by the actions of their government; some repudiate these actions, try to work against them. There is a wider sense of helplessness. This was also apparent in the period following the electoral debacle in Florida and the appointment of G.W. Bush to the presidency. It gives rise to a self-deprecatory humor. People poke fun at their own sterility and uselessness in the face of the US State or "the political machine." People avoid culpability, wanting to believe that they have no control over what is happening in

---

* This conversation was undertaken by e-mail as part of a wider set of author-led interviews originally for the publisher Hamish Hamilton who then published both authors. The point of the project was to have writers interview each other, and where possible to match authors who would tend to have certain things in common even if they worked in different areas or genres. James Kelman submitted a selection of questions that Noam Chomsky answered, and there were subsequent exchanges which have been briefly edited here. The process of the interview took about two weeks in June 2004 and was published in *The Drouth* magazine, and website, founded in Glasgow, 2001 by Mitch Miller and Johnny Rodger "to give space to writers and artists to stimulate debate on literature, film, politics, reportage, visual culture, music, and architecture." Mitch Miller and Johnny Rodger went on to publish their critical study of Kelman, *Red Cockatoo: James Kelman and the Art of Commitment* (Sandstone Press Ltd., Dingwall, Scotland 2011).

their name. At the same time they are unwilling to concede—especially to outsiders—that they are excluded from the power structure. They rather believe they have separated themselves from power, that they have conceded democratic rights, and conferred upon authority the privilege to do what it likes. Is this purely a middle-class European-American phenomenon? What happens when so-called "radical" sections of society do fight back? There has been a strong radical tradition in the United States. In the nineteenth and early part of the twentieth century this was battered into submission by the combined power of big business and the US state; and again from the 1960s and early 1970s.

Noam Chomsky: This is, I think, a recurrent cycle. There are regular periods of euphoria about "the end of history" in a utopia for the masters, with the population subdued and marginalized, but some refused to submit and shortly after were vindicated by new and more vibrant popular movements. A classic example was in the 1880s, when William Morris outraged an Oxford audience by stating that "I know it is at present the received opinion that the competitive or 'Devil take the hindmost' system is the last system of economy which the world will see; that it is perfection, and therefore finality has been reached in it; and it is doubtless a bold thing to fly in the face of this opinion, which I am told is held even by the most learned men," but if history really is at an end, as confidently proclaimed, then "civilization will die," and all of history says it is not so, he concluded. Rightly, as was soon discovered. That's not the first time or the last. Furthermore, the cycle is generally upward. It's true that popular movements have been beaten into submission since the first modern democratic revolution in seventeenth-century England, when people called for rights that have still not been won. But their struggle left a residue and raised the level from which later struggle could take place. As more freedom and rights are won, new methods are contrived to cage "the great beast," as Alexander Hamilton called the people. There's no more reason than in Morris's day, or in the 1920s, or 1950s, to accept the doctrines of "the most learned men." The sense of helplessness is more of a choice than a reality, in my opinion.

James Kelman: I heard somebody laugh and say, "We must be about the most foolish people ever to have graced the earth." This was around the same day that G.W. Bush declared the US military the greatest force for justice that the world has ever known. On national television, a famous comedian got much laughter with the comment that "we" must be the only people on earth who ever flew into someone else's country and dropped bombs from the front end of the plane while from the back "we" let loose parcels of food. This humor is surely structured on supremacy. There are few taboos. Almost anything foreign is open to a ridicule which masquerades as "healthy skepticism" and people congratulate each other for using it. Those who criticize this are themselves ridiculed. Similar attacks take place on areas of United States society that lie outside the dominant European-American culture.

Noam Chomsky: Even in totalitarian societies, satirists have had a certain space in which to articulate popular attitudes and concerns. Even more so in more free societies. It can be an evasion, but it can also be more significant. It depends on how others make use of the opportunities opened in this way.

James Kelman: Some speak of class and hierarchy as the English disease. But among European-Americans this "disease" is also discernible. For example, some of the US state's "bad decisions"—presumably including barbaric acts of terrorism—are the result of a kind of ham-fisted lack of sophistication. "How could we expect anything else from a boy from Texas?"

Noam Chomsky: When things go awry, self-designated "respectable sectors" will seek to lay the blame on people who they can dismiss as beneath them in culture and sophistication. The architects of the "bad decisions" are not "boys from Texas"—and this "boy from Texas" was born to wealth and power, attended an elite university, joined a secret society, where he was taught the manners of the rich and powerful and established the right contacts for his future career, which was based on constant intervention of sectors of great privilege and power. Rather, the architects are basically the same as in other administrations, including "the best and the brightest" of the Kennedy years, at the extreme opposite end of the very narrow political spectrum.

James Kelman: US figures of authority, whether political, religious or military, use the term "American" to signify a quality of being greater than "human": to say of someone s/he is an American is to say that s/he is a greater than normal human being. However, the term "American" is itself exclusive. European-Americans do not describe themselves as "European-Americans," they describe themselves as "Americans." They distinguish "Americans" from Native-Americans, African-Americans, Chinese-Americans, Asian-Americans, etc.

Noam Chomsky: The term *American* is, of course, problematic. It is difficult to avoid: the counterpart of *United Statesians* is commonly used in Latin America (when they are being polite), but it doesn't work well in English. The term *North American* won't work either, for obvious reasons. But apart from minor linguistic difficulties, the term does convey a kind of imperial arrogance and a special status for immigrants from Europe. That goes far back. In the nineteenth century. there was a ridiculous ideology tracing the wonders of America to their "Anglo-Saxon origins," no comment necessary. It's worth noting that those counted today as unhyphenated "Americans" include some of the most viciously repressed immigrants: Irish, "Huns" (from Eastern Europe), Wops, Kikes, etc. They may choose the hyphen today, but as a term of pride not exclusion.

James Kelman: The dominant European-American culture believes itself the pinnacle of humanity, that the history of the world has led to them. This culture is superior to the rest of the planet. The superiority is self-evident, and the rest of humanity know it though they may not admit it. If pressed on the latter, they may backtrack to the extent that when they said the rest of the world they meant the rest of the European world and were not especially including the rest of the planet Earth. The rest of the planet is not especially relevant.

Noam Chomsky: That is one of the prerogatives of power and of the success of violence. I suspect it is close to a historical universal.

James Kelman: It is assumed that the rest of the planet wants to emigrate to the USA, particularly the entire population of China. European-Americans appear to believe that their country offers the supreme welfare safety-net.

Noam Chomsky: There is some objective reality to the belief. By the eighteenth century, the English colonies were by some measures among the richest parts of the world. As they exterminated or expelled the native population, they had enormous advantages, not even closely matched elsewhere. By the late nineteenth century the US was by far the major industrial economy of the world, as well as its leading agricultural producer. After World War II, the US had about half the world's wealth, as well as incomparable security and military force. If natural advantages are taken into account, the US should be far and away the richest country of the world, with the highest quality of life for the entire population. The extent to which it falls short of that—which is substantial—is an index of the failures of the socioeconomic system and its dominant elements. One measure of the desire to immigrate to the US is given by Puerto Rico, the one part of Latin America from which immigration is not constrained (apart from Cuba, a special case, reflecting the fanatical dedication to punish Cuba for what secret documents call its "successful defiance" of the ruler of the hemisphere). Puerto Rico has an artificially inflated standard of living, for a variety of reasons. Nevertheless, probably close to half the population has come to the US, where many live in poverty and at the margins of society. The relation of the US to Latin America is not unlike that of Europe and Africa, and for somewhat similar reasons. Not attractive ones, to put it mildly.

James Kelman: Is the US a democracy? What do we mean by *democracy*? In the set of interviews published as 9/11 you referred to one act of terror perpetrated against the people of Sudan by the US State. This was the "destruction of the Al-Shifa pharmaceutical plant" in 1998, bombed out of existence by the Clinton government. Who knows how many will have died as a result. Some estimate a figure in "the tens of thousands." You upset Western commentators by referring to this extraordinarily brutal act alongside the attacks on the World Trade Center and the Pentagon. From their response, you infer that at some deep level, however they may deny it to themselves, they regard our crimes against the weak to be as normal as the air we breathe. Our crimes, for which we are responsible: as taxpayers, for failing to provide massive reparations, for granting refuge and immunity to the perpetrators, and for allowing the terrible facts to be sunk deep in the memory hole. But is there a point we can distinguish between the state and the people? The people of the US are here accountable for the actions of their government. No taxpayer is let off the hook. But what is possible?

Noam Chomsky: The only credible estimates we have of death toll is tens of thousands (the German ambassador to the Sudan, in the *Harvard International Review*; the regional program manager of the respected Near East Foundation, with field experience in the Sudan, in the *Boston Globe*; that a humanitarian catastrophe was likely was anticipated by Human Rights Watch from the moment of the bombing, for good reasons). The matter is, of course, not investigated; the powerful have no need to investigate their own crimes, at least, as long as the intellectuals maintain the standard posture of cowardice and subordination to power. The reaction would be different if, say, al-Qaeda were to destroy the major source of pharmaceutical supplies in the US or England or Israel or some other place that matters. The reaction to my mention of it is instructive. I described the attack on the World Trade Center as a "major atrocity," carried out with "wickedness and awesome cruelty," but I added that it was by no means unique in scale, mentioning the Sudan bombing, but with no further comment. That elicited enormous fury, quite naturally: the atrocities that *we* carry out against *them* are not to be compared with what *they* do to *us*. Again, probably a historical universal. Even the term *terror* is restricted to *their* terror against *us*. Long before 9/11, I had elicited much the same reactions by using the official US definitions of *terror* in reviewing the "war on terror" declared by the Reagan administration—the current incumbents and their mentors—in 1981. The immediate consequences of the use of the official definition are hardly obscure, but utterly intolerable to deeply indoctrinated intellectuals.

One cannot fairly blame the people of the United States in this case. They are carefully protected from awareness of any of these crimes. True, the facts are technically available—as just noted. But they are effectively concealed, and those who have the privilege and ability—and therefore the responsibility—to inform the public much prefer to admire themselves for their extraordinary courage in condemning someone else's crimes, while suppressing their own, a historic task of the intellectual classes, with only marginal exceptions.

A lot is possible. Quite commonly activist movements have escaped the doctrinal controls and helped create quite broad understanding of criminal acts of state and other power systems and strong resistance to them. The Vietnam War is a dramatic illustration. Among the articulate intellectuals, one would have to go far from the mainstream to find any principled criticism: after many years of war, when South Vietnam was virtually destroyed and the attack had spread to the rest of Indochina, one began to hear twitters of protest about how the noble endeavor was a "mistake" which was becoming far too costly (mostly to the US). At the same time, about 70 percent of the population regarded the war as "fundamentally wrong and immoral, not a mistake." Precisely what people mean by these attitudes—which persist until the present—is not entirely clear, because scholarly inquiries into public attitudes do not pursue the question any further, taking for granted that the responses mean that people object to US casualties. Conceivable, but hardly the obvious interpretation.

Over time, there is a notable improvement in the level of civilization of the general public, with quite striking signs, including in recent years. Much that was considered perfectly acceptable only a few years ago is intolerable today. There is a long way to go, needless to say, but also a record of success on which to build further.

Correspondence Four

November 2, 2018

Dear Noam,

I've been working to bring together a short book concerning the Self Determination event in Glasgow, back in January 1990. This begins from your participation and represents an account of the seeds of the Self Determination event, of how it came to exist in the first place, using our correspondence of that period.

There is nothing here to be added or withdrawn.

We have a full account of the correspondence in reference to the event whether by yourself directly, or via Jamie, your assistant at that time. I was not aware of this until a couple of months ago. I was surprised, but pleased. Not for my own interest; I already had most of it in my own archive which is now held by the National Library of Scotland, and the Spirit of Revolt archive. (You'd find the latter of interest, run by volunteers here: spiritofrevolt.info).

For those of us still around from the days of the event itself, it is important that the origins of the event are stated clearly. I cannot do that entirely. But I can bring to light your own participation in and within a certain context.

It is not my intention to "make a book of the event." This can no longer be done. We did try for this following the event itself, and sterling work was performed by a couple of individuals, but it never came to fruition.

The event itself became a rich thing, with a very strong list of invited speakers and participants, including George E. Davie, John La Rose, Mandla Langa, Tom Raworth, Gus John, and Viktor Krivulin.

If you recollect, you delivered two primary contributions, keynote talks on successive days. I thought you had delivered two written papers. However, I spoke to Ramsey Kanaan at PM Press a few days ago, and he is pretty certain you worked from brief notes on both days.

I do not want to take up your time needlessly. If you can answer the following questions I would appreciate it very greatly: Can you remember if you worked from notes on the two keynote contributions you made? (If so, did you ever publish them?)

Would you prefer that I did *not* go ahead with this work? I'm very aware that our correspondence of the period is absolutely essential.

For your interest here are the listed contents. I shall not send you the work-in-progress itself, but this would be available at any time. An alternative is that I forward to you the correspondence for your interest.

Crucially, and I emphasize this, if you would prefer me not to go ahead with this please advise me. There are no hard feelings whatsoever.

All the best to you and yours,
Jim

Preface (James Kelman)
Introduction (James Kelman)
Correspondence (James Kelman and Noam Chomsky)
Correspondence with George E. Davie and Others
The 1988 essay by James Kelman (edited): "A Reading from Noam Chomsky and the Scottish Tradition in the Philosophy of Common Sense"
Day One: James Kelman's Opening Address
Day Two: James Kelman's Opening Remarks
Day Two: "A Response to Noam Chomsky" by George E. Davie
Some Later Correspondence (James Kelman and Noam Chomsky)
James Kelman and Noam Chomsky: "In Conversation with Noam Chomsky" (2009?)

November 2, 2018

Great idea. The most memorable conference I ever attended. I don't have any record of talks, except for one chapter of a book, *Deterring Democracy*, which was based in part on my talks at Glasgow. Attached. There may be some things in the MIT archives, but it would take a search, and not easy—I've since moved to Arizona.

Great to know about your archives. Will look into it.

Hope that you can carry this project through.

November 11, 2018

Hi Noam,

Thanks for your response and sending on chapter 12 from *Deterring Democracy*. It turned out I have had the book for years! I have the AK publication too from 2005 with some of your essays and interviews re anarchism. Here too, in chapter 6, you make use of the papers you delivered at the conference (re Hume's paradox on submission and authority) and which brought forth George E. Davie's response. Would it be possible for me to abstract and make use of some of these for the short book I referred to earlier? Of course, I would do this work myself.

A few days ago, I picked up a 1932 biography of Mustapha Kemal Atatürk, *Grey Wolf: an Intimate Study of a Dictator* by H.C. Armstrong. Given the context, it has been a marvelous find for myself. I didn't know of its existence prior to now. I checked online, and there is a most interesting thesis which I recommend, if you don't know it already: *A Critical Discourse Analysis Perspective on Censorship in Translation: A Case Study of the Turkish Translations of Grey Wolf*, by Ayşe Saki (tinyurl.com/ymxupcxk).

I mentioned to my wife Marie that you were now working in Arizona, a beacon of hope for all we youthful seventies folk. Her immediate, and pragmatic, response was "Ah, the weather..."

All the very best in the new job.

November 11, 2018

Sure, use the materials as you like.

Took a quick look at the link. Looks very interesting. Over my head in work (as usual) but will put it aside for later reading. Thanks for sending.

Just turning ninety in a few weeks, and I won't deny that, with all the attractions of New England, I won't mind not shoveling snow or trudging through slush this coming winter. Temperature here reaches 110°F regularly over the summer, but my wife Valeria (who's from Rio, and used to it) and I found it less oppressive than in Boston summers. Out here in the desert, where Valeria found a lovely place and is turning it into a kind of desert paradise—outdoors right now, in fact, in the chicken coop she designed. A lot different from Cambridge, MA.

Afterword: Ideas and Dialogue

James Kelman

People who take an interest in the life and work of Wittgenstein will be familiar with the name of Rush Rhees, who was his chief editor in later years and one of his literary executors. They were close friends over a long period. When Rhees taught at the University of Swansea, Wittgenstein often visited him and his family. After he retired, Rhees remained in the area and is buried about two miles west of the university.[1] Between his name and this connection to South Wales, he is presumed Welsh, but he wasn't: Rush Rhees was American.

I was surprised to discover that he had been an undergraduate student at the University of Edinburgh. Why was I surprised? There was nothing secret about it. The subject just never arose. Rhees was studying philosophy in Scotland, not "the Scottish Philosophy" and not "the history of philosophy as it applied to Scotland." He is an elusive character altogether for someone who, in his own way, left a significant mark on twentieth-century philosophy.

On one occasion, Wittgenstein was asked "as to whether [David] Hume was a great philosopher or only a very clever man," and he replied, "I can't say, never having read him."[2] Later he refers to reading Hume as a "torture," which suggests he had become *obliged* to read him, eventually. Various factors could have influenced this. It is beyond my scope to discuss the philosophical writings of Wittgenstein but I can talk around the area. We all have ideas. My concern is the value of dialogue and our exploration of ideas in the company of other human beings.

I found Wittgenstein's lack of interest in Hume illuminating firstly because I had assumed Hume was a seminal figure. If Wittgenstein found no reason to read his work then it was not essential. Then I found that G.E. Moore studied the work of Thomas Reid.

Anyone who reads Thomas Reid must know something of the work of David Hume. It is impossible otherwise. Hume is always in his sights. Reid's original aim was "to restore the certainty of God and put an end to Hume's skepticism."[3] He was not alone in what he saw as his primary task but whether or not he succeeded in "putting an end to Hume's skepticism" is not so important as the basic feature that here we have a discourse in which mathematical certainty, "philosophical skepticism" and "revealed truth" are discussed in the same conversation.

Wittgenstein took on the "torture" because he found it necessary, like going to the dentist. People say "visiting the dentist" but no one *visits* the dentist, it is a case of two steps forward, one step back. We go because we have to. In reading it happens in other ways, we see something that sparks an interest elsewhere. Somebody close to us says, Oh you must read so and so. The person has heard something you've said, some idea or other, that suggests a link to something else, some other idea. Maybe we don't want to do it, but we feel the obligation. We grit our teeth and open the book. Wittgenstein and G.E. Moore had become "discussion-partners" and through Moore's influence he would have come upon the work of Thomas Reid. G.E. Moore studied the eighteenth-century philosopher to such effect that his influence on Moore is now itself the subject of study.

Nevertheless, I read someplace that without the advent of Moore nobody would have known what Thomas Reid was talking about.[4]

Not even in Scotland?

Let there be light, said the stranger, I've brought my torch.

In Scotland the natives wandered the streets using bound-volumes of printed matter to thump other natives on the head until the imperialist arrived to advise us that these were books and books also may be read. In colonized cultures, people are familiar with such phenomena. We don't even know whom we are, until the foreign stranger tells us: You are the natives. We are here now. You may leave. If your preference is to stay, please apply using the appropriate form.

Wittgenstein "rarely referred to other philosophers in his own writings, and expressed a positively cavalier attitude towards such matters[, as] in the Preface to the *Tractatus*: 'it is indifferent to me whether what I have thought has already been thought by another.'"[5] His attitude towards other sources would have resulted, partly at least, from his tangential approach to the subject: take what you need and move on. He didn't study philosophy as an undergraduate in the United Kingdom. He arrived from Germany, aged nineteen, to study aeronautical engineering at the University of Manchester. His interest in pure and applied mathematics developed into a passion, to such an extent that within three years he made the acquaintance of Gottlob Frege, one of the foremost logicians and mathematicians of the period.[6]

It was Frege who recommended that he attend Cambridge University and study under Bertrand Russell, which he did. He met another young student here, David Pinsent. They worked together, sharing a passion for mathematics and music. It is probable that Pinsent developed an early interest in aeronautical engineering through his friendship with Wittgenstein. During World War I, he was turned down for the army on physical grounds. He took on experimental work with the RAF, testing aircraft. He was killed in a plane crash in 1918, due to an engineering failure.

Pinsent and Wittgenstein are thought to have been lovers. Perhaps they were; perhaps the physical attraction was from Wittgenstein alone. There are reams to be read on his personal and family background. The depth of their friendship is incontrovertible.[7] Pinsent's mother wrote to advise him of her son's death and Wittgenstein replied that "the hours I have spent with him have been the best in my life, he was to me a brother and a friend."[8] His full name was David Hume Pinsent, and David Hume was his ancestor. I find it difficult to believe, given the circumstances, that Wittgenstein would not have made the effort to read something of Hume's work. We know our own obligations.

At the University of Cambridge, Russell had encouraged him to study philosophy. This was where he met with G.E. Moore. They became friends and "discussion-partners."[9] Through his many discussions with Moore over the years, it is "difficult to imagine that (Wittgenstein) was entirely unfamiliar with Reid's ideas."[10] It has been noted that his "later formulations and arguments often display striking, and enlightening, parallels with those of Reid."[11]

People who learn for the sake of it are not obliged to cite sources, showing that they know. If we don't know, we can continue reading until we do, or move elsewhere, following an idea, whatever we like.

When writers discuss writing, it leads to other writers. We start with the stories and it leads to the creators. The writers I enjoyed in earlier years were comfortable talking about "big things." I wanted to consider "big things" myself. Names appeared within stories, referenced in writers' diaries and autobiographical notes. I was guided by this, and occasionally I followed up on it. It mattered a great deal when the writers had a life beyond the page, had opinions on art, culture and politics, and voiced them, even when it got them into trouble with the authorities.

I just wanted to know. I was looking for whatever it was and not being forced to grasp where I was to get there, to find what it was, if anything was there or whatever. Why read "x" if you have read "y"? Is the difference between the two enough to warrant the effort? Is one dependent on the other? In nonfiction, I found it easier to skip my way through. Sometimes I found myself skipping parts of the same sentence. It seemed worthwhile to continue. It depended on the work. I remember someone saying that Tolstoi's novel *War and Peace* was good, but ye had to skip a lot. I knew that already. I had read it, and I did skip a lot, especially the long sections dealing with philosophy. In fiction, I preferred writers who forced me to read everything.

There is no doubt that the lone route leads to forms of understanding, even if it takes so damn long. In my own case this is eternal, praise be. The chase is all, and the track aye mysterious, in itself an adventure: turn a corner, whohh maan! More closed doors. Where is the key? How do we find it? Is there a keyholder? And on we blunder, ingesting information, somehow, processing a little of that, somehow, digesting a bit and making sense in, of, and from the process. We jump around discovering new data, facts and phenomena, following threads, leaping and skipping our way through, a function of our own developing capacity.

Each of us knows a few people and among them is one or more individuals with whom we can do this. It depends on the idea. Some are the concern of no one outside the family-circle. There are occasions we work our way through things alone, and see no need to go beyond the book in hand.

I bought the *Tractatus Logico-Philosophicus* by Wittgenstein before going to university. I knew his name and the book looked interesting.[12] I may have got a third of the way through, just reading. Even the layout on the page appealed to me. It was the precision: whatever else was going on, it was the precision.

Wittgenstein struck a chord with me, there is no doubt about that. I kept my wife awake at night with "sudden insights." Exclamation marks littered the bedroom. My grasp of his "picture theory" fitted with certain ideas on art and how to appraise what we do as artists. Here was the created thing, the art-object; the painting, the story, the piece of music. There was nothing to explain. Just set it down properly, the way it is. Then it exists. What you create cannot be described, let alone represented. Others may talk about it and fair enough. Artists create the work as best they can, then finish. Leave it at that. No elucidation, just leave it alone.

There are negatives as well as positives. Just about everything I early obtained in the writings of Wittgenstein was refracted by a method of singular prismaticism artists aspirational and otherwise have developed over past millennia, making use of concepts familiar to any occulture or student of neo-Heraclitean ideas; specifically those involving non-substantial mass, category and opposition as energy. The later Diyarbarkians dwelt likewise on post-Zoroastrian categories of measure qua measure, sphere and number-as-set conditional, making use of any field structured not on three being equal to one but identical to it thus requiring the one for the mystical four which enables the quantification of space and derivable quanta, infinity via...

Halt! I'm joking. I made all that up. All these ideas are a load of *ciogh*,[13] the entire paragraph.

What exactly do I know? Hardly anything at all, or not much, I think, or thought I did or thought I thought or had thought, but there you are, gone.

Apologies once again. Language, the intoxication.

Those who search out knowledge for their own purposes can move rapidly but not always in the right direction. It does not mean we miss out. There is no one way. We make sense of the data after our own fashion. There is the academic route, but others are possible. Art is one human being's perception and sense of the world as experienced at that very moment, moment, the next, moment, the next too, and the reality of that, the infinity of moments, tick tock the pulse, tick tock the pulse, refusing to stop stop stop, I beseech you!

At the age of twenty-nine, I managed to get a financial grant to attend university, flitting between classes and nursery duties, doing a three-year course in philosophy alongside one in English studies. In the second year, I took the class in logic. I considered myself hopeless at such stuff generally, mathematics and so on, and I wanted to improve. Truth tables, inference strings, the existential quantifier: I knew nothing about any of it. But I found it satisfying. Logic is functional and of value for artists. It barely matters the subject, its primary elements lurk anywhere and everywhere, a field of potential; a kind of manifold or pinball machine. Its topography comprises intellectual properties, mental attitudes, psychological positions, human signposts: precision, consistency, coherence. I was very aware of how little I knew, and I wanted to go more deeply. It was guaranteed to intrude on my own writing, and I wanted that to happen. One day, I presented a seminar paper that took me ages to prepare. Not a murmur was heard for the duration. On I went, delivering the paper. Would I make it to the end or drop the baton. . .?

The students studied the floor, heads bowed, all five of them. At the table at the head of the room sat the tutor, rolling another smoke. In those days teachers of philosophy could smoke in front of their students (although they didn't approve of students smoking in front of them). He had very long hair, it covered his eyes. Was he listening or not? I couldn't tell; sometimes he didn't.

On I droned until there it was, the flaw, the flaw—I knew it at the point of utterance and knew also that this was the end of the argument. Unless—maybe nobody was listening. . . . Maybe I could get away with it, if I just droned on. No such luck, the student sitting nearest me whispered, Ye've blown it man.

The entire edifice, seen for what it was, a debacle.

I enjoyed the class but, very much; even if its value was unquantifiable, if its only value was whatever I made of it. It was mine anyway, all mine, the entire project and its outcome.

It was a wonderful thing to have taken on and done, whatever it was, who knows. The paper I delivered related to the work of W.V. Quine. I folded it, carried the paper from the class, and sent it to oblivion en route to the Dunrobin Bar.

The third and final year, I took the class in Philosophy of Language. This centered on the work of Chomsky as well as Wittgenstein, and now I came upon concepts such as "morphophonemic structures," "nominalizing transformations," and the "accidental corpus of observed utterances." It was not a nightmare but neither was it entertaining.

I preferred Wittgenstein. He seemed more artist than philosopher. Aspects of his life, his personality and commitment, were most unlike my idea of the Oxbridge norm. But what was my idea? I don't know. Authoritarian academics, a right-wing bunch of upper-middle-class reactionary bastards, backbone of the Brit establishment; muffins with the vicar, sherry with the local landowners, bowing and scraping to distant cousins of the royal family.

When Wittgenstein taught at Cambridge University, some of his students were so taken by him that they "imitated his gestures and phrases when following him . . . on their way to the lectures."[14] He reminded me of Van Gogh. I could see him preaching the gospel to poverty-stricken miners, pronouncing ideas reminiscent of nobody so much as Dostoevsky: "If I thought of God as another being like myself, outside myself, only infinitely more powerful, then I would regard it as my duty to defy him."[15] Yes, a hundred percent, and lay odds on the outcome. "I don't care what I eat as long as it's always the same." Yes, exactly.

And he did the work, in spite of all, he did the work.

People who don't do the work don't do the work does not express a tautology, and there is always that fun to be had. I came to realize that the discussion of ideas we shared on the philosophy course was a form of missing link. In English Literature tutorials some of what was said by other students seemed fanciful and naive. On one occasion, a tutor rebuked me for "taking advantage." I was making use of arguments and knowledge derived from philosophy class.

He described it as "intellectual bullying," and I think he was correct. Students who had a basic awareness of philosophy certainly did hold an advantage. More crucially, those without that basic awareness were at a disadvantage. I raised this at a meeting between students and faculty. If the aim is learning, what is wrong with holding an advantage? This form of advantage might have nothing to do with other people, but everything to do with the ability to learn. Learning is not a competition, unless we allow it. Some achieve higher marks than others. But what that proves depends on what we seek.

Despite the intellectual disadvantage, the students uncluttered by philosophy were able to pass their English course at a high level, whereas folk with the philosophical baggage were liable to expulsion for challenging the authorities to justify their position. This indicated not that the study of philosophy was irrelevant to the study of English, but that the criteria to pass at a high level can be adjusted according to the bureaucratic needs of the department.

There is more to education than passing exams. The discussion of ideas is a powerful feature in what makes philosophy such an aid to learning. It helps spark creativity. People are stimulated, energized, ready to engage in the quest for knowledge. They discover the fun to be had. They laugh rather than gape or become angry at the question whether or not God exists is begged because of the existence of the capital letter.

It is not so much the philosophizing that makes the difference, it is the widening of perception. People are less fearful, less likely to faint at the sight of a book on theoretical physics, more willing to challenge authority.

One effect of the marginalization of the Scottish end of the Common Sense tradition in philosophy is that one of last century's outstanding philosophers was under no intellectual obligation to read the work of an outstanding philosopher of the eighteenth.

That in itself seems quite shocking. He made the point in earlier years that it didn't matter to him "whether what I have thought has already been thought by another.'"[16] This is fine for young folk, but older folk are more likely to have read the racing results; they don't go haring off in a race if someone else has reached the finishing line.

It all depends on the race, some might say, and offer Zeno's paradox in answer. My own finding here is that there were two races going on: the one where the hare races to cross the finishing line before the tortoise, and the other race is to beat the tortoise. The hare can win the first but not the second.

It seems clear that the major disadvantage for Wittgenstein was that he read the work of Immanuel Kant in German rather than English. If he had been obliged to read Kant in English, then it was impossible to escape reading Hume. This is not because Kant cited Hume as an influence. It is because the primary translators of the work of Immanuel Kant were Scottish, from the end of the eighteenth century right the way through into the twentieth.

Two of the later and more prominent were professors, one at the University of Glasgow, H.C. Paton, and the other at the University of Edinburgh, Norman Kemp-Smith. Inevitably, they took different positions. Conflict is essential. Ideas are shared, explored, and debated. This becomes a function of each individual and of that individual's intellectual history, which is unique. People come at things in their own way, unless parroting the work of "an authority," a specialist or so-called expert.

If he had read Kant in English then Wittgenstein could not have avoided the work of Kemp-Smith, and nor could he have avoided that of David Hume. Kemp-Smith was an authority on each, and wrote comprehensively on each. And finally, in this regard, Wittgenstein read and respected the work of Friedrich von Hügel, who was a close friend of Kemp-Smith.

It was in a letter to von Hügel, in 1923, that Kemp-Smith introduced Rush Rhees. He had just turned nineteen years of age. In those days Norman Kemp-Smith held the Chair of Logic and Metaphysics at the University of Edinburgh.[17] Rhees made an immediate impression on him. In the letter he describes Rhees as "a very picturesque youth . . . like a young Shelley, & rather lives up to it—though quite a nice and simple youth."[18] It is difficult to imagine Rush Rhees ever having been "quite a nice and simple youth" but that Kemp-Smith mentioned him at all is noteworthy. He wondered how his new undergraduate ended up in Edinburgh and guessed he must have "got into some kind of youthful trouble" back home.[19] He was correct. Rhees had just been expelled from Rochester University, New York.[20]

This is even more intriguing when we learn that his father was Benjamin Rush Rhees, who taught at the same university. He was "Professor of New Testament Interpretation" and for thirty-five years President of the University itself. What would possess one Professor to mete out such punishment to the son of another? There are many unanswered questions on this affair.

In its day, the story of the expulsion of the student of philosophy had a sensational impact in the US. The *New York Times* carried a startling front-page headline (telling of this) youth of "advanced ideas" (who) had been dropped from a philosophy class because he presumed to refute everything (taught by his Professor) and was guilty of shallow thinking and inordinate conceit. . . . Professing allegiance to anarchism, Rhees was quoted as saying, "I am a radical. . . . That is why I am debarred. . . . From a Puritan I have revolted into an atheist."[21]

The use of his term "anarchism" is striking. This was one of those periods in American history that are too familiar. Yet another "red scare" had developed during yet another period of "austerity," a euphemism applied by the State when they tighten the screws on lower-order folks to sustain the wealth and quality of life of the ruling elite. The attacks are carried out on working-class people and racial, ethnic, religious, and immigrant communities.

This particular "red scare" followed the end of World War I and the period known as the Great Depression. Any criticism of the American State was an act of betrayal, unpatriotic and not to be tolerated. Especially when voiced by outsiders, by people who were different. "Difference" here refers to those who don't think the same, don't sound the same, don't look the same. The same as what and whom are dangerous questions. If you don't know, you don't belong, thus, you yourself are suspect, open to accusations of difference.

The cry is "unity"! In periods of austerity, "unity" is the watchword. Unity will pull us through. Divided we fall. The survival of the nation is in peril! State authorities become even more fearful of solidarity. They never quite grasp what it is but know that it only exists in the presence of empathy, and that its effects are unpredictable. What is *empathy*? They grab a dictionary, google the word online. Eventually they find themselves dwelling on the meaning of *human being*. What does a conversation amount to? Is it dangerous?

With "unity" the cry, the US State had made the move consistent to tyrannies everywhere: they launched an attack on their own population. "Prejudice was particularly strong against [those] who espoused the radical ideas of anarchism, communism, or socialism . . . and thousands of suspected radicals were arrested in over twenty states."[22]

The authorities chose to make an example of two Italian immigrants whose politics were anarchist. They convicted Nicola Sacco and Bartolomeo Vanzetti of murder following "a grossly unfair trial."[23] A strong campaign formed, led by individuals of the caliber of defense lawyer, Clarence Darrow. The campaign had worldwide support. In spite of this, the two men were murdered by due process, put to death for a crime for which "they [had] never been proved guilty."[24] It was a travesty. Widespread revulsion greeted the verdict. American people were ashamed and outraged by it. Most people favor justice. Young people are particularly susceptible. Many fight for justice. A few die for it. This case was notorious, and it remains notorious.

Rush Rhees learned to his own cost where the pursuit of truth and justice might lead within wider society. Here, within academia, he discovered a further truth, that it was exactly the same inside as outside: humbug, lies, careerism, hypocrisy, ruthless cynicism. Only somehow it seemed worse where the pursuit of truth is sanctified. Punishment and retribution; no career, no salary, expulsion, exile. Rhees had experienced academic reality while still in his teens.

There is additional significance in his declaration: "From a Puritan I have revolted into an atheist." It suggests a family background where ideas and opinions were not forbidden. Whether or not radical politics and religious belief can coexist is a recurring question, and a seminal one historically. In Scotland, it remains pertinent to most every generation of radicals.

But from this, it appears that the one thing in which the young Rhees had faith was his own family background. It was okay to tell the truth. It was okay to have your own ideas and to work through them. Rhees and his father had the example of their ancestor who left Wales for America in the late eighteenth century: Morgan John Rhys, "a Welsh radical preacher and pamphleteer who wrote tracts on the abolition of slavery, the disestablishment of the Church, and other reforms."[25] This was during a period of intense radical activity. In the US, France, and Haiti actual revolutions had taken place. In Great Britain and Ireland, the Friends of the People and the United Irishmen had formed; class struggle and nationalist self-determination were on the agenda. The State's response was to strengthen secret-state activities to destabilize these movements. The military carried the fight to the enemy, now identified as the mob, battering those who fought back into submission, shooting them dead in the street.

Meanwhile, most but not all religious authorities in most but not all religious organizations were advising lower-order folks how wrong they were to tamper with the strictures of the State. These were natural happenings and justified. It was urged upon people how very very wicked and sinful they were for rising against their masters. Men and women were essential components of a world designed by a power of such supernatural magnitude that absolutely no evidence of its existence might be found in the entire universe. Disciplined prayer, disciplined behavior, and total obedience to authority were the only answer, avoiding eternal torture the only compensation.

A smaller band of religious authorities insisted that self-defense was no offence; monstrous injustice and murderous robbery were precisely that. Morgan John Rhys and a couple of companions traveled from Wales to revolutionary France to see how matters fared following the political upheavals. On his way home to Wales, Morgan John thought discretion the better course of action. He forsook Wales and sped to the "land of the free." A hundred and twenty years later, his great-great-grandson sped in the opposite direction, from a land become unfree.[26]

Rush Rhees's willingness to accept the term "anarchist" applied to himself demonstrates an independence of spirit, and courage, given the US State's murderous attacks on anarchists, immigrants, and those who came to their defense. Years later, and Rhees was still being described as "a strong-headed anarchist."[27] His father was abroad when his expulsion from Rochester University took place. Rhees wrote to tell him of the situation, that he was leaving America, and why he was leaving America. He wanted to study philosophy in the hope it might lead him to think "coherently." His father was supportive and "urged me to do so, saying that 'the very best thing education can give a man is the ability to think coherently.'"[28]

In America, a Professor of Philosophy had had him expelled from the course. In Scotland, he landed at the University of Edinburgh when Norman Kemp-Smith held the

Chair. Following his arrival Kemp-Smith asked the new student what he "wanted from his studies." Rhees replied, "Inspiration." "You won't get it without discipline," said Kemp-Smith.[29]

In later life Rush Rhees described this as exactly the advice he needed. Even so, it was not the Professor whose influence he felt so keenly but the Professor's Assistant John Anderson, named by George Davie as the most significant Scottish philosopher of the twentieth century.[30]

In America, Rush Rhees had dared tell the truth and suffered the consequences. He was now under the tutelage of a man who would have taken such matters for granted, political commitment as well as truth-telling. In a recent interview, the Australian philosopher David Armstrong, another of Anderson's ex-students, said: "It would have been hard to pass through an undergraduate course under [him] without having one's moral and political thought affected, and given an intellectual edge."[31]

Anderson was a man of his own time and place. The intellectual life was not of another world but inseparable from the day-to-day. His father was headteacher of his local school in the village of Stonehouse, Lanarkshire. He was also a socialist and member of the Independent Labour Party (ILP).[32] Ideas were explored in the family household. John had an elder brother, William, who became a Professor of Philosophy in New Zealand. This was at the same time John became a Professor of Philosophy in Australia.

It was an important period in radical history. Shortly before Rhees arrived in Edinburgh, the socialists had stormed through the 1922 General Election, and twenty-nine Scottish socialists arrived in the Westminster Parliament, including a member of the Communist Party.[33] They shared the position of John Anderson's father, which was that of the ILP, that radical change is possible in a set-up controlled by State authority. This was the Communist Party position, as well that of the mainstream left. The October Revolution of 1917 had had a phenomenal effect on the revolutionary and socialist left throughout the world. Lenin was a hero, not only to members of the Communist Party. The ideas laid out by him and others were of their time and influenced radicals and revolutionaries throughout the world. The anti-parliamentary position had been commonly shared until then. Lenin's attack on "Left-wing communism" just about finished it off. In Scotland, people committed to that basic, foundational position and if compromise was a part of that it was worked through theoretically, rarely to the loss of an intellectual, political, or moral position: no humbug, no hypocrisy. That was the way it was, as I see it, but this is beyond the scope of this essay.

It is enough to recognize that such was the political and intellectual environment when the young student of philosophy, Rush Rhees, arrived in Edinburgh and met with John Anderson. Not only did Anderson hold and maintain a position politically, he argued that "in philosophy, it is of the first importance to have 'a position' . . . so that what you say about one thing depends crucially on what you say about another."[34] Anderson argued "that in society there is a continual clash and struggle of opposed interests and movements, with no possibility of this being transcended in some ideal future."[35]

This particular idea is a core feature of the Scottish intellectual tradition. It appears in other forms and connects to what people in past centuries refer to as "original sin." Noam Chomsky makes the point strongly in reference to John Locke:

> what he regards as the Scottish pessimism opens the way to an optimistic view of human potential, though, to be sure, with the intrinsic limitations that are a logical consequence of capacity to achieve anything nontrivial. I think there has been a great deal of confusion about this, based, really, on careless reasoning.[36]

People will never be perfect. No matter how hard they try. What is "perfection"? Such concepts are better left for mathematics. "Utopia," in the conventional sense, is not possible. People will not move "as one;" not the masses, not the proletariat, not the mob, and not the rabble. Whether to do nothing and be led by the nose is also a decision. In law, committing to take action may be considered an action. The chain of command cannot be held accountable. War criminals must account for the omission of actions as well as actions, sometimes known as "depraved indifference."

It is significant that Marx saw humanity as individuals. Surely this is at the heart of alienation as he saw it? People are divorced from their own humanity by the exigencies and demands of ruling-class interest.

Unless we ignore the evidence utterly, it is very difficult to envisage a time when all humanity will come to grasp truth and understanding and develop together for the benefit of all, in a form of mutual dependency and regard, all moving ahead voluntarily for the good of humankind. Humankind does not march forward as one, not even to a football match, unless controlled by the police. The conflict between opposing interests won't allow it to happen.

On the other hand, that "continual clash and struggle" applies also to human beings sharing thoughts; having chats and blethers, conversations. Who knows how it will go? Ideas are tossed in, elaborated, tossed out.

The study of philosophy is the study of ideas. The study of ideas is to take part in the creation of something. This means taking stuff apart, taking old ideas to bits.

Two things are involved: the old idea and you. This is a dialogue. Old ideas are the product of other minds. You join in. You bring your own thoughts; out of that comes a new idea.

One idea is the work of many minds; add your own thoughts and you have a discussion. The people you meet socially have their own thoughts: dialogue, discussion, debate. But some of these ideas derive from centuries earlier, featuring all sorts of other minds, from all sorts of people. This was how the ancient Greeks operated. Each "school" was a meeting of minds, the Milesians, the Eleatics, the Pythagoreans, and onwards from Plato. Ideas in action: dialogue, discussion, and debate between human beings, dead and alive. The history of philosophy is the history of ideas. Nothing should hold you to ransom. Not even the teacher.

The primacy of dialogue and discussion stayed with Rush Rhees throughout his life. Alongside Wittgenstein, he named Anderson, G.E. Moore, and Alfred Katsil, the Austrian philosopher, as the most important influences on himself. It is crucial to take note that these were discussions.

There are academics who will stop to discuss with a student why some who devote their life to the struggle for social justice are imprisoned, blacklisted, and attacked by the authorities to the extent that their health is damaged irreparably, that they die in consequence. Students of law who query if the early death of a crusading theologian, reformer, or philosopher after years of persecution should be termed "bad luck," "manslaughter," or "murder" might be asked to formulate their arguments and present them in a paper.

Occasionally, young folk come across a teacher or academic who will ask them to cite an example not from history but from contemporary society and include in the list political activists who take a position against the Government or State authority. They are allowed to refer to the oppression, repression, and suppression; the disinformation, misinformation, dissembling, hypocrisy and lies; State barriers against education, creativity, imagination. How are people to cope? how may we aid others to cope? These questions are not barred. No teenager will be executed or expelled. No adult will be executed or exiled.

Socrates was executed for corrupting the youth. This particular "corruption" had nothing to do with morals, ethics, or religion. He had shown the primacy of dialogue and debate, the value of evidence and its use in establishing arguments. He showed that putting all of that forward as precisely as possible could lead to a place where one outcome was more likely than another and any decision might be made in respect of that. This was not achieved through an act of faith or obedience.

Few authorities countenance such a thing. They seek to place their right to power beyond challenge. Human variations on "the divine right to rule" are the aim. This is achieved by placing the possibility of power beyond the scope of ordinary human beings. The "right to the throne" belongs to the head of the most powerful family. I am the head male of the family. I am the leader. I am the King. This is beyond dispute. There is no discussion. No human being may challenge this. I am chosen. God has called upon me. I am authorized. My decisions are authorized.

The right to power is obtained by divine authorization. In the event of my absence, authorization is with my family and representatives. God's word is with us. Our people are chosen. We do not enslave the world. God acts through us. We are vessels. We do God's bidding. The world submits to God through us. There is no negotiation. We are authorized. No human is to challenge the word of God. There is no discussion. No question may be raised in my presence. None may speak unless authorized. No one is to talk. No one is to appear in my sight unless so requested.

Faith in the existence of the greater power is not necessary. The requirement is faith in the authorization. If you do not hold the faith, you should act as though its absence is temporary: the authorization is permanent. Decisions and judgments are a function of authority.

Socrates had shown that the power to judge was inside of all of us. These were human attributes but required to be helped along. The way to do this was through sharing and exploring ideas with other human beings. Decisions and judgments were natural conclusions after due deliberation, in consideration of the opinions and views of others, including the disputes and objections.

One example remains current after 2,500 years. This is the story of Xenophon of Erchia, an Athenian who was attached to an army of 110 thousand left stranded on the Persian border. Their leader had been killed in battle.[37] Of that army one hundred thousand had been raised by the leader himself, from Persian-occupied territories. Now he was dead, the war was over, and his army disbanded. The remainder were Greek mercenaries, foot soldiers. There was nobody to pay the wages, nobody to supply the food. Their sole objective was survival. Not only the ten thousand mercenary foot soldiers but those in their train; the women, children, elderly people, slaves, and cattle, dragging their remaining belongings and materials. They had to travel by foot from southern Mesopotamia right the way through Asia Minor, across into Greece surrounded by hostile forces under orders of the King of Persia who was determined to destroy them in one way or another, whether by guile or slaughter.

Greece was not a country in the contemporary sense. It comprised more than a thousand city-states, each in principle self-governing: "the main [ones] were Athína (Athens), Spárti (Sparta), Kórinthos (Corinth), Thíva (Thebes), Siracusa (Syracuse), Égina (Aegina), Ródos (Rhodes), Árgos, Erétria, and Elis."[38] Within the ten thousand foot soldiers were small battalions from each of those, and each had its own leadership; feuds, battles, and minor wars were not uncommon. Many of their generals were dead. The most powerful city-state was Sparta, and there were many Spartan warriors within the army. Their way of life began and ended on the battlefield. They knew the value of strong leaders in warfare and would fight to the last drop, always within the chain of command.

But there were other points of view. Different city-states had different value-systems. Xenophon was barely thirty years of age when he took on a leadership role. He was not a Spartan, not bred to follow orders to the bitter end, neither "a general, nor a captain, nor a soldier." He was from Erchia in the city-state of Athens, an ex-student of Socrates. His strengths were early in evidence in his appraisal of the situation confronting the ten thousand soldiers. He could explain matters with clarity. He considered the ideas and opinions of others. The decisions he made were based on discussion. He listened, then considered, then arrived at a conclusion that seemed sensible to those around him, and then he moved.

Athenian democracy may have been restricted to the ruling class, but that was a manufacture. It didn't have to be that way. It suited the Athenian ruling class at that particular time. Xenophon reminded the ten thousand foot soldiers of their forbears and of their own strengths, that they didn't need any more generals: they already had ten thousand. Every last man of them was a general. They were all generals. "You can find proof of all this in the trophies we have," said Xenophon, "but the greatest piece of evidence of all is the freedom of the cities in which you have been born and brought up. For you worship no man as a master, but only the gods."[39] We're Greeks, he said.

He acknowledged the humanity of the army. Each soldier was an individual; each had the power to act as befits a human being. Xenophon was of the ruling class and accepted its right to rule. During the march he was distrusted by other generals, because he spent so much time with the ordinary soldiers. None of it was a fluke. Democracy in thought, in the spirit of comradeship, empathy, solidarity.[40] The ten thousand soldiers became ten thousand generals.

Certain features are self-evident: the equality of thought and the facility to think; not the right and not the entitlement, but the facility. We don't need somebody to decide or judge on our behalf. We do this ourselves.

The proper education model begins from this recognition. How do we encourage and help it along? The classical model exists to educate a leadership. Why not the entire population?

Socrates demonstrated that the teacher was not separate from his community, never beyond society. He occupied a position within it. He lived or died by that. He belonged to that first tradition of teachers.

Once ye enter into philosophy it is difficult to stop. I don't know whether ye can jump in and out, but jumping in is important, and where it ends is up to you.

I recall a point where I thought Chomsky's work on creativity set limits to human potential. I was opposed to limits of any kind, but especially on human potential. There is only one Mozart. Sure there is, but that was never enough for me.

Later, I realized there was nothing to worry about, I had misunderstood. There is only one Kafka, and he is not Tolstoi. Now we're getting somewhere. Wittgenstein and Chomsky may appear poles apart, but this is not the case. In this primary area too, they are together. Not only are we human, we are uniquely ourselves.

A British politician made the comment in the 1980s that *the center had shifted too far to the left*.[41] She was a significant member of the authoritarian right, and I thought her comment would have become "classic nuspeak." But its absurdity was never remarked upon seriously that I ever heard. Instead of that a conceptual shift occurred. In contemporary culture people are encouraged by the State not to distinguish between fascism and "radical forms of socialism." Fascism is "far" right. Anarchism is "far" left. Each is a far something. "Fars" are unacceptable. Society teaches this. "Far" is "way out." "Far" is "extreme." "Far" is far "too far." "Far" does not rope in everybody.

What we mean by fascism and the significance of its origins is ignored and forgotten. Fascism and anarchism are now thought to share a space; each is "far out," so that makes them the same thing, more or less. "You go there, and you go there," says the State. Everybody is roped in. We all play up and play the game. The State seeks unity. Everybody is unity. The State speaks for everybody. Unity at all costs. We can relax.

The State will assume the burden. The public need not concern themselves. Exercise the intellectual faculties as you wish but restrict the critical ones; it makes the brainwashing easier. Periods of rest should be occupied in the pursuit of fantasy. Lithe bodies for those who can afford them. Go and climb mountains. Plunge into deep lochs. Matters of the body take precedence: big arms for men and doll-faces for women. Devise and develop your "personal ethic," preferably one that allows loose forms of intellectualizing without the burden of study. Play classical mood music. Relax, don't get involved. Yes, the State is corrupt; be thankful for what you've got, and live with it. Do a bit of gardening and learn from the Stoics.

The idea that a certain number of prayers a day plus the occasional donation to charity sets you free of individual responsibility, amounts to joining a mainstream political party: pay your dues, and let the politics happen elsewhere.

With Noam Chomsky I think the wrong approach is to look for answers. His analysis presents what is. Once we become acquainted with "what is" it is up to us. The world is full of information. What do we do when we get the information, when we have digested the information, what do we do then? Is there a point where ye say, "Yes, stop, now I shall move on." It is the sense of being in communication with the man and what can come from that and where it may lead. It is what we make of these ideas, how we move on from there.

There is no romance in what he does and has been doing for more than seventy years. What he offers is how things are. Perhaps you too can do something about how the world is. If so, it will be through the work you do. In Chomsky's world, there is no escaping reality. He sets out how things are. Deny them if you will. If you cannot deny them, well then, what are *you* going to do about that?

Notes

1 Rhees's archive is housed in the University of Swansea.

2 Rush Rhees, ed., *Recollections of Wittgenstein* (Oxford: Oxford University Press, 1981), 80.

3 This reads like a quotation from George E. Davie, but I cannot find the source.

4 See Kristóf Nyíri, "Wittgenstein and Common-Sense Philosophy," in *Beyond Words: Pictures, Parables, Paradoxes*, ed., András Benedek and Kristóf Nyíri, (Pieterlen, CH: Peter Lang Publishers, 2105), accessed May 18, 2021, http://www.hunfi.hu/nyiri/Nyiri_VL_5.pdf. Nyiri here quotes Nicholas Wolterstorff, *Thomas Reid and the Story of Epistemology* (New York: Cambridge University Press, 2001), 232, suggesting that "it was impossible to understand what Reid was trying to say until *On Certainty* was published." Maybe that was the case for those who were unaware of the Common Sense tradition in Scotland; those with some knowledge of that may wish to challenge the point.

5 Cited in David Stern, "Wittgenstein and Carnap on Physicalism," in *The Cambridge Companion to Logical Empiricism*, ed., Alan Richardson and Thomas Uebel (Cambridge: Cambridge University Press, 2007), 324.

6 For more on the relationship of Frege and Wittgenstein, see Juliet Floyd, "The Frege-Wittgenstein Correspondence: Interpretive Themes," accessed May 18, 2021, https://www.bu.edu/philo/files/2011/01/Frege-WittCorrespondence.pdf.

7 There is much to be read nowadays on their friendship, including David Pinsent's diaries. Good practical information on his family is available at "Wittgenstein's Birmingham Notes, 1913," Eyes v. Ears: The Blog of Mike Johnston, accessed May 18, 2021, https://mikeinmono.blogspot.com/2013/10/wittgensteins-birmingham-notes-1913.html.

8 Citing David Pinsent's diary, undated letter to Ellen Pinsent.

9 This useful phrase comes from Christian Erbacher, "Wittgenstein and His Literary Executors," *Journal of the History of Analytical Philosophy* 4, no. 3 (2016), accessed May 18, 2021, https://tinyurl.com/2xmaksyr.

10 Nyíri, "Wittgenstein and Common-Sense Philosophy."

11 Ibid.

12 Ludwig Wittgenstein, *Tractatus Logico-Philosophicus* (London: Routledge and Kegan Paul, 1975).

13 *Ciogh* is Glaswegian-Gaidhlig for *tollè*, which is Glaswegian-Français for shite which is anyone's guess.

14 From notes of a personal conversation with Sir John Bradfield, referenced in Erbacher, "Wittgenstein and His Literary Executors."

15 See M O'C Drury, "Conversations with Wittgenstein," in *Recollections of Wittgenstein*, ed. Rush Rhees (Oxford: Oxford University Press, 1984), 108.

16 Stern, "Wittgenstein and Carnap on Physicalism," in Richardson and Uebel, *The Cambridge Companion to Logical Empiricism*, 324n4.

17 Compare the impression Wittgenstein had on Bertrand Russell at a similar age.

18 In a letter to Friedrich von Hügel, November 1923; cited in Rush Rhees, *Wittgenstein and the Possibility of Discourse*, ed., D.Z. Philips (Cambridge: Cambridge University Press, 1998), 293.

19 Rhees's archive is housed in the University of Swansea.

20 See Rhees, *Wittgenstein and the Possibility of Discourse*, 291–301.

21 Rhees, ed., *Recollections of Wittgenstein.*

22 "Sacco & Vanzetti: Justice on Trial," Mass.gov, accessed May 18, 2021, https://www.mass.gov/info-details/sacco-vanzetti-justice-on-trial.

23 For a copy of the campaign poster, see, Mass.gov, accessed May 18, 2021, https://www.mass.gov/files/we_expect_justice.jpg.

24 Ibid.

25 See Rhees, *Wittgenstein and the Possibility of Discourse*, 291–301.

26 There is good work to be done on Rush Rhees. For more on his family background, see "University of Rochester History: Chapter 14, Rhees of Rochester," accessed May 18, 2021, https://rbscp.lib.rochester.edu/2320.

27 Erbacher, "Wittgenstein and His Literary Executors."

28 Rhees, *Wittgenstein and the Possibility of Discourse*, 293.

29 In a letter to Friedrich von Hügel dated November 23, 1924; see Lawrence F. Barmann, ed., *The Letters of Baron Von Hügel and Professor Norman Kemp-Smith* (New York: Fordham University Press, 1981).

30 George E. Davie, *The Crisis of the Democratic Intellect* (Edinburgh: Polygon Books, 1986). Davie also studied under Norman Kemp-Smith, and he too became his assistant.

31 Ibid.

32 In the village of Stonehouse, Lanarkshire.

33 Willie Gallacher was the Communist Party MP.

34 Rhees, *Wittgenstein and the Possibility of Discourse.*

35 See "Extended Interview with David Armstrong," Phuket News, accessed May 19, 2021, https://www.youtube.com/watch?v=ehpRFRsF3nI&ab_channel=ThePhuketNews.

36 In response to a point made by George E. Davie; letter dated April 26, 1989.

37 Cyrus, younger brother of the King of Persia.

38 For basic information, see "Greek City-States," *National Geographic*, accessed May 18, 2021, tinyurl.com/cc4xab5j.

39 Xenophon, *The Persian Expedition*, trans. Rex Warner (London, Penguin Classics, 1952).

40 Although he eventually went to live in Sparta; see ibid; also see Edith Hamilton, *The Greek Way to Western Civilization* (Dublin: Mentor Books, 1954 [1930]).

41 Margaret Thatcher, when Prime Minister.

Index

"Passim" (literally "scattered") indicates intermittent discussion of a topic over a cluster of pages.

About the Authors

James Kelman is a novelist, short story writer, playwright, and essayist. He was born in Scotland in 1946, left school in 1961, and began writing at the age of twenty-two.

Noam Chomsky is a laureate professor at the University of Arizona and professor emeritus in the MIT Department of Linguistics and Philosophy. His work is widely credited with having revolutionized the field of modern linguistics, and Chomsky is one of the foremost critics of US foreign policy. He has published numerous groundbreaking books, articles, and essays on global politics, history, and linguistics. His recent books include *Taming the Rascal Multitude* and *A New World in Our Hearts*.

Professor Gus John is an activist and academic working in education, youth work, and social justice. He was a founder trustee of the George Padmore Institute in London. In 2010, he produced *The Case for a Learners' Charter for Schools*, a charter that articulates the educational entitlement of all school students and the rights and responsibilities of all authorities engaged in the schooling process. Since 2006, he has been a member of the African Unity's Technical Committee of Experts working on "modalities for reunifying Africa and its global diaspora." In 2016, he was chosen as one of the thirty

Most Influential Contemporary African Diaspora Leaders globally.

George Elder Davie (1912–2007) was one of Scotland's most influential modern philosophers. He was Reader in Logic and Metaphysics at the University of Edinburgh, and was a Fellow of the Royal Society of Edinburgh. His work on the Generalist tradition in Scottish philosophy has been seminal in the country's intellectual development in recent years.

ABOUT PM PRESS

PM Press is an independent, radical publisher of books and media to educate, entertain, and inspire. Founded in 2007 by a small group of people with decades of publishing, media, and organizing experience, PM Press amplifies the voices of radical authors, artists, and activists. Our aim is to deliver bold political ideas and vital stories to all walks of life and arm the dreamers to demand the impossible. We have sold millions of copies of our books, most often one at a time, face to face. We're old enough to know what we're doing and young enough to know what's at stake. Join us to create a better world.

PM Press
PO Box 23912
Oakland, CA 94623
www.pmpress.org

PM Press in Europe
europe@pmpress.org
www.pmpress.org.uk

FRIENDS OF PM PRESS

These are indisputably momentous times—the financial system is melting down globally and the Empire is stumbling. Now more than ever there is a vital need for radical ideas.

In the years since its founding—and on a mere shoestring—PM Press has risen to the formidable challenge of publishing and distributing knowledge and entertainment for the struggles ahead. With over 450 releases to date, we have published an impressive and stimulating array of literature, art, music, politics, and culture. Using every available medium, we've succeeded in connecting those hungry for ideas and information to those putting them into practice.

Friends of PM allows you to directly help impact, amplify, and revitalize the discourse and actions of radical writers, filmmakers, and artists. It provides us with a stable foundation from which we can build upon our early successes and provides a much-needed subsidy for the materials that can't necessarily pay their own way. You can help make that happen—and receive every new title automatically delivered to your door once a month—by joining as a Friend of PM Press. And, we'll throw in a free T-shirt when you sign up.

Here are your options:

- **$30 a month** Get all books and pamphlets plus 50% discount on all webstore purchases

- **$40 a month** Get all PM Press releases (including CDs and DVDs) plus 50% discount on all webstore purchases

- **$100 a month** Superstar—Everything plus PM merchandise, free downloads, and 50% discount on all webstore purchases

For those who can't afford $30 or more a month, we have **Sustainer Rates** at $15, $10 and $5. Sustainers get a free PM Press T-shirt and a 50% discount on all purchases from our website.

Your Visa or Mastercard will be billed once a month, until you tell us to stop. Or until our efforts succeed in bringing the revolution around. Or the financial meltdown of Capital makes plastic redundant. Whichever comes first.

A New World in Our Hearts

Noam Chomsky
Edited by Michael Albert

ISBN: 978-1-62963-868-3
$16.95 160 pages

An interview with Noam Chomsky is a bit like throwing batting practice to Babe Ruth. What you lob in, he will hammer out.

This conversational interview by Michael Albert, who has been close to Chomsky for roughly half a century and talked with him many hundreds of times, spans a wide range of topics including journalism, science, religion, the racist foundations of American society, education as indoctrination, issues of class and resistance, colonialism, imperialism, and much more. The thread through it all is that every topic—and the list above takes us just about halfway through this book—reveals how social systems work, what their impact on humanity is, and how they are treated by the elite, mainstream intellectuals, and leftists. It gets personal, theoretical, and observational. The lessons are relevant to all times, so far, and pretty much all places, and Chomsky's logical scalpel, with moral guidance, is relentless.

"Chomsky is a global phenomenon. . . . He may be the most widely read American voice on foreign policy on the planet."
—*New York Times Book Review*

"For anyone wanting to find out more about the world we live in . . . there is one simple answer: read Noam Chomsky."
—*New Statesman*

"With relentless logic, Chomsky bids us to listen closely to what our leaders tell us—and to discern what they are leaving out. . . . Agree with him or not, we lose out by not listening."
—*Businessweek*

"Chomsky remains the thinker who shaped a generation, a beacon of hope in the darkest of times."
—Sarah Jaffe, author of *Necessary Trouble: Americans in Revolt*

Taming the Rascal Multitude: Essays, Interviews, and Lectures 1997–2014

Noam Chomsky with an Afterword by Michael Albert and Foreword by Andrej Grubačić

ISBN: 978-1-62963-878-2
$27.95 448 pages

As Noam Chomsky writes about something—US foreign policy, corporate policies, an election, or a movement—he is not only quite specific in recounting the topic and its facts but also exercises blisteringly relentless logic to discern the interconnections between the evidence and broader themes involved. This may seem mundane, but virtually every time, even aside from the details of the case in question, the process, the steps, the ways of linking one thing to another illustrate what it means to be a thinking, critical subject of history and society, in any time and place.

Taming the Rascal Multitude is a judicious selection of essays and interviews from *Z Magazine* from 1997 to 2014. In each, Chomsky takes up some question of the moment. As such, in sum, the essays provide an historical overview of the history that preceded Trump and the reaction to Trump. The essays situate what followed even without having known what would follow. They explicate what preceded the current era and provide a step-by-step revelation or how-to for successfully comprehending social events and relations. They are a pleasure to read, much like the pleasure of watching a great athlete or performer, but they also edify. They educate.

Reading Chomsky is about understanding how society works, how people relate to society and social trends and patterns and why, and, beyond the specifics, how to approach events, relations, occurrences, trends, and patterns in a way that reveals their inner meanings and their outer connections and implications. It is like reading the best you can get about topic after topic, and, more, it is like watching a master-craftsmen in a discipline that ought to be all of ours understanding the world to change it.

"Noam Chomsky is the world's most humane, philosophically sophisticated, and knowledgeable public intellectual. "
—Richard Falk, professor of international law emeritus, Princeton University

God's Teeth and Other Phenomena

James Kelman

ISBN: 978-1-62963-939-0
$17.95 384 pages

Jack Proctor, a celebrated older writer and curmudgeon, goes off to residency where he is to be an honored part of teaching and giving public readings, he soon finds the atmosphere of the literary world has changed since his last foray into the public sphere. Unknown to most, unable to work on his own writing, surrounded by a host of odd characters, would-be writers, antagonists, handlers, and members of the elite House of Art and Aesthetics, Proctor finds himself driven to distraction (literally in a very very tiny car). This is a story of a man attempting not to go mad when forced to stop his own writing in order to coach others to write. Proctor's tour of rural places, pubs, theaters, fancy parties, where he is to be headlining as a "Banker-Prize-Winning-Author" reads like a literary version of *Spinal Tap*. Uproariously funny, brilliantly philosophical, gorgeously written this is James Kelman at his best.

James Kelman was born in Glasgow, June 1946, and left school in 1961. He travelled and worked various jobs, and while living in London began to write. In 1994 he won the Booker Prize for *How Late It Was, How Late*. His novel *A Disaffection* was shortlisted for the Booker Prize and won the James Tait Black Memorial Prize for Fiction in 1989. In 1998 Kelman was awarded the Glenfiddich Spirit of Scotland Award. His 2008 novel *Kieron Smith, Boy* won the Saltire Society's Book of the Year and the Scottish Arts Council Book of the Year. He lives in Glasgow with his wife Marie, who has supported his work since 1969.

"God's Teeth and other Phenomena *is electric. Forget all the rubbish you've been told about how to write, the requirements of the marketplace and the much vaunted 'readability' that is supposed to be sacrosanct. This is a book about how art gets made, its murky, obsessive, unedifying demands and the endless, sometimes hilarious, humiliations literary life inflicts on even its most successful names."*
—Eimear McBride author of *A Girl is a Half-Formed Thing* and *The Lesser Bohemians*

Yugoslavia: Peace, War, and Dissolution

Author: Noam Chomsky
Edited by Davor Džalto with a Preface by Andrej Grubačić

ISBN: 978-1-62963-442-5
$19.95 240 pages

The Balkans, in particular the turbulent ex-Yugoslav territory, have been among the most important world regions in Noam Chomsky's political reflections and activism for decades. His articles, public talks, and correspondence have provided a critical voice on political and social issues crucial not only to the region but the entire international community, including "humanitarian intervention," the relevance of international law in today's politics, media manipulations, and economic crisis as a means of political control.

This volume provides a comprehensive survey of virtually all of Chomsky's texts and public talks that focus on the region of the former Yugoslavia, from the 1970s to the present. With numerous articles and interviews, this collection presents a wealth of materials appearing in book form for the first time along with reflections on events twenty-five years after the official end of communist Yugoslavia and the beginning of the war in Bosnia. The book opens with a personal and wide-ranging preface by Andrej Grubačić that affirms the ongoing importance of Yugoslav history and identity, providing a context for understanding Yugoslavia as an experiment in self-management, antifascism, and mutlethnic coexistence.

"Chomsky is a global phenomenon. . . . He may be the most widely read American voice on foreign policy on the planet."
—New York Times Book Review

"For anyone wanting to find out more about the world we live in . . . there is one simple answer: read Noam Chomsky."
—New Statesman

"With relentless logic, Chomsky bids us to listen closely to what our leaders tell us—and to discern what they are leaving out. . . . Agree with him or not, we lose out by not listening."
—Businessweek

The Art of Freedom: A Brief History of the Kurdish Liberation Struggle

Havin Guneser with an Introduction by Andrej Grubačić and Interview by Sasha Lilley

ISBN: 978-1-62963-781-5
$15.95 192 pages

The Revolution in Rojava captured the imagination of the Left sparking a worldwide interest in the Kurdish Freedom Movement. *The Art of Freedom* demonstrates that this explosive movement is firmly rooted in several decades of organized struggle.

In 2018, one of the most important spokespersons for the struggle of Kurdish Freedom, Havin Guneser, held three groundbreaking seminars on the historical background and guiding ideology of the movement. Much to the chagrin of career academics, the theoretical foundation of the Kurdish Freedom Movement is far too fluid and dynamic to be neatly stuffed into an ivory-tower filing cabinet. A vital introduction to the Kurdish struggle, *The Art of Freedom* is the first English-language book to deliver a distillation of the ideas and sensibilities that gave rise to the most important political event of the twenty-first century.

The book is broken into three sections: "Critique and Self-Critique: The rise of the Kurdish freedom movement from the rubbles of two world wars" provides an accessible explanation of the origins and theoretical foundation of the movement. "The Rebellion of the Oldest Colony: Jineology—the Science of Women" describes the undercurrents and nuance of the Kurdish women's movement and how they have managed to create the most vibrant and successful feminist movement in the Middle East. "Democratic Confederalism and Democratic Nation: Defense of Society Against Societycide" deals with the attacks on the fabric of society and new concepts beyond national liberation to counter it. Centering on notions of "a shared homeland" and "a nation made up of nations," these rousing ideas find deep international resonation.

Havin Guneser has provided an expansive definition of freedom and democracy and a road map to help usher in a new era of struggle against capitalism, imperialism, and the State.

Mutual Aid: An Illuminated Factor of Evolution

Peter Kropotkin
Illustrated by N.O. Bonzo with an Introduction by David Graeber & Andrej Grubačić, Foreword by Ruth Kinna, Postscript by GATS, and an Afterword by Allan Antliff

ISBN: 978-1-62963-874-4
$20.00 336 pages

One hundred years after his death, Peter Kropotkin is still one of the most inspirational figures of the anarchist movement. It is often forgotten that Kropotkin was also a world-renowned geographer whose seminal critique of the hypothesis of competition promoted by social Darwinism helped revolutionize modern evolutionary theory. An admirer of Darwin, he used his observations of life in Siberia as the basis for his 1902 collection of essays *Mutual Aid: A Factor of Evolution*. Kropotkin demonstrated that mutually beneficial cooperation and reciprocity—in both individuals and as a species—plays a far more important role in the animal kingdom and human societies than does individualized competitive struggle. Kropotkin carefully crafted his theory making the science accessible. His account of nature rejected Rousseau's romantic depictions and ethical socialist ideas that cooperation was motivated by the notion of "universal love." His understanding of the dynamics of social evolution shows us the power of cooperation—whether it is bison defending themselves against a predator or workers unionizing against their boss. His message is clear: solidarity is strength!

Every page of this new edition of *Mutual Aid* has been beautifully illustrated by one of anarchism's most celebrated current artists, N.O. Bonzo. The reader will also enjoy original artwork by GATS and insightful commentary by David Graeber, Ruth Kinna, Andrej Grubačić, and Allan Antliff.

"N.O. Bonzo has created a rare document, updating Kropotkin's anarchist classic Mutual Aid, *by intertwining compelling imagery with an updated text. Filled with illustrious examples, their art gives the words and histories, past and present, resonance for new generations to seed flowers of cooperation to push through the concrete of resistance to show liberatory possibilities for collective futures."*
—scott crow, author of *Black Flags and Windmills* and *Setting Sights*

The Sociology of Freedom: Manifesto of the Democratic Civilization, Volume III

Abdullah Öcalan
with a Foreword by John Holloway
Edited by International Initiative

ISBN: 978-1-62963-710-5
$28.95 480 pages

When scientific socialism, which for many years was implemented by Abdullah Öcalan and the Kurdistan Workers' Party (PKK), became too narrow for his purposes, Öcalan deftly answered the call for a radical redefinition of the social sciences. Writing from his solitary cell in İmralı Prison, Öcalan offered a new and astute analysis of what is happening to the Kurdish people, the Kurdish freedom movement, and future prospects for humanity.

The Sociology of Freedom is the fascinating third volume of a five-volume work titled *The Manifesto of the Democratic Civilization*. The general aim of the two earlier volumes was to clarify what power and capitalist modernity entailed. Here, Öcalan presents his stunningly original thesis of the Democratic Civilization, based on his criticism of Capitalist Modernity.

Ambitious in scope and encyclopedic in execution, *The Sociology of Freedom* is a one-of-a-kind exploration that reveals the remarkable range of one of the Left's most original thinkers with topics such as existence and freedom, nature and philosophy, anarchism and ecology. Öcalan goes back to the origins of human culture to present a penetrating reinterpretation of the basic problems facing the twenty-first century and an examination of their solutions. Öcalan convincingly argues that industrialism, capitalism, and the nation-state cannot be conquered within the narrow confines of a socialist context.

Recognizing the need for more than just a critique, Öcalan has advanced what is the most radical, far-reaching definition of democracy today and argues that a democratic civilization, as an alternative system, already exists but systemic power and knowledge structures, along with a perverse sectarianism, do not allow it to be seen.

Facebooking the Anthropocene in Raja Ampat: Technics and Civilization in the 21st Century

Bob Ostertag

ISBN: 978-1-62963-830-0
$17.00 192 pages

The three essays of *Facebooking the Anthropocene in Raja Ampat* paint a deeply intimate portrait of the cataclysmic shifts between humans, technology, and the so-called natural world. Amid the breakneck pace of both technological advance and environmental collapse, Bob Ostertag explores how we are changing as fast as the world around us—from how we make music, to how we have sex, to what we do to survive, and who we imagine ourselves to be. And though the environmental crisis terrifies and technology overwhelms, Ostertag finds enough creativity, compassion, and humor in our evolving behavior to keep us laughing and inspired as the world we are building overtakes the world we found.

A true polymath who covered the wars in Central America during the 1980s, recorded dozens of music projects, and published books on startlingly eclectic subjects, Ostertag fuses his travels as a touring musician with his journalist's eye for detail and the long view of a historian. Wander both the physical and the intellectual world with him. Watch Buddhist monks take selfies while meditating and DJs who make millions of dollars pretend to turn knobs in front of crowds of thousands. Shiver with families huddling through the stinging Detroit winter without heat or electricity. Meet Spice Islanders who have never seen flushing toilets yet have gay hookup apps on their phones.

Our best writers have struggled with how to address the catastrophes of our time without looking away. Ostertag succeeds where others have failed, with the moral acuity of Susan Sontag, the technological savvy of Lewis Mumford, and the biting humor of Jonathan Swift.

"With deep intelligence and an acute and off-center sensibility, Robert Ostertag gives us a riveting and highly personalized view of globalization, from the soaring skyscapes of Shanghai to the darkened alleys of Yogyakarta."

—Frances Fox Piven, coauthor of *Regulating the Poor* and *Poor People's Movements*

Asylum for Sale: Profit and Protest in the Migration Industry

Edited by Siobhán McGuirk & Adrienne Pine with a Foreword by Seth M. Holmes

ISBN: 978-1-62963-782-2
Price: $27.95 368 pages

This explosive new volume brings together a lively cast of academics, activists, journalists, artists, and people directly impacted by asylum regimes to explain how current practices of asylum align with the neoliberal moment and to present their transformative visions for alternative systems and processes.

Through essays, artworks, photographs, infographics, and illustrations, *Asylum for Sale: Profit and Protest in the Migration Industry* regards the global asylum regime as an industry characterized by profit-making activity: brokers who facilitate border crossings for a fee; contractors and firms that erect walls, fences, and watchtowers while lobbying governments for bigger "security" budgets; corporations running private detention centers and "managing" deportations; private lawyers charging exorbitant fees; "expert" witnesses; and NGO staff establishing careers while placing asylum seekers into new regimes of monitored vulnerability.

Asylum for Sale challenges readers to move beyond questions of legal, moral, and humanitarian obligations that dominate popular debates regarding asylum seekers. Digging deeper, the authors focus on processes and actors often overlooked in mainstream analyses and on the trends increasingly rendering asylum available only to people with financial and cultural capital. Probing every aspect of the asylum process from crossings to aftermaths, the book provides an in-depth exploration of complex, international networks, policies, and norms that impact people seeking asylum around the world. In highlighting protest as well as profit, *Asylum for Sale* presents both critical analyses and proposed solutions for resisting and reshaping current and emerging immigration norms.

Crossroads: I Live Where I Like: A Graphic History

Koni Benson. Illustrated byAndré Trantraal, Nathan Trantraal, and Ashley E. Marais, and with a Foreword by Robin D.G. Kelley

ISBN: 978-1-62963-835-5
$20.00 168 pages

Drawn by South African political cartoonists the Trantraal brothers and Ashley Marais, *Crossroads: I Live Where I Like* is a graphic nonfiction history of women-led movements at the forefront of the struggle for land, housing, water, education, and safety in Cape Town over half a century. Drawing on over sixty life narratives, it tells the story of women who built and defended Crossroads, the only informal settlement that successfully resisted the apartheid bulldozers in Cape Town. The story follows women's organized resistance from the peak of apartheid in the 1970s to ongoing struggles for decent shelter today. Importantly, this account was workshopped with contemporary housing activists and women's collectives who chose the most urgent and ongoing themes they felt spoke to and clarified challenges against segregation, racism, violence, and patriarchy standing between the legacy of the colonial and apartheid past and a future of freedom still being fought for.

Presenting dramatic visual representations of many personalities and moments in the daily life of this township, the book presents a thoughtful and thorough chronology, using archival newspapers, posters, photography, pamphlets, and newsletters to further illustrate the significance of the struggles at Crossroads for the rest of the city and beyond. This collaboration has produced a beautiful, captivating, accessible, forgotten, and in many ways uncomfortable history of Cape Town that has yet to be acknowledged.

"Crossroads *is, quite simply, beautiful. It is intellectual and appealing and everything one could hope for from this kind of project. It is a meaningful engagement with a deeply troubling and enormously significant past. Not only does it weave text and images together to their best effect, but this is also one of the most insightful studies of urban history and social movements in any medium."*

—Trevor Getz, professor of African history, San Francisco State University; author of *Abina and the Important Men: A Graphic History*; and series editor of the Oxford University Press's Uncovering History series

Re-enchanting the World: Feminism and the Politics of the Commons

Silvia Federici
with a Foreword by Peter Linebaugh

ISBN: 978-1-62963-569-9
$19.95 240 pages

Silvia Federici is one of the most important contemporary theorists of capitalism and feminist movements. In this collection of her work spanning over twenty years, she provides a detailed history and critique of the politics of the commons from a feminist perspective. In her clear and combative voice, Federici provides readers with an analysis of some of the key issues and debates in contemporary thinking on this subject.

Drawing on rich historical research, she maps the connections between the previous forms of enclosure that occurred with the birth of capitalism and the destruction of the commons and the "new enclosures" at the heart of the present phase of global capitalist accumulation. Considering the commons from a feminist perspective, this collection centers on women and reproductive work as crucial to both our economic survival and the construction of a world free from the hierarchies and divisions capital has planted in the body of the world proletariat. Federici is clear that the commons should not be understood as happy islands in a sea of exploitative relations but rather autonomous spaces from which to challenge the existing capitalist organization of life and labor.

"Silvia Federici's theoretical capacity to articulate the plurality that fuels the contemporary movement of women in struggle provides a true toolbox for building bridges between different features and different people."
—Massimo De Angelis, professor of political economy, University of East London

"Silvia Federici's work embodies an energy that urges us to rejuvenate struggles against all types of exploitation and, precisely for that reason, her work produces a common: a common sense of the dissidence that creates a community in struggle."
—Maria Mies, coauthor of *Ecofeminism*

We Are the Crisis of Capital: A John Holloway Reader

John Holloway

ISBN: 978-1-62963-225-4
$22.95 320 pages

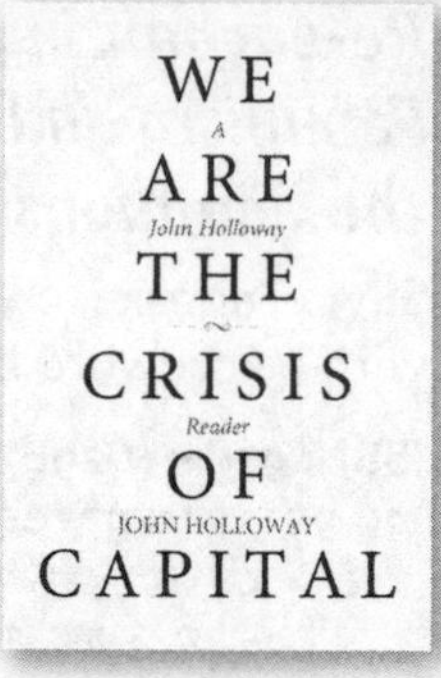

We Are the Crisis of Capital collects articles and excerpts written by radical academic, theorist, and activist John Holloway over a period of forty years.

Different times, different places, and the same anguish persists throughout our societies. This collection asks, "Is there a way out?" How do we break capital, a form of social organisation that dehumanises us and threatens to annihilate us completely? How do we create a world based on the mutual recognition of human dignity?

Holloway's work answers loudly, "By screaming NO!" By thinking from our own anger and from our own creativity. By trying to recover the "We" who are buried under the categories of capitalist thought. By opening the categories and discovering the antagonism they conceal, by discovering that behind the concepts of money, state, capital, crisis, and so on, there moves our resistance and rebellion.

An approach sometimes referred to as Open Marxism, it is an attempt to rethink Marxism as daily struggle. The articles move forward, influenced by the German state derivation debates of the seventies, by the CSE debates in Britain, and the group around the Edinburgh journal *Common Sense*, and then moving on to Mexico and the wonderful stimulus of the Zapatista uprising, and now the continuing whirl of discussion with colleagues and students in the Posgrado de Sociología of the Benemérita Universidad Autónoma de Puebla.

"Holloway's work is infectiously optimistic."
—Steven Poole, the *Guardian* (UK)

"Holloway's thesis is indeed important and worthy of notice."
—Richard J.F. Day, *Canadian Journal of Cultural Studies*